LEADING

for

SOCIAL JUSTICE

LEADING *for* SOCIAL JUSTICE

Transforming Schools for All Learners

Elise M. Frattura • Colleen A. Capper

CORWIN PRESS
A SAGE Publications Company
Thousand Oaks, CA 91320

For information:

 Corwin Press
A Sage Publications Company
2455 Teller Road
Thousand Oaks, California 91320
www.corwinpress.com

Sage Publications Ltd.
1 Oliver's Yard
55 City Road
London EC1Y 1SP
United Kingdom

Sage Publications India Pvt. Ltd.
B 1/I 1 Mohan Cooperative
   Industrial Area
Mathura Road, New Delhi 110 044
India

Sage Publications Asia-Pacific Pte. Ltd.
33 Pekin Street #02-01
Far East Square
Singapore 048763

Printed in the United States of America

Library of Congress Cataloging-in-Publication Data

Frattura, Elise Marie, 1960-
Leading for social justice: Transforming schools for all learners / Elise M. Frattura, Colleen A. Capper.
      p. cm.
Includes bibliographical references and index.
ISBN 978-0-7619-3177-5 (cloth)
ISBN 978-0-7619-3178-2 (pbk.)
   1. Inclusive education—United States. 2. School management and organization—United States. I. Capper, Colleen A., 1960- II. Title.
LC1201.F73 2007
371.9'0460973—dc22

                                                            2006101266

This book is printed on acid-free paper.

07   08   09   10   11   10   9   8   7   6   5   4   3   2   1

Acquisitions Editor:	Hudson Perigo
Editorial Assistant:	Jordan Barbakow
Production Editor:	Libby Larson
Copy Editor:	Teresa Herlinger
Typesetter:	C&M Digitals (P) Ltd.
Proofreader:	Dorothy Hoffman
Indexer:	Rick Hurd
Cover Designer:	Scott Van Atta

Contents

List of Figures

List of Tables

Appendices

Preface

This book joins the education conversation at the nexus of two powerful educational movements underway in this country. The first is the accountability movement, spurred on by the No Child Left Behind (NCLB) Act and its revisions. Though we expect this act to be continually revised, the premise of the act we predict will remain intact for years to come, regardless of the political whims of politicians—that is, the premise that we need to raise the achievement of all students, particularly students who have traditionally been underserved by schools (i.e., students of color, low-income students, students for whom English is not their first language, and students with disabilities). In fact, we argue that the achievement of students who typically struggle should be the primary focus of all educators—that educators should be held accountable for the high achievement of literally all students, regardless of whether federal or state policy supports that goal.

Though the intentions of NCLB were in part to raise student achievement, especially for marginalized students, in practice, the perhaps unintended result of this act is not only the continued but the increased segregation of marginalized students in schools. That is, school districts are now required to report on the achievement of low-income students, students of color, students for whom English is not their first language, and students with disabilities. When districts learn that these students are not scoring as high on the achievement tests as their white, middle-class counterparts, they are then required to raise the achievement levels of these students. Unfortunately, to do so, districts and schools are segregating and tracking these students into at-risk programs, summer school programs, afterschool programs, tutoring programs, and literacy and math programs, to name a few. Thus, in their efforts to eliminate disparities in achievement for traditionally marginalized students, well-intentioned educators in schools and districts end up segregating these students and in so doing, marginalizing them from the school community. Thus, a federal policy with a goal to mitigate against educational discrimination for traditionally marginalized students results in schools and districts discriminating against these same students in efforts to meet the policy goals.

The second powerful education movement providing the context for this book is constituted by the teaching and leadership for social justice movement. Heralded primarily by progressive educators, in the past decade a plethora of literature has emanated about how to educate students for whom English is not their first language (Lopez, Gonzalez, & Fierro, 2005; Portes & Hao, 2004; Rolstad, Mahoney, & Glass, 2005), how to educate students of color successfully (Conchas, 2006; Ladson-Billings, 1994, 1995, 2001), educational programs that address students who are at-risk (Slavin, 2002; Wasik, Bond, & Hindman, 2002), and myriad books and articles on how to include students with disabilities (Friend & Bursuck, 2006). The field has also gained from the literature on differentiated instruction to address the array of student learning needs in classrooms (Tomlinson, 2001; Tomlinson & Allan, 2000; Tomlinson & Reis, 2004). Moreover, the scholarship that directly addresses teaching for social justice at the PreK–12 level of education has contributed in significant ways to understanding the challenges and opportunities of this work (Allen, 1997; Darling-Hammond, French, & Garcia-Lopez, 2002, Darling-Hammond & Youngs, 2002; French, 2002; Gaudelli, 2001; Hunt, 1998; Lewison, Flint, & Van Sluys, 2002; Makler, 1994; Traudt, 2002). Another body of literature also describes the challenges and opportunities of preparing teachers to teach for social justice (Adams, Bell, & Griffin, 1997; Ayers, Hunt, & Quinn, 1998; Cochran-Smith, 1995, 2004; Darling-Hammond, et al., 2002).

Unfortunately, not even the literature on teaching or leading for social justice addresses the importance of integrated learning environments for all students. For example, the literature in the field of educational leadership provides empirical studies on the success of "high-achieving schools" for low-income students and students of color (Oakes, Quartz, Ryan, & Lipton, 2000; Perry, 1997; Scheurich, 1998; Scheurich & Skrla, 2003; Vibert & Portelli, 2000). These schools and the people that lead them are hailed as "high achieving"; "highly successful"; and indeed, embodiments of schools where social justice and equity prevail, and where these individuals are regarded as social justice leaders. Yet, this same social justice literature is silent about where the students in these schools are educated. In fact, whether or not students of color, of low income, with disabilities, or for whom English is not their first language are educated with their peers is not a criterion for these to be considered social justice schools.

This is the point at which we depart from many of our colleagues who are oriented toward social justice. We argue that a school cannot be considered a social justice school, or a high-achieving school, or a highly successful school, or a school that is led by a social justice leader, unless that school has also eliminated segregated pullout programs.

Thus, when we use the term "transforming" in this book's title, we mean that to truly lead for social justice will require a full transformation of our traditional beliefs and practices about schooling. Leading for social justice requires transforming the structure of the school, not dismantling existing segregated, pullout programs and creating new separate programs. To accomplish this revolutionary feat will require transforming beliefs and practices about leadership; transforming teaching and learning; transforming teacher capacity to teach to a range of students; and transforming how to acquire and how to reallocate resources.

We also are intentional about our use of the phrase "all learners" in this book's title. To lead for social justice requires school leaders to be advocates for literally all students in their schools. Many equity-related books either implicitly or explicitly make this statement. However, because we argue that leading for social justice demands the integration of literally all students with each other, in this book, rather than discuss particular groups of students in discrete categories (e.g., gender, sexual orientation), we instead include chapters that focus specifically on those students who most school leaders find it difficult to educate in heterogeneous, mixed-ability classrooms: students with severe cognitive disabilities, students with challenging behaviors, and students for whom English is not their first language.

While it is positive that educators in many schools are including students with disabilities more often in general education than they have in the past (most educators believe their school is "an inclusive school" even when students are segregated for parts of the day), this book moves far beyond these "inclusive" practices to include more than just students with disabilities. We describe what we mean more specifically in Chapter 1.

In short, what both the accountability and social justice movements and associated literature do not address is the importance of educating all students in heterogeneous learning environments. In other words, *where* students learn (the actual location of student learning), and associated with that, with *whom* students learn (who the traditionally marginalized students are learning with) matter a great deal. We have had some educators counter to us that where students learn does not matter, that if students are being pulled out of the classroom into small groups in another part of the building, as long as they are learning to high levels, then segregating them from their peers for this period of time is fine.

As we discuss more thoroughly in Chapter 1, where students learn should matter to a social justice leader for many reasons. First, the students who are routinely removed from the general education setting are typically students of color, low-income students, students for whom English is not their first language, and students with disabilities. These students cease to become integral to the classroom community—they are viewed as dispensable, flawed, and blamed for their own lack of achievement. In so doing, we end up marginalizing and discriminating against these students in our efforts to help them succeed. When these students are required to disrupt the continuity of their day to leave the classroom for instruction, they leave behind their white, middle-class peers to benefit from the smaller class and the continuity of one teacher who can meet their needs. These white, middle-class students do not waste instructional time wandering down the halls to receive instruction elsewhere. Second, research shows that student achievement increases when students learn in heterogeneous learning environments, and that student achievement decreases when students are segregated from each other (Peterson & Hittie, 2003; Rea, McLaughlin, & Walther-Thomas, 2002). Third, where students learn also matters because educating students in segregated pull-out settings is more expensive than integrated education (see Chapter 1).

Thus, in a sense, this book reconceptualizes and redefines the accountability movement to address the fact that all educators do have a responsibility to increase the achievement of literally all students, and they also are responsible for ensuring that they do so in integrated educational environments. Indeed, we argue that educators who move toward what we term Integrated Comprehensive Services (ICS)™ must also remember that the goal is to increase student achievement. Merely creating heterogeneous learning environments without also raising student achievement is not enough.

In addition, this book reconceptualizes and redefines education and leadership for social justice. We argue that a definition of education/leadership for social justice must include educating students in integrated, heterogeneous environments. Even more strongly, we argue that a school in which educators are not working toward the principles and practices of Integrated Comprehensive Services cannot be considered a school that is engaged in social justice work, no matter how high their student achievement. A school or district in which the educators are moving toward ICS principles and practices (whether or not they refer to it as ICS) is the embodiment of a social justice school or district. Hence, throughout each chapter, we clearly distinguish how leading toward Integrated Comprehensive Services is different from what is described in the existing social justice education literature.

Though many books have been written about special education administration or student services administration, these texts typically perpetuate the problems in schools for typically marginalized students. While it can be useful for educators to learn about the various federal and state policies and programs that have been developed for typically marginalized students (i.e., special education, alcohol and other drug programs, homeless programs), learning the uniqueness of each policy and program only serves to perpetuate the segregation of students philosophically and in practice. That is, educators learn about these separate programs, but do not learn how to draw from these policies and associated funding in ways that can serve students in heterogeneous settings. We describe in Chapter 13 the movement toward a merger of federal policies and offer suggestions for doing so.

For an educational leader to take on the dismantling of segregated programs, the most entrenched, normative, standard practice in public education, is no small thing. In fact, by pursuing the dismantling of these programs, leaders can predict they will be accused of taking resources and support away from students. They may be called racist, or be attacked by families with and advocates for students with disability labels for working against the rights of these individuals. These attacks come about because segregated, separate programs are the most visible reminder that someone, somewhere, is doing something for a particular child. Even if little is being accomplished in these programs, or program effects are not even measured (as is typically the case), administrators, other educators, and politicians can point to these "special programs" as evidence that something is being done for students who struggle. In fact, in states in which interdistrict public school choice is allowed (public school students have a right to attend any school they want in the state, without charge), many schools tout the high number of "special programs" in their district as evidence that theirs is a high-quality school district. This book turns this premise on its head. From ICS principles and practices, we would argue that if the schools in that district at their core were being successful with students, then the extensive array of special programs would not be necessary.

Thus, though many educational policies and practices today are intended to eliminate discrimination, their implementation results in segregating students from their peers. In school systems across the country, we have constructed a normed group entitled "general education students." By using this phrase, "general education students," we in fact create another group of students, loosely titled non–general education students. Non–general education students are those who do not meet the criteria for academic, physical, emotional, social, or behavioral success of the normed or dominant group, the general education students. Consequently, when a student has deviated from the dominant group, educators look for another subculture in which to track and marginalize the student who does not meet the normed parameters. In so doing, we continue to increase the number of students we send to special programs, located on the sidelines of our educational institutions (Thurlow, Elliott, & Ysseldyke, 1998; U.S. Department of Education, 2000; Ysseldyke, 2001; Zhang & Katsiyannis, 2002). Such programs include, but are not limited to, special education programs, at-risk programs, English as a second language (ESL) programs, teenage parent programs, reading and math programs, and Title I, among others. These programs are intended to be of educational value. However, because they are separate from the core of the school, these programs result in questionable student outcomes—socially, emotionally, and academically. In this book, we challenge all educators to move beyond the maintenance of general education and its proliferation of segregated programs to a second-order shift in thinking and practice that will challenge the core of the education system as we know it. Via an educational planning process, this book offers a way for educators to conduct a formative analysis in their schools to move from programs that marginalize children in need to one of proactive services of support for all students.

SOURCES OF OUR IDEAS AND INTENDED AUDIENCE

This book is not about ivory tower or armchair theorizing about how schools should be. The ideas in this book are a culmination of our work over the past 22 years with schools and educators across the country. We both draw from our practical experience as teachers and administrators in public schools—in extreme rural poverty settings, in suburban schools, in small rural districts, and in quite large urban districts. We both have first-hand experience with implementing the ideas behind ICS in every school and district in which we have worked.

A second source for our ideas is our extensive experience, more than 50 years combined, in preparing future school leaders. The students in our courses are typically full-time teachers or school or district leaders pursuing their administrative licenses. Our courses require these students to collect extensive equity data on their own schools and to describe their current service delivery model for students who struggle in their schools. Then, based on ICS principles and practices, students are required to establish goals and an implementation plan to bring ICS to fruition in their own districts. As a result, we have over 15 years of equity data from literally hundreds of schools and districts. This has helped us keep in touch with current practices and outcomes of educators' efforts. We have also heard students' stories of the barriers and supports to working toward ICS in their schools/districts. Most rewarding to us are the majority of students who take these ideas and implement them in their own classrooms, schools, and districts, and report back to us the gains they have made in this direction. Some of these students have focused their doctoral dissertation research on topics associated with ICS in their own schools and districts, and we have greatly benefited from these studies.

A third source for our ideas is our continued work with educators in the field as we are asked by their schools and districts to analyze their current service delivery models and help them redesign their education for students who typically struggle. We have worked with over 100 schools and districts in this way. In addition, we have conducted research with schools that have significantly increased student achievement for students with disabilities, students of poverty, students of color, and students for whom English is not their first language—and they have increased this achievement while also dismantling their segregated programs.

Thus, our intended audience for this book is educators in schools including teachers, support staff, teacher leaders, school principals, district administrators or superintendents, directors of special education and student services, directors of curriculum and instruction, and business managers. We also believe this book can be quite useful in leadership and teacher preparation programs.

We know most educators put in long hours in their efforts to educate all students, and there is little time to digest theoretical ideas that are distant from the day-to-day practice of education. With this in mind, we purposely have written this book to be easily accessible, in the language we use and in our style of writing. We do not mince words and have tried to write directly to the point regarding what we think school leaders need to believe, understand, and know how to do to meet the needs of all learners in integrated heterogeneous environments. Though we draw from the research literature, and where it is useful we reference this literature in the event the reader would like to read further, the reader will not find extensive reviews of the literature in this book. Again, rather, we have chosen to be parsimonious and practical in our writing, and have included helpful checklists and an evaluation form at the end of each chapter as ways to help busy educators determine the current status of serving students who typically struggle and where they need to focus their efforts. In addition, though we are conscious of the theoretical and epistemological underpinnings of our ideas, again, we have chosen not to make these underpinnings explicit, in favor of sharing as many practical ideas as possible.

We made these writing decisions out of a sense of extreme urgency and a great sense of care and concern for students who typically struggle in school, and also for the educators who valiantly show up each day to try to make a difference in these students' lives. As one of our grandparents would say, "Time is a-wastin'." We have too many students who are struggling each day in school, who do not want to go to school, for whom school has always felt like a foreign land to them. These students feel left out and unsuccessful; they do not feel good about themselves, nor do they feel excited about learning. This is a travesty of modern society, and we each need to take personal responsibility to put an end to this situation.

In addition, many educators show up to school each day putting in their maximum effort, and trying with the best of intentions to help students who typically struggle. The data and research show, however, that often all the effort, time, and resources are not bearing the hoped-for academic fruit. In frustration, educators may turn to blame the students themselves, their families or communities, or the state and federal governments for the lack of student progress. It is time to put down the blame game and to focus our educational efforts in a way that can maximize them in the most cost-effective way possible, to the benefit of all students.

THE USE OF THIS BOOK WITH OUR FIRST BOOK

In 2000, we published the book, *Meeting the Needs of ALL Abilities: How Leaders Go Beyond Inclusion* (Corwin Press). In the first chapter of that book, we explained the current status of efforts to help traditionally marginalized students (typically segregated, pullout programs) and explained the problems with such programs (along with figures that explained our ideas). In Chapter 1 in this book, we greatly expand on that chapter with a more thorough explanation of the problems with segregated programs, and we explain what we mean by Integrated Comprehensive Services as a transformative way to meet the needs of all learners in schools.

In the second chapter in our first book, we explained one way to get the process started—by asking questions, and then by forming a service delivery team at the school level to initiate the process. This team would, in part, collect data and information about the school to move the process forward. In this book, we have greatly expanded on these ideas.

Specifically, in this book, our major premise is that meeting the needs of students who typically struggle requires that these efforts form the central core of the school planning process. That is, these efforts will not succeed if they are relegated to the student services or special staff alone. Moving to ICS means changing the core of the school, and thus the core of the school educators must be involved in the effort. To this end, we have devoted an entire chapter (Chapter 5) to identifying and describing the school- and district-level teams that can initiate and move the process along.

In our first book, we suggested the teams should collect additional data to ascertain the current status of how the school is meeting the needs of students who typically struggle. Since publishing that book, we have found that this data collection forms the foundation of all the other efforts to work toward ICS. Hence, in this book, we devote all of Chapter 4 to data collection, and we have included a revised version of the data collection instrument from our first book.

In our first book, we devoted an entire chapter each to the role of the principal and district office staff in service delivery change. We continue to believe strongly that these leadership positions and roles must evolve to reflect ICS principles and practices. In Chapter 2 of this book, we focus on the importance of leadership and just what kind of leadership it takes to implement and sustain ICS.

Our first book included a chapter on standards for student safety, which we continue to believe is critically important to ICS. The first book also included an entire chapter on student behavior and working proactively with students with challenging behaviors. Again, given that students with challenging behaviors are often the ones most excluded in schools, we consider these ideas to be vitally important for ICS. In this book, we devote an entire chapter to students who significantly challenge our teaching, students with severe disabilities. We have found that it is these students who most typically are the exceptions to inclusive efforts in schools.

In short, this book does not replace our first book. Our intention is that our first book lays the foundation for ICS (though the term ICS was born out of the present book) and includes specific practices related to how to bring ICS to fruition. This current book greatly expands on the practical ideas, adds information that will help ICS be fully embodied in schools, and provides more extensive details about ICS—specifically how ICS can form the core of the school planning process. We detail these contents in the introduction to this book.

Acknowledgments

We wish to acknowledge the assistance of the following people in producing this book. First and foremost, the Milwaukee Public Schools in allowing Elise to be part of their transition from programs to services—your dedication and perseverance make it impossible for any of us to give up. Our students from both Administrative Leadership Programs at the University of Wisconsin–Milwaukee and the Department of Educational Leadership and Policy Analysis at the University of Wisconsin–Madison, you asked the difficult questions and were willing to be the test pilot—your feedback has been invaluable. To Beverly Luckenbill with the Milwaukee Collaborative who is currently piloting our book with the Charter Schools across the Milwaukee Metropolitan Area, and who seeks to create equitable schools of choice in urban cities, without harming the city schools—your care for the whole is clear. To Martin Scanlan, assistant professor at Marquette University, Milwaukee, Wisconsin, we truly appreciate all your time and efforts in the final weeks of producing the book that helped us cross the finish line, in particular your coauthorship of Chapter 10 and tracking down countless references. We are indebted to you. In addition, we would like to sincerely thank Luciana Ugrina for assisting in the last edits of the book, and Teresa Herlinger, copyeditor extraordinaire. Your quality of work speaks for itself. We would also like to thank Corwin Press for their patience as we restructured our book; we truly appreciate your continued support and enthusiasm for our work. To those administrators, teachers, and parents with whom we work every day, thank you for creating schools where social justice prevails as a result of changing the structural organization of service delivery for all students.

About the Authors

Elise M. Frattura is an assistant professor in the Department of Exceptional Education and Educational Administration and associate dean for the School of Education at the University of Wisconsin–Milwaukee. She spent 5 years as a public high school teacher and 13 years as a district student services and special education administrator. While working as a school practitioner, she also served as an adjunct lecturer at the University of Wisconsin–Madison, teaching courses related to student services and diversity in elementary and secondary administration. Currently she is teaching courses in administration of student services, organizational leadership, and special education law. Dr. Frattura researches and publishes in the area of nondiscrimination law, Integrated Comprehensive Services for all learners, and the theoretical underpinnings of educational segregation. In addition, Dr. Frattura works with school districts across the country to assist in the movement from programs to services for all learners. In 2000, she coauthored *Meeting the Needs of All Learners: How Leaders Go Beyond Inclusion* with Dr. Capper.

Colleen A. Capper is a professor in the Department of Educational Leadership and Policy Analysis at the University of Wisconsin–Madison. She has written or cowritten four books (published or in press) and over 120 chapters, and refereed journal articles and conference papers related to the intersection of educational leadership and equity. She is currently working on a book with Michael Dantley that addresses the intersection of educational leadership, spirituality, and social justice. Prior to her work at Madison, she served as a special education teacher, administrator of special programs, and founding director of a nonprofit agency for preschool children and adults with disabilities in the Appalachian region of southeastern Kentucky. She works with schools and districts on redesigning service delivery for all students and raising achievement for typically marginalized students in inclusive ways, particularly those with disabilities and English language learners. She also consults with nonprofit and for-profit agencies across the country on ways to integrate social justice, equity, and spirituality into their daily work.

Introduction

*L**eading for Social Justice: Transforming Schools for All Learners* is the result of our work in urban, rural, and suburban school districts over the past two decades as teachers, administrators, and researchers. This book has been conceptualized to assist educational leaders in developing Integrated Comprehensive Services (ICS) for all learners, especially those learners who have been labeled to receive services from federally mandated programs (special education, Title I, English as a second language, at-risk, etc.). We believe that oppression in our society is perpetuated through our schools by the "slotting and blocking" of students with differing needs into self-contained programs and separate schools for their perceived own good. As Freire stated in 1970 in his book, *Pedagogy of the Oppressed,*

> it is in the interest of the oppressor to weaken the oppressed still further, to isolate them, to create and deepen rifts among them. This is done by varied means, from the repressive methods of the government bureaucracy to the forms of cultural action with which they manipulate the people by giving them the impression that they are being helped. (p. 141)

The population of oppressed or dehumanized students in our schools is growing. If we continue to function in the same manner as we have over the past five decades, we will continue to create schools composed of students who belong and those students who do not. To overcome the dismal outcomes of segregated programs, school leaders (i.e., principals, school-based steering committees, site councils, etc.) require clarification of what the current program delivery structure looks like and results in, knowledge of how integrated comprehensive service delivery can make a difference, and clear guidance to bring the concept of integrated services to fruition. This book is aimed toward this end.

Time and again, to achieve educational equity for students who have been pushed to the margins of our educational institution, we use program-specific initiatives, such as the inclusion initiative for special education, truancy initiatives, and bilingual education initiatives, only to perpetuate the fragmentation of services. No Child Left Behind (NCLB) high-stakes testing does assist in bringing about data-driven reform efforts, but school district personnel do not take into consideration the structure of how services are arranged within the school as they make their data-based decisions. Often we measure student performance and assume that the structure of services, staff design, staff development, and teacher evaluation plans are not part of the inquiry. Thus, we continue to segregate students, and the cycle of failure is perpetuated (Burrello, Lashley, & Beatty, 2000; Capper, Frattura, & Keyes, 2000; Sailor, 2002).

Historically, school leaders attended to the use of instructional techniques, building teacher capacity, advancing curricular practices, and developing policies based on new legislation. However, little if any time has been spent on the structure of how schools service the growing population of students who are labeled through federal nondiscrimination regulations. This book is a means to address this gap.

We also know that school district leaders across our nation are under extreme pressure to assess, collect, and report student achievement data as part of the No Child Left Behind legislation. Concurrently, those same school district leaders are under significant mandates to collect compliance data in the area of special education under the Individuals with Disabilities Education Act (IDEA). Such data collection is completed under the assumption that it will bring about quality education for all learners. A second assumption is that school districts that meet compliance on all standards in relation to IDEA are providing quality services for students with disabilities. Both these assumptions are incorrect. If we aim for compliance, we will never find quality; however, if we aim to achieve Integrated Comprehensive Services, we will find not only quality, but equity, and compliance will follow.

This book has been developed to assist educational leaders to engage in a multidimensional analysis of schools and districts. In this book, we address the nitty-gritty, step-by-step process that is required to change service delivery in schools. Most important, however, we tie these changes into the school educational plan. That is, these changes cannot be a special education endeavor, but must form the core of schoolwide change. The book also asks educators to collect data on and analyze their own school. The school plan that results from this process stands apart from other plans for school change in three ways:

1. This plan is based on an Integrated Comprehensive Services philosophy that is defined in detail in Chapter 1 of this book.

2. This plan ties in 15 major components of a school educational plan.

3. This plan aligns both qualitative and quantitative points of inquiry to each section of the school education plan tied to each chapter of this book to assist school teams in asking the necessary questions to develop Integrated Comprehensive Services.

THE FOUR CORNERSTONES

We have divided the book into four primary sections, defined as "cornerstones" of Integrated Comprehensive Services: Focusing on Equity, Establishing Equitable Structures, Providing Access to High-Quality Teaching and Learning, and Implementing Change (see Figure 0.1). School committees may decide to begin with one cornerstone as they begin their formative analysis, then move on to the next three.

These four cornerstones serve as the four primary goals to achieve Integrated Comprehensive Services, and each cornerstone builds on the one before it (see Figure 0.2). Each of these cornerstones comprises a section in the book. Within each section, we describe specific actions that must be taken that will accomplish that cornerstone goal. Each of these 15 actions should constitute the primary sections of a school education plan (see Figure 0.3), and each action comprises a chapter in this book.

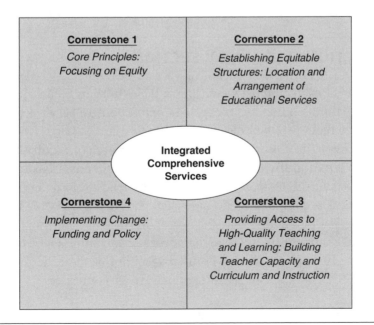

Figure 0.1   Four Cornerstones of ICS

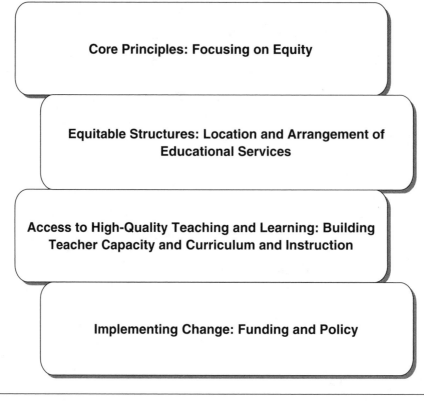

Figure 0.2   Building Blocks to ICS

COLLECTION OF DATA BY SECTION

At the end of each chapter, we include a table that can guide educational leaders as they conduct an Integrated Comprehensive Services formative analysis of their school or district. The ICS formative analysis (see Figure 0.3) addresses three points of inquiry: the focus area of inquiry, the comment section, and the phase of application. The focus areas reflect the main points in the chapter and can help the leadership teams prioritize their work. The comment section for each focus area gives team members the opportunity to address the focus area in their own setting and write additional comments to describe their progress toward implementing ICS. The phase of application can be used to quantify the school's process toward ICS. Definitions for specific ratings are as follows:

Phase 1:   Little to no discussion has occurred regarding this specific focus area.

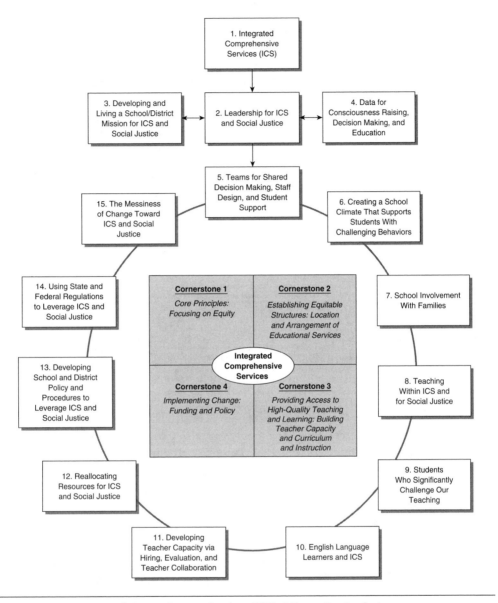

Figure 0.3   Integrated Comprehensive Services (ICS): A Formative Analysis

Phase 2:   Faculty are beginning the discussion regarding this specific focus area.

Phase 3:   Faculty are working toward success regarding this focus area.

Phase 4:   Faculty have met this focus area in spirit but are working on quality of the application.

Phase 5:   Faculty have met this focus area in spirit and application.

After completing all the end-of-chapter evaluations and determining phases for each focus area, it is important to regroup the data by phases and then by chapters or sections. For example, the team could decide to focus on all the areas that are rated Phase 1 as a way to prioritize their work.

Many school and district administrators report confusion about how to connect their student demographic data and school achievement data with their school mission, staff development plan, teacher retention issues, and so on. Data seminars typically only connect student achievement data with standards and curricular alignment, often resulting in more segregated programs to "fix" the problem. Over time, such a process only serves to create a large division and more student failure (as described in Chapter 1). For example, often school personnel collect data on student performance and then disaggregate the subpopulations and determine that students of African American ethnicity and those receiving free and reduced lunches are performing lower in achievement than their same-age white counterparts. Often, educators then develop new programs and other separate supports for the students who are low achieving. The problem with this scenario is twofold. First, the low-achieving students are viewed as defective, requiring special resources to fix them, while the institution as a whole is not questioned. Second, schools continue to perpetuate the cycle of oppression and status quo, with the positive intent of increasing student achievement. In contrast, through this book and the formative analyses at the end of each chapter, school teams can recreate school structures in support of high student achievement for all students. School leaders must move forward in the development of Integrated Comprehensive Service delivery practices and away from the "slot and block" program method that has done nothing but generate more students in need. Moving toward ICS will assist in reducing the number of students who are educated separately from our public school arena in the name of nondiscrimination. In so doing, we will increase the number of school graduates who feel a sense of belonging to our greater society as a result of high-quality Integrated Comprehensive Services and instructional practices. In Chapter 1, we explain in detail what we mean by Integrated Comprehensive Services and why changes in service delivery are vitally necessary.

Elise

Sydney and Addyson, may you grow in a world where children are not marginalized to the periphery of our educational institutions to receive individualized instruction and support.

I love you.

Colleen

I dedicate this book to all the students in my courses, all my dissertation advisees over the years, and the educators in schools and agencies across the country with whom I have worked, who know in their hearts the ways our practices marginalize students, who steadfastly refuse to accept that that is the way it has to be, and who get up every day with courage and hope that they can and are making a difference. Blessed be.

CORNERSTONE 1

Core Principles: Focusing on Equity

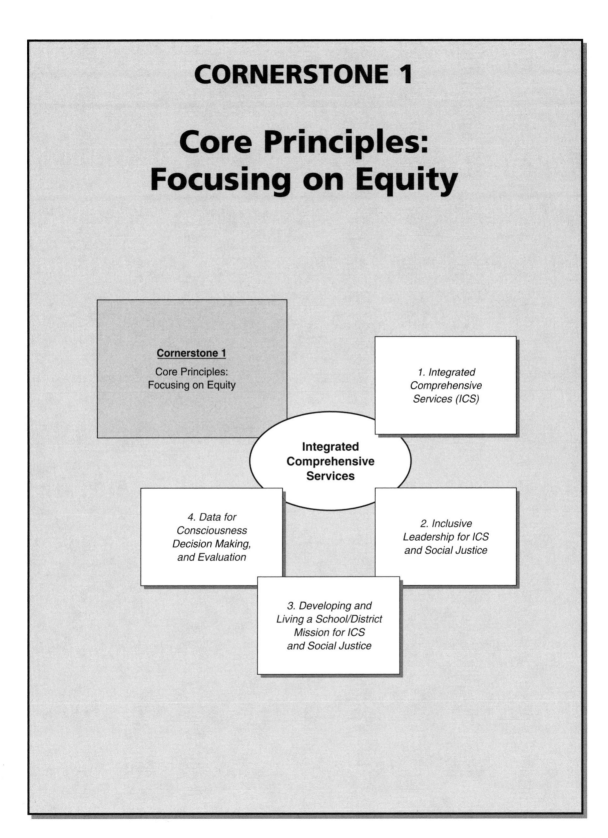

Cornerstone 1
Core Principles:
Focusing on Equity

1. Integrated Comprehensive Services (ICS)

Integrated Comprehensive Services

4. Data for Consciousness Decision Making, and Evaluation

2. Inclusive Leadership for ICS and Social Justice

3. Developing and Living a School/District Mission for ICS and Social Justice

Integrated Comprehensive Services (ICS)

Throughout the past decade, the research and literature on inclusive education has increased significantly (Peterson & Hittie, 2003). This literature predominantly positions the unit of analysis at the classroom level. For example, many researchers have focused their attention on the social and academic outcomes of integrated education (Peterson & Hittie, 2003; Rea, McLaughlin, & Walther-Thomas, 2002), on collaborative teaching arrangements (Thousand, Villa, & Nevin, 2002), on the role of paraprofessionals (Doyle, 2002), on including students with disabilities in district and state assessments (Thurlow, Elliot, & Ysseldyke, 1998), or on ways to integrate curriculum (Rainforth & Kugelmass, 2003). Others have offered a conceptual and ideological analysis of the literature in support of or against inclusive education (Brantlinger, 1997). However, literature that focuses specifically on the role of school leaders with students who typically struggle (Riehl, 2000), or organizational, structural, and cultural conditions necessary for inclusion, is significantly less comprehensive. Even book-length works whose titles suggest a focus on whole-school restructuring to serve students (e.g., Sailor, 2002) do not address the school- or district-level organizational and structural implementation intricacies of serving students in heterogeneous classrooms. Exceptions to this include work by Burrello, Lashley, and Beatty (2000); Capper et al. (2000); and McLeskey and Waldron (2000). However, this literature focuses primarily on students with disability labels and does not take into account how providing services for such students is similar to and different from addressing the needs of other students who may struggle in school, such as students for whom English is not their primary language, students considered "at-risk," students considered gifted, or students with lower reading levels.

The recent comprehensive school reform (CSR) models by design come closest to taking such a whole-school approach to raising the academic achievement of all students (Borman, Hewes, Overman, & Brown, 2003); however, even CSR does not specifically address the needs of students with disabilities. Though this literature explains how lower achieving students can experience academic success, the research does not articulate how students with disability labels have experienced similar success, nor do we know from this literature to what extent students with disabilities are included in heterogeneous class environments in these models of reform. In addition, none of the CSR models make disability the focus.

The purpose of this book is to address this gap in the literature by taking each school as the unit of analysis, and focusing on specific school-level organizational conditions necessary for schools to deliver what we call *Integrated Comprehensive Services* (ICS) in heterogeneous environments for all learners. Integrated environments are the settings that all students, regardless of need or legislative eligibility, access throughout their day in school and nonschool settings. That is, in these settings (e.g., classroom, playground, library, field trips), students with a variety of needs and gifts learn together in both small and large groups. Comprehensive services refer to the array of services and supports, centered in a differentiated curriculum and instruction, that all students receive to ensure academic and behavioral success. By all learners, we mean especially to include those learners who have been designated to receive services such as those labeled with a disability or labeled at-risk, gifted, low readers, or English language learners (ELL).

We will first address why changes in service delivery are vitally necessary, pointing to the current status of special education, including the growing incidence of students labeled with disabilities, the historically poor school and post-school outcomes of special education efforts, and the enormous outlay of financial and other resources into activities with such poor outcomes. We follow this with a description of the differences between providing programs for students and bringing services to students via ICS, and the principles that should guide the delivery of educational services to all students. What we mean by service delivery are the ways in which students are provided educational services, including curriculum, instruction, assessments, and any additional supportive services that are necessary for the student to be successful in heterogeneous learning environments.

OUTCOMES OF SEGREGATED PROGRAMS

The number of students labeled with a disability has increased 151% since 1989 (Ysseldyke, 2001). In addition, students of color are significantly overidentified for and overrepresented in special education (Donovan & Cross, 2002; Hosp & Reschly, 2002; Losen & Orfield, 2002; Quality Counts, 2004; Zhang & Katsiyannis, 2002). Unfortunately, these students often spend the largest part of their day away from their classroom receiving special instruction, resulting in a disconnected and fragmented school day (Capper et al., 2000). Moreover, these special programs have failed to result in high student achievement as measured by postschool outcomes or standardized scores. For example, in the United States, despite extensive efforts at providing special education for more than 25 years since the implementation of federal disability law, 22% of students with disability labels fail to complete high school, compared to 9% of students without labels (National Organization on Disability, 2000). For a more specific example, in one Midwestern state, 13.8% of students with disability labels drop out, compared to 8.2% without labels (Wisconsin Department of Public Instruction, 2005). Of these students, 50% of those who are labeled with emotional disturbance drop out. In addition, 21.7% of students with learning disabilities, 25% of students labeled for speech/language issues, 24.9% of students with mental retardation, and 9.5% of students with autism all fail to complete high school. Further, 11.68% of students with disability labels are suspended, compared to 5.15% of students without labels (Wisconsin Department of Public Instruction, 2005).

Equally alarming are the poor long-term outcomes of these special education efforts. For example, according to a study by Blackorby and Wagner (1996), "nearly 1 in 5 youth with disabilities out of school 3 to 5 years still was not employed and was not looking for work," while 69% of students from the general population over that same period of time were employed (pp. 402–403). After providing special education to students for at least 18 years in public schools and in many cases for 21 years as mandated by the special education law, these school and postschool outcomes are indeed dismal.

Not only are the special education outcomes dismal, the amount of money educators have put forth to support these failing efforts is staggering. Special education in special programs costs 130% more than general education. That is, if a school district spends $5,000 per student, then each student labeled for special programs costs districts $11,500 (Odden & Picus, 2000). In the 1999–2000 school year, "the 50 states and the District of Columbia spent approximately $50 billion on special education services, amounting to $8,080 per special education student" (Chambers,

Parrish, & Harr, 2002, p. v). In comparison, in 1998, total instructional expenditures for students at the elementary/middle school level who are served in the general education classroom was $3,920 (Chambers, Parrish, Lieberman, & Wolman, 1998).

Relatedly, the more students are served in restrictive, segregated placements, the higher the cost of the education. For example, Capper et al. (2000) note that

> if we serve students with disability labels 25% to 60% outside the regular class, then the cost for this education increases to $5,122. If we provide a program for these students in a separate public facility, like many charter and alternative schools, then the cost increases to $6,399 per student. (pp. 7–8)

That is, the data clearly show that the more students are segregated from their peers for instruction, the more costly is that instruction. The reason for this is that "a separate program means that students often require separate space, separate materials and infrastructure, a separate teacher, and an administrator not only to manage the program but also to spend time and money on organizing the program" (Capper et al., 2000, p. 7).

Though separate alternative and charter schools are quite costly, as of January 2004, a total of 1,996 charter schools were operating across the United States (see http://www.uscharterschools.org). Just as separate programs within public schools track disproportionate numbers of students of color and lower income students into these programs (see Capper & Young, in press), charter schools suffer the same problem. For example, these charter schools

> enrolled higher percentages of Black and Hispanic students as well as lower percentages of White students than traditional public schools. A higher percentage of these charter schools than traditional public schools had more than 75 percent enrollment as well as more than 75 percent of students eligible for free or reduced-price lunch. (National Center for Education Statistics, 2004)

Similarly, during the 2000–2001 school year, 10,900 public alternative schools and programs for so-called "at-risk" students were in operation, and 59% of these programs were housed in a separate facility (National Center for Education Statistics [NCES], 2004, p. 33). Districts with high percentages of students of color and low-income students tended to have higher enrollments in alternative schools (NCES, 2004, p. 33).

Moreover, educators spend an inordinate amount of time and resources deciding exactly for which program a student may qualify. In the Verona (Wisconsin) school district in 1999, "it cost more than $2,000 to evaluate one student to determine eligibility for special education. [In this case,] a district of 4,500 students averages 225 (5%) evaluations per year for a total of $443,713 spent on evaluations alone" (Capper et al., 2000, p. 7).

According to the U.S. Department of Education (2000), "Slightly under half [of students with disability labels] between the ages of six and seventeen are served in general education settings with their [typical] peers for more than 89% of their school day . . . and the number of students served in general education classrooms is increasing each year" (cited in Causton-Theoharis, 2003, p. 7), due in part to the Individuals with Disabilities Act (IDEA) 1997, which created "a legal presumption in favor of regular class placement" (Huefner, 2000, p. 242, cited in Causton-Theoharis, 2003, pp. 6–7). Research suggests that educating students in these general education environments results in higher academic achievement and more positive social outcomes for students with and without disability labels (McLeskey & Waldron, 2000; see Peterson & Hittie, 2003, pp. 37–39 for additional studies; Rea, McLaughlin, & Walther-Thomas, 2002), not to mention that it is the most cost-effective way to educate students.

In sum, more students are being labeled with disabilities, due in large part to the failure of the education system. Though more of these students are being educated in heterogeneous educational environments than in previous years, increasingly students who are labeled "at-risk" are being placed in segregated, alternative classrooms and schools. Many students are not served in their neighborhood schools (or the school they would attend if they did not have the disability or other program label) and spend large parts of their days out of the general education classroom. Not only are these practices failing to meet the needs of these students, resulting in significantly high percentages of students dropping out of school or not being employed after secondary education, but these practices also exact an exorbitant financial toll on schools and districts.

To overcome these costly, dismal outcomes of segregated programs, school leaders (i.e., principals, school-based steering committees, site councils, etc.) must focus their efforts on preventing student struggle and must change how students who struggle are educated. In so doing, fewer students will be inappropriately labeled with disability or educational at-risk labels, and more students will be educated in heterogeneous learning environments, resulting in higher student achievement and more promising post-school outcomes.

Placing students in special programs is quite the opposite of providing services to students (i.e., ICS). The two approaches differ in the following ways: core principles, location, educators/staff, curriculum and instruction, and funding (see Table 1.1). In our work with educators across the country and with our students, we also hear persistent assumptions about the factors that inhibit change toward ICS. As we describe the differences between special programs and ICS, we will also identify these assumptions and describe the evidence-based practices that refute them.

Table 1.1 Differences Between Segregated Programs and Integrated Comprehensive
Services (ICS)

Segregated Programs	Persistent Assumptions That Inhibit Change	Integrated Comprehensive Services
Core Principles: Focusing on Equity		
• Source of student failure is student, hence student needs to be fixed to fit the system		• Source of student failure is the system, hence system needs to accommodate the student
• Students not helped until after they fail		• Primary aim of teaching and learning is prevention of student failure • Primary aim of all educators is building teacher capacity
• Overlooks individual needs, slots student into "program"	• Administratively easier to plug a student into an existing program, than to creatively plan how to best meet a student's needs	• Student needs met on an individual basis
Equitable Structures: Location		
• Separates students either at the classroom level, or forces students to attend a school they would not attend if they did not have a label	• More cost effective to cluster students with similar labels in schools and then bus them to those schools • Easier on staff if students with similar labels are clustered in schools and classrooms • Educators can provide individual attention and support only in a setting or situation separate from the student's peers	• Students receive services with neighborhood peers or school of choice. (They do not have to go someplace else in the district or in the school to receive support.)
• Fragments a student's day by moving from location to location to receive support		• No rooms/schools set aside for labeled students (e.g., LD, ED, special education resource, ESL, at-risk)

Segregated Programs	Persistent Assumptions That Inhibit Change	Integrated Comprehensive Services
Location (cont.) • Prevents transfer of educator and student knowledge • Students homogeneously grouped by like categories (LD, CD, ESL, etc.) • Tracks and marginalizes students of color and lower social class students • Students segregated with those with similar labels for extended periods of time • Students move in homogeneous groups from class to class		• Flexible grouping patterns used throughout day depending on content and student needs (i.e., 1:1 or small or large group)
Access to High-Quality Teaching and Learning: Building Staff Capacity and Educator Roles		
• Staff adhere to their professional, expert roles • Staff develop territories and "program identification" (e.g., "my kids, my at-risk program, my specialty")	• Certification in a specialty area means that the person has some magical skills that no one else can ever learn • What specialist teachers do (ESL, special ed., GT) is something other than good teaching • If staff who are not professionally certified to support students succeed in doing so, it undermines the professionalism of staff and threatens job security	• Requires teachers/staff to share knowledge and expertise with each other and with students • Staff are organized by the needs of each learner • Staff build each other's capacity to work with a range of students
Access to High-Quality Teaching and Learning: Curriculum and Instruction		
• Separate from the core teaching and learning of the school	• If students fail, it is the students' fault	• Supports and builds on culturally relevant, differentiated curriculum and instruction

Table 1.1 (Continued)

Segregated Programs	Persistent Assumptions That Inhibit Change	Integrated Comprehensive Services
Curriculum and Instruction (cont.) • Requires students to be identified and labeled for them to receive help • Students denied access to content-based instruction, which adversely affects performance on standardized assessments • Instructional techniques developed using group norm rather than individual goals and objectives • Instruction often driven by available supports, classes, and instructional resources	• Core teaching and learning need not or cannot be changed • Schools are incapable of changing to meet student needs	• Based on principle of universal access— curriculum is differentiated to address range of needs instead of developed and then adapted after the fact • Students do not have to qualify or be labeled to receive a curriculum and instruction that meet their needs
• Requires students to be identified and labeled to get "help"	• Special education teachers cannot support students who do not have labels • Educators are incapable of differentiating curriculum and instruction	• Students do not have to be qualified for nor labeled to receive an education that meets their needs
Implementing Change: Funding		
• Separate funding and resources focused on fixing student deficits • Separate policies that are compliance, not quality driven • Separate programs are costly due to replication of staff and materials	• We cannot merge funds and resources • The problem is with students	• Funding and resources are merged to build teacher and system capacity with a focus on prevention of student struggle • Policies are unified around all learners in a proactive/supportive manner

CORE PRINCIPLES: FOCUSING ON EQUITY

One core principle of segregated special programs is that students do not receive help for their learning needs until after they fail in some way. This practice is akin to parking an ambulance at the bottom of a cliff to assist people who fall off the cliff. Special programs are the ambulance at the bottom of the cliff. Students are placed in them after they fail, academically, socially, or behaviorally.

In contrast, with ICS, the primary aim of teaching and learning in the school is prevention of student failure. Referring again to the analogy above, ICS works at the top of the cliff, setting up supports that not only prevent students from falling off the cliff, but also keep them from nearing the

**Core Principles:
Focusing on Equity**

- Source of student failure is the system, hence the system needs to accommodate the student
- Primary goal of education is to prevent student failure
- Seamlessly tied to and grounded in core teaching and learning
- Considers the range of learners within every classroom and across the grades

**Access to High-Quality
Teaching and Learning:
Building Teacher Capacity**

- Requires teachers and staff to share knowledge and expertise with each other and with students
- Staff are organized by the needs of each learner
- Staff build each other's capacity to work with a range of students

**Access to High-Quality
Teaching and Learning:
Curriculum and Instruction**

- Supports and builds on culturally relevant differentiated curriculum and instruction
- Based on principle of universal access—curriculum is differentiated for needs of all students versus developed and then adapted after the fact
- Students do not have to qualify or be labeled to receive an education that meets their needs

**Equitable Structures:
Location and Arrangement of
Educational Services**

- Students receive services with neighborhood peers or at school of choice (they do not have to go someplace else in district or in school to get services)
- No rooms/schools that are set aside for labeled kids (e.g., LD, ED, special education resource, ESL, at-risk, discipline schools)
- Flexible grouping patterns used throughout day depending on individual needs of students and content
- Flexible configurations of learning are used for all learners throughout the day (1:1, or small or large group)
- Students are not segregated and slotted into silos to receive services

**Implementing Change:
Funding and Policy**

- Funding and resources merged to build teacher and system capacity with focus on prevention of student struggle
- Policies are unified around all learners in a proactive and supportive manner and leveraged toward ICS and social justice

Figure 1.1   Cornerstone Details of ICS

cliff in the first place. It is astounding to us how so few educational practices are considered preventative. One activity we conduct in our graduate leadership preparation classes is to have students map out their response to this question: "What happens in your school or classroom when a student struggles, academically, socially, or behaviorally? What are all the practices in place to address this?" Invariably, students easily list a wide range of "ambulances" numbering up to a couple of dozen even in small schools and districts. The list includes items such as homework club, learning centers, peer tutors, adult volunteers, Title 1 reading, Reading Recovery, school-within-a-school programs, small-group tutoring, Saturday morning remedial club, summer school, calling parents, in and out of school suspension, and the list goes on. Then, we ask our students to list all the actions their school or districts take to prevent student academic or behavioral failure or struggle in the first place. This request is usually followed by several minutes of quiet, as such efforts do not readily come to students' minds. Finally, students will list a few practices such as focused, intensive reading instruction in the early grades or differentiating instruction.

According to Deschenes, Cuban, and Tyack (2001), historically, public schools have dealt with student failure in similar ways—blaming the student, or factors beyond the school (e.g., families, communities, and so forth; see Valencia, 1997, on deficit theory). With ICS, the onus of student failure is on the school, and any student failure is viewed as something that is askew in the educational system. The way educators frame student failure (i.e., whether student failure is seen as a student or a systems issue) is the pivot point of all the remaining assumptions and practices in schools.

As such, the primary aim of ICS is the prevention of student failure, and student failure is prevented by building teacher capacity to be able to teach to a range of diverse student strengths and needs, a second core principle. Every single decision about service delivery must be premised on the extent to which that decision will increase the capacity of all teachers to teach to a range of students' diverse learning needs. Segregated special programs, by definition, diminish teacher capacity. When the same student or group of students is routinely removed from the classroom to receive instruction elsewhere, the classroom teacher is released from responsibility for learning how to teach not only those students, but all future students with similar needs over the rest of that teacher's career. At the same time, students with and without special needs are denied the opportunity to learn and work with each other, while the students who leave the room are denied a sense of belonging in the classroom.

A third core principle of separate programs is that these efforts do not address individual student needs. Instead, students are made to fit into yet another program. Even the language used often reflects this idea. That is, we use language such as, "we need to program for this student." "We held a meeting to program for this student." "We can place the student in the CD program." "That school houses the ED program." The forcing of students to fit into a program is a supreme irony of programs that are created under the assumption that students do not fit into general education, hence they need something unique and individual, but are then required to fit into yet another program. A persistent assumption with this principle is that it is administratively easier to plug a student into an existing program than to creatively plan how to best meet a student's academic or behavioral needs (both of which are mandated in special education legislation).

When educators in a school have made significant progress toward restructuring based on ICS principles, one practical way to avoid placing students in prepackaged programs and to meet individual student needs can take place in IEP meetings. In these meetings, practitioners who are working toward dismantling segregated programs and moving to ICS have found it helpful to assume that no separate programs exist in their schools. They ask themselves the question, if no such program existed, how would we best meet this student's needs? And how can that decision ultimately build teacher capacity?

In addition to the core principals that distinguish ICS from segregated programs, these two different models of service delivery also differ from each other based on location—where students are taught—curriculum and instruction, staff roles, and funding. We discuss these next.

EQUITABLE STRUCTURES: LOCATION AND ARRANGEMENT OF EDUCATIONAL SERVICES

Location, where students are physically placed to learn, is a central distinction between segregated programs and ICS. Under a segregated program model, educators believe that the primary reason for student failure is the student him- or herself, that students cannot be helped until they fail and receive a label of some sort (e.g., at-risk, disability, low reader), and then the student is placed into a separate program that is removed from the core teaching and learning of the school or tracked into lower ability classes. These beliefs and practices require students to be separated from their peers either by requiring students to leave the general education classroom to attend a pullout program, to enroll in lower level or tracked classes at the high school level, or to attend a school not in their neighborhood or a school they would not attend if they did not have a special label.

Further, students with a particular label are "clustered" in a classroom or program in numbers greater than their proportion in the school.

In the case of students with disabilities, typically a special education teacher is then assigned to support the students in this classroom and perhaps two to three other classrooms where students with disabilities are clustered. In one high school we studied, students considered "at-risk" were all placed in the same "transition" English and "transition" Math classes their freshman year, taught by a "transition" teacher in a "transition" room. In the case of ELL students, they are often clustered together and assigned a bilingual or ESL teacher for nearly their entire day.

The problem with clustering students is that often special education or student services staff are assigned to the students with labels in these classrooms. Though the special education or student services staff may assist other students in the classroom without labels, his or her primary role is student support. That is, in a segregated, clustering arrangement, the primary goal is student support, not building the capacity of general education teachers to teach to a range of students. The result of such an arrangement is that students with labels and the general education teacher become increasingly dependent on the student services staff. Including students with their peers is dependent on the presence of these staff. In nearly every situation we have studied, because of budget cuts, student services staff time in these classrooms must be reduced, and general education teachers then claim that they cannot fully meet the needs of students with labels in their classrooms. This occurs especially in coteaching models, where a special education and general education teacher are assigned to coteach a class or course together—arguably one of the most common (and most expensive) practices in schools today.

In addition to educator convenience, segregated practices persist because many educators believe it is more cost effective to cluster students with similar labels in particular classrooms or particular schools. Research cited previously in this chapter refutes this belief. Moreover, this particular administrative arrangement makes little sense with the current federal support for cross-categorical services. That is, now state departments of education are issuing special education teaching licenses for teachers to be able to teach across categories because these teachers are expected to be able to teach to a range of student needs. Thus, no longer can school districts use the argument that only certain teachers can provide the needed support for particular students.

Moreover, with segregated programs, educators persistently assume that they can provide individual attention and support to students with labels only in a setting or situation separate from a student's peers. Reasons for this assumption include several arguments—for example, that a middle school student would feel embarrassed to receive speech articulation training in front of his or her peers, or that if elementary students require intensive reading instruction, then this instruction demands a separate setting, like a Title I or Reading Recovery room. Educators reason that this saves students the embarrassment of reading in front of their more able peers and that a separate room cuts down on classroom distractions. To be sure, it may be appropriate at times when a student who requires assistance with, for example, speech articulation could benefit from individual instruction outside of the classroom that does not disrupt his or her school day. At the same time, when schools and classrooms function with teams of diverse educators in support of flexible groupings, a student's need for one-on-one instruction is part of the general movement of the day and does not force the student to be the only one exiting the classroom, for example, during science class. In the reading example, at the elementary level, successful teachers are able to meet the individual needs of students without those students needing to leave the room.

At the middle school and high school level, teachers are often faced with students with low reading levels who may need intensive reading instruction. A computer-assisted reading program such as Read 180 may be used in such cases (see www.teacher.scholastic.com/products/read180). However, following ICS principles, students must be allowed to choose to access this course or class, and should not unilaterally be placed in it. In addition, under ICS, students who receive this instruction are not assigned to it based on their label. That is, educators should not assign "all students who are LD" or "all seventh-grade students who are at-risk in reading" to programs like Read 180. Instead, students should be able to volunteer to participate in the program, whether they have a label or not, which will result in a heterogeneous group of students receiving such instruction based on student need, not labels. This group of students who participate in Read 180 should be dispersed throughout the school rather than assigned to other classes together (e.g., all assigned to take the same science class, etc.). Grouping these students in the same classes would effectively create tracking, with all the lower readers grouped together throughout the day.

Referring again to our high school example, another way that educators attempt to raise student reading levels is to assign low-reading students to the same language arts class as freshmen. To illustrate, educators at one high school placed all these students together in a freshman "transition" language arts class. With good intention, these educators believed that in so doing, they would be able to use curriculum materials suited to the reading levels of these students and in turn, raise their English achievement, enabling these students to be integrated with their peers after their freshman year. However, this example is counter to ICS principles because it is segregating and grouping students by ability, creating a lower track for these students. We do know that teachers in highly successful schools that use ICS principles are able to effectively teach language arts and other subjects to a range of different learners in heterogeneous classrooms (see Jorgensen, 1998).

Ironically, under segregated program assumptions, we have seen inclusive practices evolve into another segregated program—i.e., the segregation of inclusion. Segregated inclusion happens when students with disabilities are disproportionately assigned to, or clustered in, particular classrooms. For example, in a school with four third-grade classrooms, students with disabilities are clustered into one or two of these classrooms, resulting in a higher percentage of students with disabilities in these classrooms than their percentage in the school. Some educators argue that these practices are legitimate because it then becomes more convenient for special education staff to support students across fewer classrooms. We have witnessed educators in these schools calling these "the inclusive classrooms" and the students with disabilities in these classrooms "inclusion students." In so doing, these classrooms and students, under the guise of inclusion, inherit yet another set of labels. These educators reason that if a practice is more convenient for staff, then students will receive higher quality services in these segregated arrangements. Unfortunately, in the schools we have studied, while clustering students may be more convenient for staff, this model does not build teacher capacity. That is, although the "inclusion" and "transition" teachers increase their capacity to teach to a range of students, all the other teachers in the school are "off the hook," with no incentive to gain these skills, resulting in higher costs and less effectiveness in the long run.

In contrast, under ICS, all students attend their neighborhood school or the school they would attend if they did not have a label. This is a basic civil right. Students do not have to leave their peers in their classroom, school, or district to participate in a curriculum and instruction that meets their learning needs. All students are then afforded a rich schedule of flexible small-group and large-group instruction based on learning needs, interest, and content areas. With ICS at the district level, particular schools would not be designated the "ESL school" or "the school where all the elementary students with severe disabilities attend" or "the middle school that houses the students with severe challenging behaviors." At the school level, ICS does allow students with labels to be clustered in particular classrooms, but only to the extent that their numbers in any one classroom do not represent a higher percentage than what is found in the school as a whole. Accordingly, with ICS, a school does not have rooms labeled or even used as the "Resource Room," "LD Room," the "CD Room," the "ESL Room," or the "At-Risk Room." With ICS, students are flexibly grouped based on the individual needs of the learners in that particular classroom and grade.

With ICS, all student learning takes place in heterogeneous environments. This means that students are not grouped by similar characteristics in the same way all the time. Teachers use flexible grouping patterns throughout the day depending on the instructional content and student needs. Hence, when a group of students travels on a field trip, it should not just be those with disabilities or students who are "at-risk" who are attending. Nor should it just be students without labels who go on the trip. The leader will look at any situation and always ask if there is a mix of students involved, and if not, why not.

Under ICS, students are placed in classes according to their natural proportions in the school. For example, if ELL students comprise 20% of a school population, then any classroom in that school (e.g., special education) should be composed of no more than 20% of students who are ELLs. Similarly, if students with disabilities comprise 15% of the school population, then no classroom should have more than 15% of its students labeled with a disability. Likewise, using these same numbers and the principle of natural proportions, at least 20% of the student council, 20% of the band and other extracurricular activities, and 20% of the advanced placement courses or gifted programs should be composed of ELL students, while 15% of these same curricular and extracurricular areas should be composed of students with disabilities.

To further illustrate, in one integrated middle school we studied, students who are ELLs were clustered in two of the four seventh- and eighth-grade classrooms. However, the percentage of ELL students in these classrooms was less than their percentage in the school. Under ICS, in the high school example, instead of clustering students into a freshman transition class, students in need of additional support are dispersed among the freshman English classes. When students are placed in natural proportions, it sets the expectation that all school staff can successfully teach all students with a wide range of academic skills in their classrooms. The goal of support staff is to initially support students in these settings, but ultimately to build the general educator capacity to teach to a range of student abilities. Over time, one goal of support staff is to gradually reduce their involvement in the classroom because the general classroom teacher has strengthened his or her teaching and learning strategies to meet the diverse range of student needs.

We cannot overemphasize the critical role that location—where students are placed—plays in ICS. As long as segregated settings, classrooms, courses, and schools exist, educators will find reasons to place students in these settings. With segregated programs, these settings reinforce negative assumptions about students and teaching and learning, and not only does this model not build teacher capacity, it also breeds teacher and student dependency. Even more important, segregated programs are the most expensive and least effective way to serve students (see discussion earlier in this chapter). ICS becomes a proactive means to break the vicious cycle of negative beliefs that require segregated programs that in turn reinforce negative assumptions and beliefs. The core principles of ICS suggest that the system needs to adapt to the student; that the primary aim of teaching and learning is the prevention of student failure; that the aim of all educators is to build teacher capacity; that all services must be grounded in the core teaching and learning of the school; and that, to accomplish this, students must be educated alongside their peers in integrated environments. Student location dictates teacher location, and the location of teachers and students in integrated environments lays the groundwork for all the other aspects of ICS.

ACCESS TO HIGH-QUALITY TEACHING AND LEARNING: BUILDING TEACHER CAPACITY

Educator roles in segregated programs are based on teacher specialization and student labels. In segregated programs, staff adhere to their professional, expert roles, which limits adult learning opportunities and professional growth. Moreover, when structures isolate students, they also isolate educators. When educators are isolated from each other, they do not share knowledge and expertise, precluding the development of teacher expertise across a range of learners. For example, in one urban high school we studied, support staff in a program model were comfortable teaching segregated math and adapted language arts classes but were hesitant to provide support in general education classes in math because they were unsure of their ability to do so. Therefore, students with needs were placed in segregated math classes due to the teaching abilities (or lack thereof) of staff and denied a rich curriculum in the regular math content classes. Subsequently, students performed quite poorly on the math section of the statewide accountability assessment.

A persistent assumption that fuels this adherence to expert roles is a belief that certification in a specialty area means that an educator possesses highly specialized, "magical," esoteric skills that no one else can ever learn. Professional associations and accreditation or certification bodies reinforce this expert view. (For a complete history of how the professions reinforce segregation, see Skrtic, 1995.) For example, in segregated programs, a social worker can be the only person who conducts personal history reviews with students and makes contacts with families, and no other staff person volunteers or is assigned to share in those duties. Likewise, a middle school guidance counselor provides career guidance to individuals and groups of students, facilitates support groups for students, and meets individually with students who have various problems. Rarely do other staff members share these duties.

If, in such segregated programs, other staff not certified in these areas were to assume some of these duties, the social worker or guidance counselor would view these persons as undermining his or her professionalism and perhaps even threatening the person's job security. In addition, with these assigned duties, neither the social worker nor the guidance counselor is involved in the core curriculum and instruction of the school. In this context, professional development is often targeted to particular staff (i.e., all special education staff), while others are excused, which further segregates staff from each other and prevents the sharing of expertise.

In contrast, with ICS, in one middle school we studied, the roles and responsibilities of the guidance counselor and school social workers were drastically changed. One guidance counselor was assigned to support the sixth grade and the other was assigned to the eighth grade, while the social worker was assigned to the seventh grade. The roles of the guidance counselor and social workers changed to include the following tasks: home visits; door duty; readmitting of students; representation on all special education team meetings; support staff; collecting and disseminating data on achievement, attendance, and behavior; handling all special education reevaluations; teaching units on identity (e.g., race, ethnicity, etc.) and bullying; coordinating of interns; and coordinating mentoring with local high school students. These roles and shared expertise, tied to the core curriculum and instruction, stand in great contrast to what occurs in segregated programs.

Location, defined as where students are assigned, and staff roles, are inextricably linked. In segregated programs, the limited expertise of staff contributes to where students are placed, and where students are placed limits the expertise of staff. All students require small- and large-group instruction, and at times, one-on-one instruction is needed for a student with more severe needs; however, rather than expecting students with educational or behavioral needs to leave the classroom to receive instruction, ICS requires educators to share their knowledge across disciplines (e.g., special education, bilingual education, behavior management, reading), with their peers and with the students they teach, in a range of educational environments.

As such, with ICS, staff roles pivot around developing teacher capacity to teach a range of learners in their classrooms. Given that only 21% of teachers feel well prepared to address the needs of labeled students (U.S. Department of Education, 2000), building teacher capacity becomes the primary goal in ICS. All staff development and all decisions about service delivery are aimed toward building staff capacity to work with a range of student needs.

ACCESS TO HIGH-QUALITY TEACHING AND LEARNING: CURRICULUM AND INSTRUCTION

In segregated programs, the curriculum and instruction is separate from the core teaching and learning in the school. For some programs, at one end of the spectrum, if a student is failing, it is assumed that the curriculum and instruction did not succeed with a student; hence, the student needs an entirely different curriculum and instruction. Again, the assumption made is that the school curriculum does not need to change, that it works for most students, and that there is something inherently different about some students who thus need something entirely different. Moreover, this principle assumes that staff are incapable of teaching to a range of students, that schools are incapable of changing to meet student needs, and that students who struggle and who then are removed from the classroom for a special curriculum are more alike as a group than they are different. Segregated programs also assume that students need to be identified and labeled to access a curriculum that meets their needs. In so doing, these programs deny student access to a content-rich curriculum—a curriculum that is necessary for significant achievement gains (Peterson & Hittie, 2003). Thus, given the lack of achievement for students with disabilities and students who are ELL and the post-school outcomes cited earlier in this chapter, we know that these separate programs are not effective (Peterson & Hittie, 2003). In separate programs, instruction is based on the classroom majority rather than on individual needs. Alternative schools, whether within schools or out of school buildings, are often created based on this principle. Students who receive "specialized" math, English, or other academic subjects in resource rooms, or in classrooms tracked using a homogeneous purpose, are also supported by this principle of teaching to the majority.

At the other end of the spectrum, special education staff assist students who struggle by helping them learn the general curriculum, but this learning takes place outside the general education classroom, in resource rooms, study centers, or study halls. It could be argued that these practices are not really separate from the core teaching and learning of the school. However, again, these practices typically do not build teacher capacity to teach to a range of students. Though students are assisted, support staff typically do not share ideas with classroom teachers who then do not learn new strategies that would prevent students from needing additional assistance in the first place. In contrast, in ICS, students receive their instruction with their peers in large and small, flexible, heterogeneous groups in integrated school and community settings and are supported to do so. As such, ICS is seamlessly tied to and grounded in the core curriculum and instruction of the school.

In ICS, the curriculum and instruction are built on a culturally relevant (Ladson-Billings, 1995) and differentiated curriculum (Tomlinson, 2001). A culturally relevant curriculum addresses the various families, cultures, races, and ethnicities of students in the classroom, not as added components, but as seamlessly woven into the curriculum. Differentiated curriculum means it is designed to address a range of learner needs and achievement levels within the classroom. Such a curriculum is developed under the principle of *universal access* (Bremer, Clapper, Hitchcock, Hall, & Kachgal, 2002), meaning that a lesson is initially designed for a range of learner needs in the classroom, rather than developing a lesson or curriculum, then deciding as an afterthought how students with different learning needs may access that curriculum. With these principles, students do not have to be tracked into high-level classes to receive access to a rich and engaging curriculum.

IMPLEMENTING CHANGE: FUNDING AND POLICY

In segregated programs, separate funding sources are accessed and policies are written to support each program for each eligibility area, causing replication of services and soaring costs. These policies and programs are focused on fixing student deficits. Often, policies are compliance driven and not quality driven, resulting in meeting the letter of many nondiscrimination regulations but never reaching the spirit in which the regulations were written. As discussed previously, separate programs are expensive due to the costs involved in identifying students and the duplication of staff and materials between and across schools and programs.

Educators persistently assume that particular funds or resources cannot be comingled, and this only reinforces the creation of segregated programs. For example, in one of the high schools we studied, educators established a learning center that any student could access throughout the day to receive additional support. The center included processes to enable teachers assisting in the center to provide feedback to students' teachers on effective strategies to help students in the classroom, as well as suggestions for curriculum changes to reduce the number of students who accessed the center. However, the principal was concerned that because students with disability labels also accessed the center, this practice in some way violated special education law or the use of special education funds, which it did not. Hence, he dismantled this service and in its place established a separate support program for students with disabilities.

With ICS, funding sources and policies are merged with a focus on prevention of student struggle. Resource reallocation forms the basis of funding decisions (see Odden & Archibald, 2001). That is, a school leader takes into account sources of funding at the federal, state, district, and school levels (minority student achievement, gifted and talented, alcohol and other drug abuse, special education, Title I, at-risk, bilingual, special education, and so on) and then combines these funds in a way to best serve students in heterogeneous learning environments. Staff are also viewed as resources—staff skills and expertise are considered when placing students—and staff are assigned to students and classrooms based on ICS core principles.

SUMMARY

To summarize, segregated programs result in some students receiving support, while others do not. Students who need the most routine, structure, and consistency in their day experience the most disruptions when placed in separate programs, become fringe members of their classroom community, and miss valuable instructional time when traveling to and from these programs. Once in these separate programs, students are denied access to a rich and engaging curriculum that could boost their academic achievement. Segregated programs inadvertently blame and label students as well as marginalize and track students of color and those of low income. Segregated programs prevent sharing of knowledge and skills by educators, prevent any particular educator from being accountable to these students, and enable educators to not change their instructional, curricular, and assessment practices. The costs involved in identifying students for these programs, as well as the programs themselves, are quite high.

In contrast, the principles and practices of ICS contribute to five non-negotiables for service delivery: they are the least restrictive, least intrusive, least disruptive, least expensive, and least enabling. These five non-negotiables refer to location (where students are placed), the curriculum and instruction they experience, and the role of educators in their lives. All students should have the opportunity to attend their neighborhood school (or preferred school in school choice systems), and be placed in heterogeneous classrooms at their grade level alongside their peers. This placement is the least restrictive, least intrusive, and least disruptive in their daily lives; encourages independence in learning and not being over-helped (i.e., it is the least enabling); and ultimately is the least expensive. The curriculum and instruction they receive in these environments should address their learning needs and, at the same time, open the window to a rich, creative, nonrestrictive learning experience. With ICS, individual learning needs are met in the least intrusive, most respectful, and least disruptive way, and students are challenged to reach their maximum learning potential. A curriculum and instruction that reflects these four non-negotiables is ultimately the least expensive option as well. Finally, with ICS, educators themselves move out of segregated, restrictive teaching environments and provide high-quality curriculum and instruction in ways that tap each learner's gifts (i.e., that are the least intrusive and least disruptive), that foster student self-esteem, and that encourage students' positive sense of self as a learner (are the least enabling). Educators engaged in teaching in this way save district resources that can be reallocated to the benefit of all in the school community. (See Appendix A for a list of questions to determine to what extent a school or district is oriented toward ICS principles and practices.)

Given the high cost of special education in these times of budget crises and the dismal outcomes of segregated programs, educators can no longer ethically justify segregated service delivery. Continuing to label students and place them in segregated programs is indefensible. This is particularly so when these programs are not effective academically and socially and draw resources away from other effective practices. As confirmed by the research, ICS can meet the needs of all students. The core principles, combined with the indisputable importance of location— where students learn—the curriculum, and moving educators out of their traditional roles, all supported by creative reallocation of resources, can pave the way for educational success for all students.

Table 1.2   Chapter 1. Integrated Comprehensive Services (ICS)

Focus Area	Focus Area Inquiry	Comments: What We Have	Phase of Application (See p. xxx)
	Core Principles: Focusing on Equity		
1.	All staff and administration believe that the source of the student failure is the system; hence, the system needs to accommodate the learner.		
2.	All staff and administration believe that the primary goal of schools is to prevent student failure.		
3.	All staff and administration believe that the primary way student failure is prevented is to build teacher capacity to teach to a range of diverse student needs.		
4.	All administration and staff believe that ICS meets individual student needs—students are not slotted into predetermined programs.		
	Equitable Structures: Location and Arrangement of Educational Services		
5.	All students attend their neighborhood school or school of choice.		
6.	No rooms or courses are set aside for students with specific needs (ESL, special education, at-risk). If there are separate rooms or courses for particular labels, how many rooms serve this purpose?		
7.	The district does not have any schools that are set aside for particular students (e.g., ESL schools) or schools for particular categories of disabilities (e.g., students with LD all attend particular schools).		

Focus Area	Focus Area Inquiry	Comments: What We Have	Phase of Application
8.	Students with similar labels or needs are not clustered together in the school for extended periods of time or if so, the percentage of students clustered by label does not exceed their percentage in the school.		
9.	Particular classrooms are not designated "inclusive classrooms" while other classrooms are not labeled this way.		
10.	None of our students who could attend this school are sent to other schools in the district or outside the district. If this is not true, how many are tuitioned out?		
	Access to High-Quality Teaching and Learning: Building Teacher Capacity		
11.	Staff are organized (staff design) based on the needs of each learner in an integrated comprehensive manner.		
12.	All staff value the importance of sharing knowledge and expertise with each other and with students.		
13.	All staff build on each other's capacity to work with a range of students.		
	Access to High-Quality Teaching and Learning: Curriculum and Instruction		
14.	Based on the principle of universal access, curriculum is differentiated by the needs of all students rather than making accommodations after the fact.		
15.	Educational services support and build on culturally relevant differentiated curriculum and instruction.		
16.	Students do not have to qualify for a label to have their needs met.		

(Continued)

Table 1.2 (Continued)

Focus Area	Focus Area Inquiry	Comments: What We Have	Phase of Application
17.	**Curriculum and Instruction (cont.)** Flexible configurations of learning groups are used for all learners throughout the day (1:1, small- and large-group instructional arrangements, etc.).		
	Integrating Change: Funding and Policy		
18.	Funding and resources are merged to build teacher and system capacity with a focus on prevention of student struggle.		
19.	Educating students is based on the five non-negotiables: least restrictive, least intrusive, least disruptive, least expensive, and least enabling.		

Leadership for ICS
and Social Justice

2

As discussed in Chapter 1, children who do not adhere to the PreK–12 academic scope and sequence have been isolated at the margins of our educational system for special services to catch them up, modify their education, and make them fit the norm. If educational leaders and policy developers are not careful with the measurement of student progress as required by federal and state mandates, we will continue to divide and separate our children. The pressures of accountability, compounded by our educational practices of slotting and blocking of those students who do not adequately match the normed group, will only perpetuate the educational failure of the student populace that functions at the academic and behavioral margins. To reverse such an educational practice that continues to perpetuate the status quo in our society requires leadership for ICS and social justice.

Several authors have described characteristics of those who lead for equity, excellence, and social justice (Scheurich & Skrla, 2003, is one example). However, as we discussed in the preface to this book, this literature fails to address the importance of where students learn and the peers with whom they learn. Thus, we will not reiterate these leadership characteristics from the literature. Instead, in this chapter, we focus on the specific kind of leadership required for the successful initiation, implementation, and sustainment of ICS for the benefit of all learners. First, we discuss key characteristics of leaders for ICS and social justice. Then, we discuss how or in what ways these leaders carry out their leadership in schools.

The number one leadership characteristic necessary for ICS is that leaders must believe in their core that students learn best when they are educated in heterogeneous educational settings, period. If the leader does not have this belief, then nothing else really matters. If the leader does not truly believe this, then we see a wide range of contradictions with ICS practices, which are discussed further in this chapter. The second most important leadership characteristic necessary for ICS is that the leader has the knowledge and skills to ensure that this belief is carried out in practice, with absolutely no exceptions—none whatsoever.

To be sure, to implement ICS as an integral aspect of social justice leadership is no small undertaking. Social justice leadership, by its nature, can be rife with complexities and inconsistencies in practice. We are not sure a "true" social justice educational leader exists—that there is a perfect social justice ICS school out there. However, we are aware of schools that have made great strides in these efforts and are continuing to do so. From the leaders of these schools, we draw inspiration and hope.

Here we offer some examples of leadership that does not fully grasp the first core characteristic of ICS—that all students, without exception, deserve to be educated in heterogeneous learning environments. We will draw from these examples to identify additional characteristics of leadership for ICS and social justice.

Our first example is a high school principal who has had great success in addressing the needs of students for whom English is not their first language as well as gay/lesbian/bisexual/transgender youth at his school. In addition, a few of the Advanced Placement courses at his school include students with disability labels. This principal also believes in inclusive education and views himself as a social justice leader. However, in this small, rural high school, nearly 25% of the students have some sort of label such as at-risk, having disabilities, ESL, gifted, and students who attend an alternative school outside the school district. The principal does not fully comprehend the problem with such a high percentage of students being labeled, and thus has not taken steps to reduce this number. The school and district have received a federal grant for their at-risk program, where students are removed from core classes and clustered in at-risk English, math, social studies, and science classes. The district and the principal are proud of their at-risk program.

Moreover, at this same high school, students entering the ninth grade who are considered "at-risk" are clustered together in "transition" classrooms for math and English. Again, this principal does not view this as a problem, and in fact, touts this practice as a particularly transformative one in his school.

In this example, though some of the leadership practices reflect ICS principles, we have identified at least five practices that are incongruent with ICS. The problem areas are as follows:

1. Far too many students are labeled at this school. The number of students labeled should be reduced to 10%–12% of students with disabilities.

2. Students should not be labeled "at-risk." If students are struggling, their needs should be met within heterogeneous classrooms.

3. Students should not be bussed outside the district to receive services.

4. Students should not be clustered in homogeneous groups of "at-risk" students in transition classrooms at ninth grade.

5. The federal government provides competitive funding to districts that supports and encourages segregated at-risk programs.

This example illustrates that although this leader views himself as inclusive and oriented toward social justice, many of the school practices contradict this identity. These contradictions stem from the fact that this principal does not hold a core belief that all students should learn in heterogeneous settings. It is also possible that this principal does not have the knowledge or skills to make this happen at his school.

We take as a second example another highly regarded high school principal. This principal strongly believes in inclusive schooling of students with disabilities, and these students are included throughout a range of courses in the high school. At the same time, students for whom English is not their first language are clustered in particular courses where they are overrepresented compared to their percentage in the school population. Many students considered at-risk attend an alternative high school in the district. Though the school includes a gay-straight alliance (GSA), no school faculty is willing to sponsor the group, and many LGBT students at the school report feeling isolated and not included. In addition, the achievement of African American students is quite low, and these same students are underrepresented in all extracurricular activities at the school. Importantly, the principal is not as concerned about African American student achievement, believing that the family situations of these students prevents them from achieving at her school.

From an ICS perspective, it is clear that this principal is not adhering to the belief that heterogeneous settings are non-negotiable; otherwise, ESL students would not be clustered in specific courses, and particular at-risk students would not be placed at an alternative school site. A leader for ICS and social justice would also target the low achievement of African American students and their underrepresentation in extracurricular activities without blaming their families or buying into cultural stereotypes. Finally, based on the principle of student safety in school, a leader for ICS and social justice would support LGBT students and faculty, and faculty would more likely feel comfortable sponsoring the GSA at the school.

For a third example, we draw from a district perspective. In this district, the superintendent has been instrumental in implementing some aspects of ICS. Students with disabilities are more fully included in this district than in many districts in the country. The superintendent has made concerted efforts to reach out to the African American community. However, this superintendent decided to cluster all students who are English language learners (ELL) into particular schools. Again, though many might view this superintendent as a social justice leader, and he has implemented many aspects of ICS, his leadership regarding English language learners contradicts this.

These examples show just how entrenched and normative it is to segregate students. Even leaders who care deeply about social justice and equity routinely segregate students without seeing these practices as contradictory to their core beliefs and values. Thus, a third characteristic of leadership for ICS and social justice is the ability to imagine schools functioning differently from how they currently do. One of the primary reasons why leaders and other educators are often unable to bring ICS to fruition is that they simply cannot imagine schools functioning without segregated pullout programs. ICS requires leaders to imagine schools working quite differently.

To reiterate, the first characteristic of ICS leadership is that leaders must hold a core belief that all students should be educated in heterogeneous settings, while the second characteristic is that these leaders possess the knowledge and skills to put this belief into action. The third characteristic requires leaders to be able to imagine schools where all students belong, and students are not segregated from each other to have their learning needs met.

A fourth characteristic of leadership for ICS and social justice is that these leaders are able to see the similarities across student differences. That is, unlike the examples presented here, leaders for ICS and social justice know that whether the student is labeled as having a disability, or being at-risk, a slow reader, a poor math student, ESL, gifted, or whatever the label, the core value regarding heterogeneous learning environments is the same across all these different kinds of learners, again without exception. Similarly, regardless of disability label, whether the student has a label of a learning disability, emotional disability, physical disability, cognitive disability, or severe and profound cognitive and/or physical disability, the principle of heterogeneous learning environments holds for all. These leaders are able to see the similarities in the ways students should be treated, respected, and educated across the range of student differences in their schools.

A fifth and related characteristic of leadership for ICS and social justice requires leaders to be advocates for students who struggle in their school. They understand that if they do not look out for these students and advocate for them, perhaps no one else in these students' lives will do so. In fact, they view their advocacy for these students as core to their calling to be educational leaders. To that end, leaders for ICS and social justice look out for and take a special interest in students from low-income families, students with disabilities, students of color, gay/lesbian students and students from gay/lesbian families, and students whose first language is not English, as well as any other students who may be struggling in school. They deeply respect, nurture, and believe in the abilities of these students. As such, they accept no excuses from anyone for the lack of achievement from these students. Keep in mind that being an advocate for students who struggle, in and of itself, does not constitute leadership for ICS and social justice. In our previous examples, all three leaders would argue that they are strong advocates for students who struggle in school, but their advocacy meant they felt the best education for some of their students should occur in segregated environments. To lead for ICS and social justice, advocating for students who struggle in school must be paired with a core belief in heterogeneous learning environments.

A sixth characteristic of leadership for ICS and social justice is that these leaders are not defensive about their limitations, are honest about where they are in the process, and are doggedly determined to push ahead for the full realization of ICS principles and practices. These leaders will never put a positive spin on their school and district data for the sake of community support. They fully report achievement and other discrepancies among students in a way that takes full responsibility for their learning, and does not blame students or their families. What is troublesome to us about the previous examples is that in all three, none of the leaders admitted to any discrepancies in their practices. In fact, some of what we view as discrepancies they pointed to as positive examples of what they were doing for students. In our experience, the larger the school district and the longer the person has been in a formal administrative leadership role, the more likely that person will put a positive spin on an unjust situation in their school or district. Leadership for ICS and social justice requires rigorous personal and public honesty about the equity status of the school or district, with no exceptions.

A seventh characteristic of leadership for ICS and social justice is that these leaders are continually educating themselves about the areas of equity and diversity that they may lack knowledge in, striving to become experts across student differences. For example, a leader may have had extensive success with African American students and their families, but less experience with students with disabilities and their families. A leader for ICS and social justice would push him- or herself to become knowledgeable about students with disabilities and their families to ensure that these students receive the full benefits of ICS principles and practices.

To this end, we argue that most leaders lack knowledge about not only students with disabilities, but also students for whom English is not their first language. Again, the learning for ICS and social justice leaders is never over, and they push themselves to be as up-to-date as possible about the best evidence-based practices for all students.

As we described in the preface to this book, leaders for ICS and social justice can expect enormous resistance to implementing ICS. For this reason, an eighth characteristic of leadership for ICS and social justice requires the continued development and sustainment of the leader's ethical core regarding heterogeneous schooling so that it can withstand the pressures to do otherwise. We have found that these eight leadership characteristics are key to implementing ICS. Next, we discuss how these leaders lead.

HOW LEADERS FOR ICS AND SOCIAL JUSTICE LEAD

We have witnessed a variety of leadership styles (which we will return to) of those working toward ICS in their schools and districts. These leaders often find themselves swimming against the leadership current when most districts function under a regime of autocratic leadership based on position power (see Figure 2.1). Educators live in tough times where decisions are frequently based on adult needs more than those of students. Educational administrators often operate from their positional power and the need to appease the constituents and get them to vote positively on referenda. Such situations seem to demand that leaders be adult-centered and politically aligned to specific power bases in the community. Time and again, responding to outside political pressures, district personnel make quick decisions that are easily implemented—but not always in the best interest of children. In such situations, those students with the least amount of power within a system receive the least amount of decisions made with them in mind.

In schools where all decisions are aligned with ICS principles and practices, the typical organizational pyramid is inverted so that the child is first, teachers are second, the school principal is third and supports the teaching staff to enable them to do their best on behalf of each child, followed by central office administrators who assist building principals in the process of supporting teachers and students (see Figure 2.2). The result is an entirely different reporting mechanism. Teachers report to students and families, school principals report to teachers, and central office administration reports to principals and teachers. In such a school, ICS principles and practices are used when making all decisions. instead of being based on educational politics, competing factions of stakeholders, and groups of parents that may unknowingly marginalize some children.

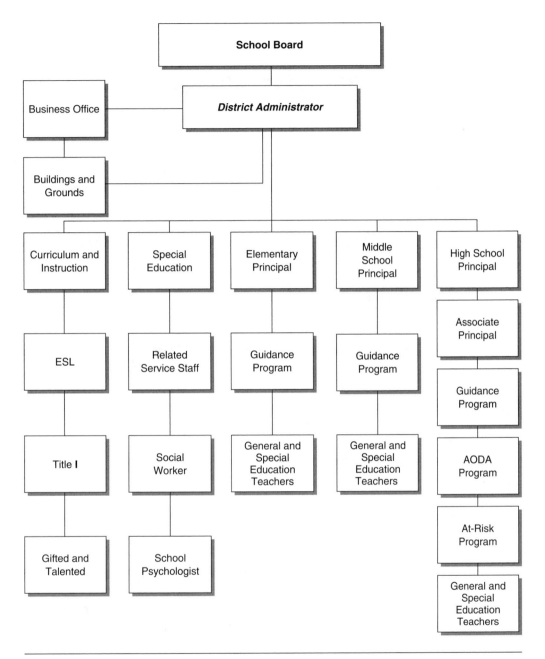

Figure 2.1 Autocratic Organizational Chart

Thus, regardless of the leadership style of individual principals, the transformation to ICS suggests rethinking the decision and organizational structure in schools and districts.

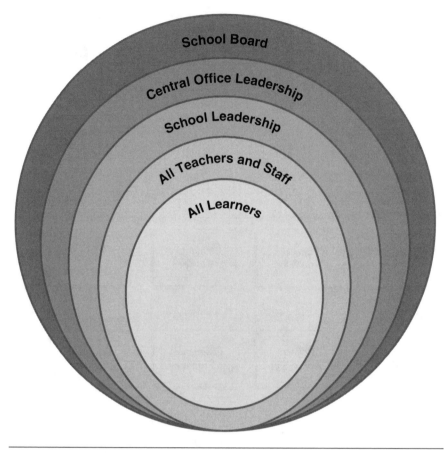

Figure 2.2   Organizational Structure for ICS and Social Justice

In this model, the school board is a support mechanism, but does not have top-down authority. It actually is at the bottom of the heap, wrapped around the central office as a support. The student and family remain the center and the teachers serve as educational leaders with an emphasis on the "to serve" perspective, aligned with ICS principles. This perspective is based on the unequivocal premise that we must support the current and future generations of children in their sense of belonging and the sharing of their gifts with each other and our greater society. Most important, in this model there are no students without gifts, including those students labeled with severe and profound disabilities.

Reshaping a school or district to support ICS rests with superintendents and districtwide reform efforts that include the reconfiguring of service delivery from special programs to services for all learners; the director of student services and special education as they move beyond federal and state regulation compliance toward the restructuring of services for all learners; school principals as the staff move from an expert/specialized program model to shared responsibility for all students; curriculum and instruction leaders as they cast a broader net to include those children who once were the sole responsibility of the student services administrator; and it especially rests with teacher leaders as they work together in the sharing of resources and talents in support of services that are brought to students rather than pushing students out into segregated programs. In such a transformed educational environment, leadership to serve must come from those individuals who are directly involved with student learning on a daily basis as well as those assigned to facilitate the growth of the institution toward specific outcomes.

INDIVIDUAL LEADERSHIP STYLES

Leading toward ICS may first require a high-profile leadership style to initiate change and then a low-profile style to facilitate the development of the vision by all stakeholders—parents, teachers, students, and community members. In schools with a history of low achievement, leaders for ICS and social justice may need to boldly take the lead—in some ways, to engage in autocratic leadership to move the school out of the quagmire of failure. Other school situations may require leadership where shared decision making occurs at the outset. Regardless, with the eight core characteristics intact, over time, leaders for ICS and social justice will need and want to develop the leadership capacity of their staff.

No matter the leadership style, autocratic/high profile or shared/low profile, leaders for ICS and social justice never waver on the eight characteristics we previously described. These characteristics are never up for negotiation or shared decision making (see Figure 2.3). Often, leaders believe that other school initiatives or state and federal regulations should take precedence over developing ICS, when in actuality, other initiatives or regulations must be leveraged to support ICS (discussed fully in Chapter 14). If, in fact, the legislation is in opposition to ICS, then the legislation must be leveraged or changed in support of ICS. Leaders for ICS and social justice do not alter their ethical core to meet the requirements of particular federal, state, or district regulations or initiatives.

Likewise, leaders for ICS and social justice understand the need for ICS to form the core of the school planning process. When ICS becomes "another fad" that is added on to a preexisting model, it will fail. As the eight leadership characteristics illustrate, ICS is not only a way of providing non-fragmented services to meet the individual needs of all learners in

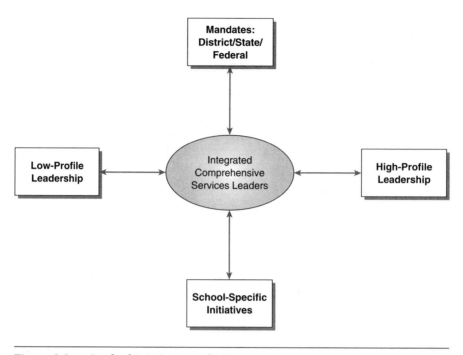

Figure 2.3   Leadership in Support of ICS

diverse environments, but is also a way of thinking and believing about education.

The centrality of beliefs and values has emerged in the most recent literature regarding leadership that has emphasized the importance of leading with the heart, or caring, ethical, servant-based leadership (Greenleaf, 1977). For example, Greenleaf states,

> Caring for persons, the more able and the less able serving each other, is the rock upon which a good society is built. Whereas, until recently, caring was largely person to person, now most of it is mediated through institutions—often large, complex, powerful, impersonal, sometimes corrupt. If a better society is to be built, one that is more just and more loving, one that provides greater creative opportunity for its people, then the most open course is to raise both the capacity to service and the very performance as servant [leader]. (p. 49)

We agree that to realize ICS requires leaders who view themselves as advocates for students who typically struggle and requires a leader with a deep heart, soul, and affinity for these students. At the same time, "caring" or "servant" leadership can be used to justify wholly unjust leadership and educational practices. As the examples we shared earlier in this chapter illustrate, these leaders were not being intentionally malicious by segregating and separating students. They truly cared for the students in their schools, and fully believed that, for example, clustering their ESL students in particular schools and classrooms, or placing their students labeled at-risk in particular classrooms or in schools outside the high school, was the caring and right thing to do. Even further, one of these leaders aligned these practices with his spiritual beliefs and values. As Capper (1993) has written, it is precisely because educators and leaders "care" that they label students and place them in segregated programs, because they truly believe that this is the right thing to do for them.

Thus, though we believe that implementing the principles and practices of ICS can certainly be supported by caring, serving, and spirited leadership, it must be aligned with the eight characteristics of leaders for ICS and social justice described earlier in this chapter. Otherwise, caring, serving, and spirited leadership can be used to justify all kinds of unjust educational practices.

Leadership for ICS and social justice requires that we learn from the past about what has and has not worked for students who struggle. Leaders for ICS and social justice are competent at the managerial tasks of the job, but they also hold a vision for ICS, adhere to the principles and practices of ICS, and have the courage to take the steps to live that vision. These leaders embody the conviction, resolve, and pure heart to lead on behalf of learning for all children in integrated, heterogeneous environments. These leaders need to maintain such a position, even when different constituents with economic power think that there is something inherently unfair about giving students what they need when they need it.

Beyond the eight characteristics of leadership for ICS and social justice we describe, and the ways that leaders lead and take into account their individual leadership styles, the remainder of this book lays out the dimensions that must be considered to implement ICS across schools and districts. This leadership begins with setting a school/district mission for ICS and social justice (Chapter 3), and is followed by collecting data for consciousness, decision making, and evaluation (Chapter 4). It also requires leaders to develop teams for shared decision making (Chapter 5).

These leaders understand the connection between adult and student behavior, and they know how to create a school climate that promotes positive behavior from adults and students, especially students who have a history of challenging behaviors (Chapter 6). Leaders for ICS and social justice move beyond blaming families for student failure, and take it upon themselves to be proactively involved with families (Chapter 7).

Leadership for ICS and social justice demands an eagle eye that is focused on student achievement—in the midst of all the distractions in and around schools, student achievement is the primary focus for these leaders. Thus they are experts on teaching within ICS and for social justice (Chapter 8). These leaders never relegate any students to the sidelines, and never draw a boundary around who should be included or not. Regardless of their educational background, these leaders understand and implement evidence-based practices for students who significantly challenge our teaching (Chapter 9), and for students who are English language learners (Chapter 10). Importantly, they view the development of teacher capacity toward these ends as their most significant role and as their number one priority in the school (Chapter 11).

To accomplish these goals, leaders for ICS and social justice know how to analyze current supports and barriers to ICS and have the ability to create a joint plan that is both attainable in steps and clearly multidimensional in application. Leadership for ICS and social justice requires financial expertise, budget savvyness, and a keen knack for accomplishing goals without spending more money by reallocating existing resources (Chapter 12). Leaders for ICS and social justice understand policies and regulations enough to determine what to circumvent and what to use in support of ICS (Quinn, 2000) (Chapters 13 and 14).

In addition, we know that change is difficult and transition from a traditional program model to a service-based model is time consuming—but once completed is time saving and reaps higher quality services for all children without the price of fragmentation and devalued subcultures of children (Chapter 15). These ICS leaders possess a moral consciousness, grounded in a belief in integrated, heterogeneous learning environments, where their chief goal is to cocreate schools where literally all children belong; political savvy to understand the factions of those who want to maintain the status quo and those who know that it is inherently wrong; financial resourcefulness to make it work and not quickly determine that it is too expensive to ensure equality—pragmatic resolve is imperative to allow the time necessary, without losing sight of the vision; and the courage to ask the questions and facilitate the action. The next 13 chapters provide school leaders with the opportunity to determine the appropriate course of action to lead change through the school educational plan. Using the multidimensional formative analysis outlined in this book will provide school leaders with a sense of direction and a place to begin the journey toward Integrated Comprehensive Services for all learners.

Table 2.1   Chapter 2. Leadership for ICS and Social Justice

Focus Area	Focus Area Inquiry	Comments: What We Have	Phase of Application
1.	All leaders believe in their core that students learn best when they are educated in heterogeneous environments.		
2.	All leaders have the knowledge and skills to carry out this belief in practice, with no exceptions.		
3.	All leaders are able to imagine schools without any segregated programs, where all students feel like they belong.		
4.	All leaders are able to see the similarities in the ways students should be treated, respected, and educated in heterogeneous environments across all student differences (i.e., "at-risk," ESL, disability, etc.).		
5.	All leaders view themselves as advocates for students who struggle.		
6.	All leaders are honest about their own equity limitations, acknowledge the inequities in the school/district, and are determined to do something about it.		
7.	All leaders continually educate themselves about marginalized groups and individuals, seek to become experts across student differences, and seek to be up-to-date about evidence-based practices for all students.		
8.	All leaders continue to develop and sustain their ethical core regarding heterogeneous schooling.		

(Continued)

Table 2.1 (Continued)

Focus Area	Focus Area Inquiry	Comments: What We Have	Phase of Application
9.	The decision and organizational structure of the school positions the students at the center, rather than taking an autocratic approach to leadership.		
10.	Leaders do not let legislation or initiatives disrupt or distract them from their ethical core.		
11.	ICS forms the core of the school planning process.		
12.	All leaders are able to analyze current supports and have the ability to recreate a joint plan with attainable steps.		
13.	All leaders understand that policy and procedures must be aligned to the mission in support of ICS.		
14.	All leaders are fiscally savvy to build a budget in support of all learners.		
15.	All leaders have student achievement for all learners as their primary goal.		
16.	All leaders use data to help them become aware of the state of equity within the school.		
17.	The leaders all hold high expectations for their colleagues and staff.		

Reflective Question:

Based on your responses to the focus areas, how will your team assist in developing the leadership capacity of staff to have the beliefs, knowledge, and skills to lead for ICS and social justice?

Developing and Living a School/District Mission for ICS and Social Justice

Many authors (Conzemius & O'Neil, 2001; DuFour, Eaker, & Karhanek, 2004; Fullan, 1999; Reeves, 2004) have described the importance of developing mission statements to build a unified community of adult and student learners. According to Conzemius and O'Neil (2001), "Goals, values, missions—and vision—are what help keep educational organizations focused on the critical factors that will determine whether students succeed or fail" (p. 19). School mission statements are often developed by a small group of school personnel who, with all good intent, want to create a mission that sets the stage for a series of strategic objectives. When school goals are developed from school mission statements without shared values and a clear vision, then the goals and actions plans will be nebulous and the mission will, again, not address the needs of all students in the school.

Hence, the first step in developing a mission statement that will support Integrated Comprehensive Services requires the school planning team (see Chapter 5), along with the school community, to agree on their values and vision. Our values drive everything we do or say and, in turn, inform our vision. As such, it is essential that educators hold a unified vision of Integrated Comprehensive Services as defined in Chapter 1. For ICS to be successful, the school community must be intentional about two particular values regarding (1) "all learners" and (2) segregation.

First, the school community must hold a clear understanding and shared values about "all learners" in the school. Many mission statements begin with the phrase, "All learners" or "All students" and proceed with statements such as that "all such learners will be proficient at or above grade-level standards as measured by the state standardized assessment." When most educators use the words "all learners," they really think they mean *all* learners. However, what we have found all across the country is that they actually mean "most learners, and we don't know what we are going to do about those who meet eligibility for federal programs." School mission statements must be applicable to literally *all* the students in the school.

Second and related, educators must consider their values regarding segregated education. One of the greatest deceptions schools create is that of belonging. Fifty years have passed since *Plessy v. Ferguson* and the "separate but equal" doctrine that was reversed through *Brown v. Board of Education*. Chief Justice Warren delivered the opinion that "separate facilities are inherently unequal . . . [and that] segregation, with the sanction of law, therefore, has a tendency to [retard] the educational and mental development of children and to deprive them of the benefits they would receive in an integrated school system." Yet we continue to place students in separate classrooms and schools. This is not to say that students in such programs have not experienced some success. It *is* to say that the success experienced does not outweigh the oppression created for the student who is segregated or the symbolism suggested to the other students "who still belong." By segregating students, we are promoting a caste system in that we know that the students who meet eligibility for special education, at-risk, ESL, and title programs are often typically from low-income families or are racially nonwhite (U.S. Department of Education, 2000). We then unintentionally teach all children that typically functioning white students and those of the middle class belong to the normed group, and every once in a great while someone of poverty or nonwhite status has the opportunity to learn with "the norm."

In our work with students in our classes and with educators across the country, we have often heard that, "conceptually ICS is great for all learners, but I can't see how it would work for students with severe and profound cognitive disabilities. If those students are suppose to be placed in a general education classroom, 100% of the day—this is no different from full inclusion." Often, in statements similar to this, the individual has already answered his or her own question. Of course students with severe and profound disabilities should not spend 100% of their day in a general education classroom, but for that matter we do not know one student who should spend 100% of his or her day in one classroom! One of the primary principles of Integrated

Comprehensive Services is that all students are placed with their same-age peers and, based on their individual needs, they weave in and out of flexible small-group, large-group, and individual instruction throughout the day. Therefore, it is essential that individuals drafting the school's mission statement understand conceptually how students with a range of needs can work together. The planning teams must have a shared understanding that ICS is not about taking students who have attended pullout programs in the past and placing them back into the confines of general education. Rather, ICS requires consideration of all services, including and especially general education, and restructuring them to better meet the needs of the range of learners within our schools.

Segregating students can also occur in seemingly benign ways. For example, we often symbolically segregate students, and in turn, deny access to all learners through our "ceremonies." When we celebrate student success, we sometimes inadvertently define who is part of the norm and who is not, who belongs and who does not. For instance, some schools use field trips as reinforcements for academic performance and an incentive for students to achieve. On the day of the field trip, often 70% to 80% of the students are slated to go to the amusement park and are excited about their day, while leaving the other 20% to 30% of the students back in the school to be miserable. When we carry out these kinds of symbolic rituals, we usually reinforce the low morale of the struggling learner. Typically, the response from the students who did not get to enjoy the trip is not, "I will do better next time," but, "Screw them. I don't care. I don't need a lame trip to Six Flags anyway!" Ironically, often the students that are left behind are the same ones who may not have the opportunity to go with their families to Six Flags Amusement Park. Therefore, it is extremely important to consider in what ways rituals, ceremonies, and reward structures in our schools reinforce the segregation of students (Oakes, 1985).

Given our social responsibility to not limit who belongs in our society, school personnel must begin to understand how such segregation perpetuates discrimination. When school personnel believe that we have a responsibility not to segregate those who are typically functioning from those who require a broader range of supports, then they understand the importance of developing a mission that can set the stage for meeting the needs of each and every learner without segregation. When a school site council, professional learning team, can go around the table and say, "I understand how segregation of students for differing needs can be detrimental to them as well as society, and I am interested in setting forth a mission that will minimize segregation and unify our students," then the team can move on to define what such a school community may look like.

COMMUNICATING THE VISION
THROUGH A MISSION STATEMENT

Once the vision is defined, the next step is writing a school mission statement that can be easily communicated and used to move toward a future where all children may be honored and supported. Below are a few examples of school and district mission statements that are written in support of ICS for all learners.

a. We will strive to meet the individual needs of each and every learner through an integrated and comprehensive mix of large-group, small-group, and one-on-one instruction to assist students in becoming proficient at grade-level standards and beyond as determined by a range of differing standard-based, performance-based, and functional assessments.

b. The children of Central Elementary School will be supported in becoming unique, productive, and loving individuals through a school society of social justice. We will provide our children curriculum, instruction, and assessment techniques that acknowledge their individual differences while supporting their need to belong.

In addition to the points expressed in the first mission statement above about addressing the needs of all learners and shared values regarding the ineffective and unethical practice of segregating students, educators can consider five additional ideas to explicitly or implicitly inform the mission statement. First, the mission statement should support the four cornerstones and the guiding practices within each cornerstone of Integrated Comprehensive Services as described in the introduction to this book (i.e., focus on equity, locate education in heterogeneous settings, provide access to high-quality teaching and learning, and merge policies and funding). In addition, the mission statement should support a range of student assessments to determine student learning. Third, the mission statement should not be long, and it should be simple enough to understand that all school community members, including students, their families, and the greater community, understand its essence. This aspect requires that the mission statement not only be easy to understand, but that educators also share the mission statement via a variety of media with all members of the school community.

Fourth, the mission statement should be revisited as part of an annual evaluation of the school and its progress toward ICS—indeed, the mission statement should serve as the guidepost for this annual evaluation. Finally, the school mission should inform every decision made at the school. Educators need to constantly ask themselves if the daily decisions they are making reflect the spirit and intent of the school mission.

ARTICULATING THE GOALS AND OBJECTIVES NECESSARY TO EMPOWER THE MISSION OF ICS

The school planning team (see Chapter 5) can use this book to establish goals and objectives to support its mission. These goals and objectives can be determined by the formative analysis questions at the end of each chapter. The end-of-chapter evaluations include focus areas that are addressed in the chapters. The team members can determine which focus areas require the most immediate attention (based on the phase for each focus area) and then determine their goals and objectives accordingly (see the introduction to this book for a detailed description of the process).

In sum, developing and living a school mission for ICS and social justice require educators and individuals who are members of decision-making teams (see Chapter 5) to all agree on the values and vision of ICS. Most important, educators must agree on the idea that the mission needs to apply to literally every single student in the school—that all learners truly means *all* learners. In addition, educators need to agree on the negative outcomes of segregating students by any group or label, for whatever reason, and in turn clearly understand the value of all students learning from and with each other in a variety of instructional arrangements. When these values are agreed upon, then the mission statement can be written. The mission statement should consider the four cornerstones of ICS; it should be simple, easy to understand, and easily communicated to families, students, staff, and community members; it should be revisited annually to determine to what extent the actual practices align with the mission; and this mission should be referenced and returned to, and thus inform every single decision made in the school. From the mission statement, goals and objectives can be established. The formative analyses at the end of each chapter in this book can help you prioritize these objectives.

Table 3.1   Chapter 3. Developing and Living a School Mission for ICS and Social Justice

Focus Area	Focus Area Inquiry	Comments: What We Have	Phase of Application
1.	The majority of individuals in the school community agree on their values and vision that align with ICS principles.		
2.	The school team shares an understanding that the mission statement should address all learners, which includes learners with the most severe learning and behavioral challenges.		
3.	The school team shares an understanding that segregating students is not an effective or ethical educational practice, and the school mission reflects this belief.		
4.	The school team has reviewed the end-of-chapter evaluation for Chapter 1 and considered to what extent each item and each of the four cornerstones of ICS are reflected in the mission statement.		
5.	The mission statement supports a range of student assessments to determine student learning.		
6.	The mission statement is not long and is easy to understand.		
7.	The mission statement is shared through a variety of media.		
8.	The mission statement is revisited as part of the annual evaluation.		
9.	The mission statement informs all school decisions.		

Data for Consciousness Raising, Decision Making, and Evaluation

4

In our first book (Capper et al., 2000), we suggested a service delivery team be created at the school level. One of the tasks of that team was to collect and analyze school- and district-level data, in part to determine the current status of student services and student opportunities for learning. In Appendix B of that book, we included a list of equity-related questions for each area of student difference, including social class, race/ethnicity, disability, gender, and sexual orientation. One purpose of those questions was to help educators determine to what extent students who are typically marginalized are either over- or underrepresented in programs and services. Adult learners in our courses as well as many practicing educators have found those equity-related questions from our first book to be invaluable as a means to conduct an equity audit of their own schools. For these educators and adult learners, hearing us discuss the status of traditionally marginalized individuals in the United States offered one perspective. However, to gather data in their own schools and districts that showed, for example, that low-income students were vastly overrepresented in special education and grossly underrepresented in gifted and talented programs brought a whole new perspective to their understanding of equity and diversity. These data helped adult learners and educators see that issues of equity and social justice were not just some far off urban issue, but in fact, permeated every classroom and program in their own schools, regardless of how rural, homogeneous, or just they thought their schools to be.

From the time of publishing our first book to this one, the need for data to uncover, explain, and help solve educational inequities has only heightened (see Johnson, 2002, and Skrla, Scheurich, Garcia, & Nolly, 2004, for additional ideas on data and equity audits). Thus, in this book, we devote this entire chapter to the topic, as we believe that the appropriate use of data is a key aspect of social justice leadership as discussed in Chapter 2. We have also updated and revised the data questions from our first book and included them in Appendix B. In our revision, we have included questions for each demographic area that pertain specifically to academic achievement. We have also added questions to the disability section, and included school- and districtwide questions concerning student discipline, as well as participation in and results of SAT, ACT, and advanced placement exams. A far bigger change is the addition of a separate set of questions for English language learners.

In this chapter, we ask that you bring together the data required by federal, state, and district reporting mechanisms with additional data that will flesh out the equity picture in schools and districts. For example, most states already ask that student achievement data be disaggregated for students labeled for special education and those who are learning English as a second language. However, federal, district, and state monitoring does not require examining student representation in particular programs (e.g., at-risk, gifted, honor roll, advanced placement, etc.). Yet, student participation in these programs determines which students are given access to particular learning opportunities and which ones are not. In turn, student participation in these learning opportunities directly impacts student achievement. As such, it is critical that data be collected on these learning opportunities. The questions in Appendix B lead toward that end.

Unfortunately, in response to low test scores of students from typically marginalized groups, school personnel are establishing more separate, segregated, remedial instructional programs—not fewer. This is why collecting equity data in and of itself is not enough. This equity data collection and analysis must be joined with the formative analyses regarding ICS at the end of each chapter in this book. Joining the two aspects of data collection will facilitate the implementation of ICS as a whole—to avoid establishing additional segregated programs in response to low student achievement, to help dismantle the segregated programs already in place, and to assist in the restructuring of student services in support of integrated comprehensive environments for all learners. To assist with the implementation of ICS, the equity data and other data can be collected and analyzed for three different purposes: consciousness raising, decision making, and evaluation. We discuss this next, followed by a discussion on communicating data.

DATA FOR CONSCIOUSNESS RAISING

Data can raise the consciousness of educators about the strengths and the inequities happening in their own schools and about the myths that continue to be perpetuated about particular traditionally marginalized groups and individuals. This consciousness-raising aspect of data collection is critical. We cannot make changes regarding inequities if we do not know about those inequities. To use the data questionnaires in Appendix B, we suggest the school planning team (described in Chapter 5) collect data from one demographic section at a time. For example, first collect basic school data (such as the number of students in the school and demographic data) and data in the social class areas. When collecting the data, it is critical to collect the number of students, the fraction as a part of the whole student group, and then the percentage from that fraction. As an example, if a question asks for the number of students labeled with a disability, it is important to report that number—say, 100—but also report the fraction; that is, 100 students out of 500 in the school are labeled with a disability, or 100/500. Next, it is important to convert this fraction to a percentage—in this case, 20% of the students in the school are labeled with a disability. Reporting the fraction is important, as it leaves a number trail for others to ascertain how the resulting percentage was obtained. Others can then follow up if they want to check on the numbers obtained to ensure they are the correct data. Reporting the percentage is also quite important as it is impossible to compare numbers unless they are converted to percentages. For example, if an educator reports that in a school of 500, a total of 125 are students of color, 100 are labeled with a disability, 93 are receiving a free/reduced-price lunch, and 37 are English language learners, that does not tell us much. However, if we know that 25% of the students in this school are of color, 20% are labeled with a disability, close to 19% are receiving free/reduced-price lunches, and 7% are English language learners, we are able to compare student populations within a school, note how those demographics have changed over time, and measure how the school demographics compare to other schools.

We would like to offer a couple of words of warning about the social class data. These may be the most difficult data for educators to gather. Many educators believe they cannot collect social class data based largely on the number of students receiving free and reduced-priced lunches in their schools because these data are confidential. Importantly, the social class questions in the equity audit data form in Appendix B in this book do not ask for information about particular students or individual families. The questions only seek information in the aggregate about these students.

For the social class data, educators will also find it difficult to uncover, for example, the percentage of students in special education receiving free and reduced-price lunches. We believe the fact that the federal or state departments of education do not even request that information is a problem. Again, educators typically report that their school or district does not report such data, citing confidentiality reasons. In some districts, supervisors of the hot lunch program are willing to review the list of students labeled for special education, and count the number of these students who also receive free/reduced-price lunches, without reporting these names to anyone. What we have learned from the schools and districts that have collected these data is that in every single case, students from low-income families (as measured by students receiving free/reduced-price lunches) are far overrepresented in special education and in at-risk programs. (We realize that reports of free/reduced-price lunches are probably underestimates of the actual number of students in poverty because of the reluctance of some families to apply for support.) That is, for example, if the percentage of students receiving free/reduced-price lunches in a school is 25%, then no more than 25% of students in special education should be receiving free/reduced-priced lunches. However, thus far, in literally hundreds of schools and districts from which adult learners in our courses have gathered data, if a student is from a poor family, he or she is more likely to be placed in special education or at-risk programs and is far less likely to be placed in gifted options than other students (Brantlinger, 1993).

We have had adult learners report that their school leaders or school board members argue that it should be expected that a higher percentage of low-income students would be placed in special education and at-risk programs, and fewer in advanced or gifted options. They cite the lack of "environmental stimulation" and other myths and stereotypes about low-income families (see Brantlinger, 1993). We have had other educators argue that because low-income students are overrepresented in special education and at-risk programs and underrepresented in gifted programs at most schools and districts across the country, then that is the norm, and therefore it is not a problem if that is the way it is in their own school or district. However, the principles of ICS as well as the research suggest that low-income students are just as intelligent as any other students in the school and that the white, middle/upper-class curriculum and culture of the school works against them (see Chapter 8, Teaching Within ICS and for Social Justice). Thus, the number and percentage of low-income students in special education and at-risk programs should not exceed their percentage in the general population, and advanced curriculum options such as advanced courses or programs (which would not exist in a full implementation of ICS in the first place) should include the same proportional representation of low-income students as the school (i.e., if 25% of the students are receiving free/reduced-price lunches, we could expect 25% of these same students to be on the honor roll or in the gifted program).

Educators also uniformly find that low-income students are underrepresented in extracurricular opportunities (e.g., band, sports, school clubs, etc.), and their families are underrepresented in school functions. Yet, we know from research (Holloway, 2002; Young, Helton, & Whitley, 1997) that students who participate in extracurricular options gain a stronger sense of belonging and connection with the school, which in turn increases student achievement across subject areas. Finally, given that students from low-income families are overrepresented in special education and at-risk programs, underrepresented in advanced and enriched curriculum opportunities, and underrepresented in extracurricular programs, and that the school is less involved with their families (see Chapter 7), is it any wonder that when educators collect achievement data, they find that low-income students achieve far less in reading and math and other academic areas compared to their peers?

When asked to disaggregate the data for students placed in at-risk or gifted programs, some educators report that their school does not have formal at-risk or gifted programs. We then suggest that educators think about the hidden or not-so-hidden pockets in their school where students who struggle are disproportionately placed. Though students may not be formally identified as "at-risk," students who struggle are often clustered, for example, in lower level academic subject areas (e.g., consumer math, general science, Reading Recovery, Title I reading or math, reading remediation, homework club, tutoring programs, or summer school, to name a few possibilities). Thus, though a school may not formally label students as at-risk, it is important to disaggregate the data in the program areas where students who struggle are clustered to determine if low-income students, students of color, or students for whom English is not their first language are disproportionately placed in these programs.

Likewise, some schools do not formally identify students for gifted programs. However, similar to the previous example, we ask educators to brainstorm for other pockets in the school where students considered higher achieving might be congregated. Possibilities include advanced placement courses, upper level math and science courses at the middle and high school level, academic decathlon, honor roll, SAT/ACT prep courses and camps, and honor societies—all places where these students may be clustered. Again, educators should disaggregate the data on participation in these programs and determine if typically marginalized students are proportionately represented.

This discussion of the gathering and understanding of the social class, "at-risk," and "gifted" data illustrates how one purpose of data collection and analysis is to raise the consciousness of the status of equity in a school or district. Educators invariably find similar data regarding students of color or English language learners in their schools. These data point out the unequal educational opportunities available to students that are typically marginalized—that these students are typically relegated to classrooms and programs outside the general education classroom where they engage in rote memorization of discrete facts. In turn, they are deprived of the rich and engaging curriculum that most other students receive. Then educators mystify the entire process, with a good heart and good intentions, saying and believing that siphoning these students off to separate programs is indeed helping them. That is the primary educational myth ICS seeks to fully uncover and dismantle.

One of the most exciting outcomes from gathering such data in schools and districts is the resulting conversations that ensue between educators when collecting and analyzing the data. School personnel become curious when they are being asked these questions; thus, questions and conversations can occur at the point where data are being collected. In addition, most educators are surprised by the data—that these inequities exist in their own districts, schools, and classrooms. This often leads to sharing these data with other educators in their settings, asking additional questions, and having deeper conversations about why these inequities are happening in their school and district. One of the central premises of ICS involves asking questions about why certain practices are happening and their effects on students, families, and educators and engaging in rich conversations about these issues. Collecting equity data can be one grand avenue for initiating these questions and conversations that lead to a greater equity consciousness among educators, students, community members, and families.

DATA FOR DECISION MAKING

For each area of student difference in the equity questionnaires in Appendix B, we require adult learners in our courses to conduct an analysis of these data. For example, they take the social class data they have collected, and then analyze it by writing (briefly—one single-spaced page) about the strengths and weaknesses regarding the education of students from lower social classes based on the data. They also write specific, concrete strategies to address areas of weakness. For example, if the data show that low-income students are not represented in extracurricular activities, then they make concrete suggestions about how the school or district can encourage students to become more involved in these activities (e.g., by offering activities during the school day when students can attend, providing transportation for afterschool events, securing additional funds to pay for fees and equipment required by the activity, etc.). If student achievement is an area of weakness, they also write specific, concrete suggestions to raise achievement. Global, vague, generalized suggestions are not acceptable (see Chapter 8 where we discuss the use of data with curriculum and instruction). For example, suggestions that include making the school climate more positive or increasing teacher collaboration are not specific enough to raise the math achievement of low-income students.

After collecting data across all the areas of difference; analyzing each of the sections of data for strengths and weaknesses; and making concrete, specific, practical suggestions to remedy weak areas, the school planning team can review the formative analyses at the end of each chapter in this book, examine their analyses of the data they have collected, and then write and prioritize concrete, specific goals for the school. Invariably, educators learn that there are many areas of weakness that need to be addressed, but a good leader knows how to facilitate team members to help them make decisions and prioritize their goals over a specific period of time.

These goals should be written in clear, measurable, and observable terms. Obviously, everything worth doing cannot be measured, and everything that can be measured may not be worth doing. But leaders and school teams need to hold themselves accountable for making measurable differences in their school. For example, vague goals such as "increase teacher collaboration," or "increase parent involvement," or "raise student achievement" are not enough—leaders or school teams could possibly provide anecdotal evidence that these goals have been met, but if we are serious about raising student achievement, in particular for students who struggle in school, vague goals such as these will never suffice.

In addition, all goals should relate directly in some way to student achievement. Schools are swirling vortexes of distractions—ironically, away from academic achievement. Educators can be easily seduced into jumping onto the nearest bandwagon, pouring thousands of dollars and hours of time into the latest "fix-it" scheme. Unfortunately, we have witnessed this even with "equity based" initiatives that require an enormous amount of resources and time, yet are no substitute for the hard work of changing perspectives and being task focused at the school, classroom, and student level.

In addition to being measurable and focused on student achievement, the goals should contain the current equity status within it. For example, a goal might be to increase the math achievement of English language learners in the school from 30% basic and 20% proficient to 0% basic and 60% proficient by the end of the school year. This makes the current status clear as well as the end-of-year goal. It would be quite easy to measure this goal and know at the end of the year to what extent it was achieved. It can also be helpful to have a longer term goal, say over 3 to 5 years, and then to divide this goal up into measurable increments for each year. For example, if the goal is to raise the math achievement of English language learners as stated previously, perhaps the 3-year goal is to have these learners at 40% proficient and 60% advanced. Then, the school leader and planning team can break down this goal into three 1-year increments, with the percentages being increased by one-third each year.

This is just one example of how data can be used for decision making. In another example, we worked with a school where the high school students in one English course collected data on harassment that they hear in the hallways and classrooms. They analyzed and reported these data to their school board, which resulted in changes to the anti-harassment policy and procedures in their high school.

As we pointed out in the preface to this book, time is quite precious. Students are struggling, daily, and educators are pouring massive amounts of time, energy, and resources into the educational enterprise. This reality behooves us as educators to be as efficient with our time and efforts as possible. When decisions are made about how to handle a problem, educators need to ask *why* the decision is being made, what data exist to describe the problem, and how will the efforts be measured to know if the problem has been addressed. We owe this level of efficiency to ourselves, to the taxpayers, and, most important, to the students.

DATA FOR EVALUATION

To be honest, you could show us any program out there of any sort—segregated, pullout—and we could probably produce data that could show the program is "working" in some way. This could include sharing anecdotal stories from families and students about how great the program is and how it has benefited their education and life. We could probably find data that showed how students may not have made it through school or graduated without the program, or how they would not have learned how to read or learned vocational skills if they had not attended the segregated program. We could gather similar data from educators in these settings.

We could interview administrators in other schools who would also praise these programs and how they shift students out of the general education settings in ways that help the students who are shifted, and how they leave space and time for those left behind to receive a good education. These educators would argue that one school cannot fit all, should not fit all, and that all students need options.

However, just because data can be produced about a practice to show its supposed effectiveness does not mean that that practice should continue. As such, it is not useful to collect survey data on whether or not students, families, or educators believe particular programs should continue. That is not the point. Of course, if some students feel unsafe, unwelcomed, or their learning style is not addressed in the typical school, these students and their families will argue for their own separate setting away from a typical school. ICS principles and practices would suggest asking, instead, what can be done to change the typical school to meet these students' needs.

It is a rare case to find a school that has collected outcome and effectiveness data on its segregated programs. Our study of the literature and our time in schools suggest strongly that such programs are grossly ineffective and quite expensive to boot. Some adult learners in our courses have collected outcome data from their segregated programs such as Title I, Reading Recovery, and others. Many have been surprised to learn that the outcomes of these programs have never been measured in their own schools, and many have learned that the costs (financial and human) far outweigh the benefits. Again, we can find evaluation data, for example, that Reading Recovery programs work—for some students. But at what cost? How many students are left out? How is the capacity of all teachers to teach reading increased as a result of the program? What has been the politics around keeping these programs in schools, where highly paid teachers work with a quite small, select group of students?

School leaders must become adept at evaluating the outcomes of their current practices in quantifiable ways. While student, family, and educator anecdotes can enrich the quantitative data, social justice leaders know how to establish measurable effectiveness criteria for their practices on a routine and ongoing basis. Again, as leaders for social justice and as stewards of public money and support, these leaders feel responsible for the prudent use of public resources. Even more important, just as ethically a doctor would prescribe only medicines that have been proven to work, a social justice leader will never place students in situations on a whim and without first rigorously collecting data on student outcomes. The days of educators expecting the public to simply trust educator decisions based on respect or anecdotal information should be plain and simply over.

COMMUNICATING DATA

In addition to collecting data for consciousness raising, decision making, or evaluation, ICS leaders for social justice know how to communicate in ways that make the data clearly visible and understandable to anyone in the community (see Johnson, 2002). They know how to arrange the data in easy-to-read graphs and charts that make the equity strengths and areas for improvement quite visible. We have witnessed a variety of effective ways that leaders can communicate data, including using software such as PowerPoint and making brief presentations to faculty, school board members, and families and community members, and publishing these data in their school newsletters and in districtwide report cards. We have walked into schools where, for example, achievement data on reading are displayed prominently on the main hallway bulletin board, showing grade-level improvements in reading from the beginning of the year to the present, comparing current data to last year, and showing the achievement-level goal for that grade. These data displays are easy for anyone walking into the school to read and understand. Bulletin boards include samples of student work taken from their portfolios that are examples of a particular learning standard that was met or exceeded. In addition, in these schools, students learn to collect, analyze, display, and explain their own learning data.

In sum, leaders for ICS and social justice must become data experts in their schools and districts. We argue in Chapter 12 that leaders for ICS and social justice must become financial experts and not back away from learning the details of school finance and funding. The same holds true for data. Leaders should take advantage of university courses and other professional development opportunities that will help them tool up on quantitative data collection and analysis. Today, software packages are available that can greatly assist in quantitative data analyses. Data collection and analyses are critical for raising consciousness about the inequities in schools and for making decisions about what actions to take to ameliorate these inequities. Finally, leaders for ICS and social justice must endeavor to carefully and systematically weave evaluation into the core of all their efforts and then learn to share these results with others in clear, easily understood ways. Social justice work demands no less.

Table 4.1   Chapter 4. Data for Consciousness Raising, Decision Making, and Evaluation

Focus Area	Focus Area Inquiry	Comments: What We Have	Phase of Application
1.	We have collected and analyzed the equity audit data in Appendix B of this book as one way to raise our consciousness about and identify inequities in our setting.		
2.	We collect and analyze equity data to trigger and sustain conversations and questions about equity in our setting.		
3.	We use data to inform all decisions in our setting.		
4.	The goals we write based on the data are specific, concrete, and measurable, and contain the current equity status within them.		
5.	The goals we set based on the data are clearly linked to student achievement.		
6.	The goals we set based on the data lead to measurable gains over a specific period of time.		
7.	We routinely include ongoing, quantifiable evaluation measures in all our education practices.		
8.	We communicate our data to a wide range of constituents, simply and clearly, using a variety of media.		

Reflective Questions:

1. Reflecting on the data you collected, what data points stand out as areas of significant concern?

2. As you go through the analysis in this book, keep in mind those areas that draw concern to begin to create opportunities for resolution.

CORNERSTONE 2

Establishing Equitable Structures: Location and Arrangement of Educational Services

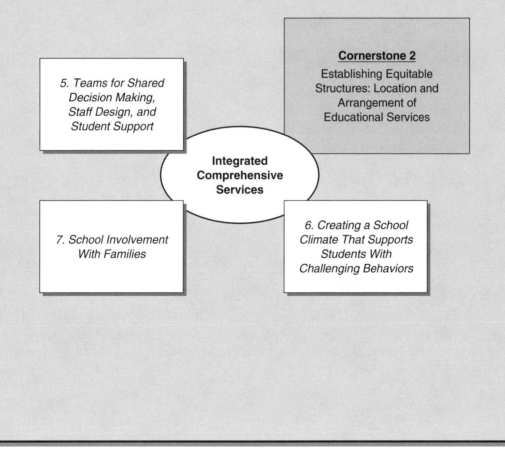

5. Teams for Shared Decision Making, Staff Design, and Student Support

Cornerstone 2

Establishing Equitable Structures: Location and Arrangement of Educational Services

Integrated Comprehensive Services

7. School Involvement With Families

6. Creating a School Climate That Supports Students With Challenging Behaviors

Teams for Shared Decision Making, Staff Design, and Student Support

For Integrated Comprehensive Services to be sustainable and benefit all learners, we suggest the creation of four teams within the school and school district that can assist in the development and implementation of ICS: the School Planning Team, School Service Delivery Team, Grade-Level Design Teams, and a Districtwide Service Delivery Team. The purposes of these teams are threefold: (1) shared decision making, that is, to provide opportunities for individuals in the school community to be involved in implementation decisions; (2) staff design, that is, to strategically assign teachers and staff to students and classes in ways that build teacher capacity and that maximize student learning; and (3) student support, that is, to strategically assign students to classes in ways that do not segregate them, that maximize student opportunities to learn in heterogeneous groups, and that thus create the conditions for optimal student learning. Frequently, school district personnel focus on instruction and curriculum and assume that they do not have control over structure or policy and procedures. The work of these four teams disrupts this assumption. In the following sections, we first briefly describe each team. Then, we detail the goals of each team, its membership, steps that the team can take to implement ICS, and ways to evaluate the team's efforts.

In schools with shared leadership, often a schoolwide team functions as an oversight committee for many school decisions. This team may be known as a school learning team, site council, school planning team, shared decision-making team, or educational planning committee. For the purposes of ICS, we will use the term "School Planning Team"(see Figure 5.1). In a school with shared decision making, such a team must be established as one of the essential teams to "care for the whole" of the school. The School Planning Team is primarily responsible for assessing every section or component of the ICS formative analysis (see the end of each chapter) and for developing an action plan based on the results obtained from the analysis. Through the use of the ICS formative analysis, the School Planning Team will delineate a step-by-step process to set annual or long-term goals for the school.

A second key decision-making team for the initiation and implementation of ICS is the School Service Delivery Team (see Figure 5.1). This team functions as an offshoot of the School Planning Team to specifically analyze and redesign the structure of how services are offered. Moreover, the Service Delivery Team is responsible for identifying the necessary changes in school- and district-based policy and procedures for the implementation of ICS.

The third key decision-making teams are Grade-Level Design Teams (see Figure 5.1). Team members include teachers who are responsible for setting up the specific staff design for each grade level as well as the instructional and curricular services for a specific grade. These teams include one representative from the School Service Delivery Team who functions as a conduit between that team and the Grade-Level Design Teams.

The Districtwide Service Delivery Team represents the fourth key decision-making team for the initiation and implementation of ICS (see Figure 5.1). This team's primary function is to ensure that service delivery is consistent across the district. A representative from each School Service Delivery Team, the director of student services, and the curriculum and instruction administrators comprise this team. The team's primary responsibility is to share information from the individual school teams to develop consistency and fluidity across the district for all students. For example, the team may want to confirm that a child moving from fifth to sixth grade is able to maintain services in a similar fashion based on his or her individualized service plan (ISP) or individualized education plan (IEP). This team is the glue that holds the service delivery model together at the PreK–12 level.

A first consideration for all four teams is team membership. We describe the specific roles or positions in each team in the sections that follow. In addition to role-specific membership, teams should ensure that the broad range of individuals who typically support students who struggle in the school are represented (i.e., ESL teacher, at-risk teacher, Title 1 staff, special education teacher, etc.). In addition, team membership should ensure that persons of color and persons for whom English is not their

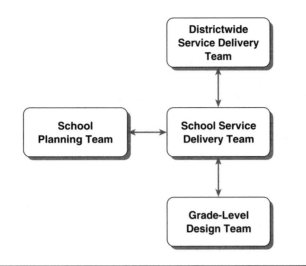

Figure 5.1 Teams for Shared Decision Making, Staff Design, and Student Support for ICS

first language are represented on all the teams in the same proportion that they are in the building and in the district. Relatedly, when community members or families are included as team members, for example on the School Planning Team, they should represent the diversity of the school and district in terms of families of color and low-income families.

All four of these teams need to set ground rules for discussion and decisions. In addition, all of the teams must decide in what ways and how frequently they will communicate their progress with the other three teams and with the other staff in the school. For example, it will be critical that, when the School Service Delivery Team discusses ICS and agrees on its principles and conducts the "All Learners Learn Best When . . ." activity (detailed in Appendix C), the results of these decisions and activities be shared with the other teams and with the other staff in the school. As a second example, when this same team completes their drawing of the current service delivery model in the school (detailed in Appendix D), they need to share this current status of service delivery with the other teams and with the other staff in the school. Further, all four teams must decide how they will receive specific feedback from the other three teams and from the other school staff about their work. The remainder of this chapter is dedicated to the specific teams and their membership, team goals, process to meet targeted goals, and evaluation strategies.

SCHOOL PLANNING TEAM

The School Planning Team is responsible for completing the ICS formative analysis described in this book. The team may choose to complete the analysis or put together an ad-hoc committee to be responsible for completing the 15 sections of the analysis. The team then analyzes their results by phase and begins to build their plan in response to those questions they determined are Phase 1. By taking the information and disaggregating the data by phases, the team is better able to develop a long-range plan responding to each item within the analysis. Often, team members define their response plan as a reconstructive plan in support of successful schools for all learners.

Membership

Team membership must include representatives from all stakeholders of the school community. These stakeholders will include but are not limited to the following: the school administrator, teacher representatives, parent representatives, student representatives, other staff representatives, and community representatives.

Goals

Typical goals of the School Planning Team include, but are not limited to, the following (Conzemius & O'Neil, 2001):

- Focus on student learning at the site.
- Serve as a forum for diverse perspectives from the school, home, and community to ensure the exchange of a variety of viewpoints.
- Provide participatory, shared decision making at each site to create the individual school's structure and culture (within the district mission).
- Promote communication between parents, community members, professional and support personnel, students, and administrators.

The School Planning Team can be responsible for curricular, instructional, and personnel budgets and then must make difficult decisions in support of the school and district mission. The ICS formative analysis is a useful tool for a School Planning Team to make data-driven decisions on behalf of all learners. The team can also use the ICS formative analysis to develop specific short-term objectives. An example is delineated below:

Our school staff will focus on Phase I areas of need defined through our ICS formative analysis. For the next school year, the following major categories will be our focus areas for immediate action:

- All students will make progress toward grade-level standards and beyond.

- Teachers will increase their skills to document individual student accomplishments using multigrade-level standards and assessments.
- Teachers will be provided three hours of collaborative time per week to work in their grade-level staff design teams to collectively meet the needs of all learners in an integrated comprehensive manner.
- All choice and neighborhood students will be accepted and educated in our school.
- Funding at the school level will be comingled in support of our ICS delivery model.

Process to Meet the Goals

Often, a School Planning Team analyzes student scores and discuses areas of concern and resolution and then creates comprehensive school goals. The ICS formative analysis is an ongoing assessment process to assist the School Planning Team in moving forward to create schools where all children have the right to Integrated Comprehensive Services.

Evaluation

Evaluation is inherent within the ICS formative analysis. As the School Planning Team moves from one phase to the next, the progress toward meeting specific goals will be clear to all stakeholders. The other three teams will also have their own goals and evaluation strategies that will be shared with the School Planning Team.

SCHOOL SERVICE DELIVERY TEAM

The School Service Delivery Team is composed of groups of teachers and administrators whose primary focus is to assess how services are being offered to and for all learners. As we discussed in Chapter 3 regarding school mission, when we refer to all learners, we mean each and every learner who lives in the neighborhood or whose family has chosen the school through school choice options. Therefore, the School Service Delivery Team's primary responsibility is to assess the quality of Integrated Comprehensive Services on an ongoing basis, using all four cornerstones of ICS: focusing on equity, structure of services, access to high-quality teaching and learning, and developing appropriate funding mechanisms and policies.

Membership

Membership on the School Service Delivery Team is based on services/programs provided within the school. A representative from each unit, grade level, department, or academy is imperative to give voice to all stakeholders and represent all children with and without labels. In addition, teachers representing the different programs currently offered in the school (e.g., ESL, Title I, at-risk) should make up the remainder of the teacher leaders on the team. As many studies confirm, the participation of the school administrator is essential to the operations of the team (Fullan, 1999). The school administrator should be an equal member of the team, with little to no veto power, but certainly the opportunity to use his or her persuasive skills. In many schools that have functioning School Service Delivery Teams, the districtwide administrator for student services and special education and the director of curriculum and instruction may participate as equal members of the team. Often, these individuals have the ability to obtain and reallocate resources to assist in the movement from programs to services, i.e., the comingling of funds in support of all learners. All that being said, the School Service Delivery Team should not exceed 10 to 12 members—primarily in order to give adequate voice to all participants. Individuals on the team should feel strongly about the need to provide educational services for all learners.

Goals

The goals of the School Service Delivery Team are clear:

To better meet the needs of each and every learner in a comprehensive manner in integrated school and community environments

To take a clear look at the structural barriers in providing the most comprehensive integrated services and reconstruct a model of service delivery that will provide students with little to no fragmentation within their school day

To attend to those symbolic and procedural practices that perpetuate the division between the "haves" and the "have nots," i.e., field trips, school ceremonies, banquets, and so forth

Next, we describe eight specific steps and processes that can help this team achieve its goals. First, the team must have the opportunity to discuss what Integrated Comprehensive Services are and what they are not. They may want to share readings either in support of or refuting the concept of ICS. At this time, the team can reflect and think about what it means to move toward ICS for all learners and come to consensus regarding what it could mean.

Second, there must be agreement among all team members about the importance of adopting a philosophy of Integrated Comprehensive Services. Many school teams make decisions without having consensus regarding the core principles of Integrated Comprehensive Services. When such assumptions occur, we default to a traditional structure of programs and compliance-driven policy that undermines the growth and education for students who require additional services. Never force change. If team members cannot generate enough interest in ICS at their school, they should continue to ask questions such as, Why do the children who have the least ability to generalize have the most fragmented schedule? Could we do more for "all learners" if we worked together instead of in our own separate silos? When we say "all learners," do we really mean all?

Third, the team needs to conduct the "All Learners Learn Best When . . ." activity described in Appendix C. This is one activity that can help teams reach consensus on learner needs and how the school can best meet those needs.

Fourth, the team should draw a picture of how the school currently meets the needs of children who are challenged—or who challenge how we teach. That is, they should draw a picture of their current service delivery model (see Appendix D for a sample of an urban high school's current delivery model). This picture should address the question, What programs are currently in place for students who struggle in our school? The picture of this current delivery model should be portrayed in as much detail as possible.

Fifth, with this information, the team should conduct a gap analysis. That is, the team members should compare their list of "All Learners Learn Best When . . ." with the list of ICS activities comprised in the ICS four cornerstones and with the current service delivery model that was drawn. The team can then determine where the gaps are between what ICS would entail, how the teams think all learners learn best, and what is currently happening in the school with the service delivery picture. For step six in the process, participants should list current practices in their school that focus on prevention and determine if they are comprehensive, integrated, and effective to build success for each and every learner. If these practices align with the ICS principles, then they should be continued in the new service delivery model.

For step seven, the School Service Delivery Team members brainstorm their vision and hopes for service delivery in their school, based on the principles of ICS, and then they draw this future service delivery model on paper. This vision and these hopes should be listed without any budgetary concerns, as these will limit future recommendations. Certainly we understand that every district has budget limitations. On the other hand, we know, as administrators and facilitators, that we are often able to creatively rectify financial concerns to support an ICS model through comingling of funds or reallocation, which would never have been recommended had the team members limited their future model using a financial formula. Often, staff find drawing the picture of the new model difficult and instead use a table or diagram to outline the new service delivery model (see Table 5.1).

The new service delivery model begins with engaging in staff design. Staff design starts with listing the number of students by learning needs (e.g., behavioral, intellectual, learning, at-risk, ELL) for each grade level. Based on these student needs, for each grade level, the team also lists educators who are typically responsible for students who are labeled in schools (e.g., students with disabilities, ELL, students with reading needs, to name a few). The School Service Delivery Team determines how many and which of these educators should be members of each grade-level team that supports these students in general education. These students will receive large-group, small-group, and one-to-one instruction based on their individualized education plan (IEP) or individualized service plan (ISP) goals and objectives. The School Service Delivery Team also assigns support staff to each grade level. These support staff will "loop" with the classes they are assigned to. This means that, for example, if a special education teaching assistant is assigned to support students in the ninth grade one year, the next year, this teaching assistant will support the same group of students in the tenth grade. The following year, this support staff will return to the ninth grade to support students at that level, and so on. Support staff may loop in this way with students at the ninth and tenth grade, and then also between the eleventh and twelfth grade.

The School Service Delivery Team then needs to take step eight, which is to develop a plan for how to achieve their new service delivery model. At this point, the decision making needs to move to the Grade-Level Design Teams who will be responsible for setting the vision into motion.

Evaluation

The School Service Delivery Team should meet as often as necessary in the beginning of the change process, but may reduce their meeting schedule as the Grade-Level Design Teams begin their work. The School Service Delivery Team is then primarily responsible for evaluation activities and will convene to collect feedback or a major concern regarding the efficacy of the model. In so doing, the members of the School Service Delivery Team should examine what is working and what is not and determine options for creative solutions without reverting back to an old model of segregation of children. For example, if a teacher who has typically taught students with mild learning disabilities is now responsible for a much broader range of learners (a child with autism and one whose first

Table 5.1   Staff Design for Non-Label-Driven Services by Grade Level—2006-2007 Projection

Need	Ninth Grade	Tenth Grade	Eleventh Grade	Twelfth Grade	Second-Year Seniors
Behavioral	20	22	9	3	
Intellectual	22	27	18	8	13
Learning	80	77	39	21	
At-risk	35	42	22	12	15
ELL	18	12	10	7	
Total	175	180	104	35	
Number of Specialized Support Educators	8.5	8.5	6	3	1.5
Needed Specialization	LD (3), ED (2), CD (2), ELL (.5), At-Risk (1)	LD (3), ED (2), CD (2), ELL (.5), At-Risk (1)	LD (2), ED (1), CD (2), ELL (.5), At-Risk (.5)	LD(1).ED(1) DVI (.5) ELL, BRS At-Risk (.5)	CD (1) DVI (.5)

CD = Cognitive Disability

ELL = English Language Learner

LD = Learning Disability

ED = Emotional Disability

BRS = Bilingual Resource Specialist

DVI = Designated Vocational Instructor

language is not English, as well as two students struggling with behavior issues), then short-term support may need to be established for this teacher and the students. In this case, a consultant might provide onsite support for two hours a week for four weeks. When the School Service Delivery Team engages with challenges, the pendulum must not swing back to segregation—we have a responsibility to educate the next generation of children, in a way that structurally, symbolically, and academically honors each of them. Nonetheless, we cannot discount the fact that there will be strife in the process. Change is difficult, and there will be times when teachers and administrators need support from the School Service Delivery Team members.

GRADE-LEVEL DESIGN TEAMS

As described in the previous section, most School Service Delivery Teams provide recommendations that result in a grade-based model of service delivery—for example, teams of teachers and staff work with a range of learners at the eighth-grade level, or at the tenth- and eleventh-grade levels. As long as schools are primarily structured by grades, it makes sense to structure a support model by grades. If the school is structured by small learning academies, then it would make more sense to provide services based on the academy structure. Either way, what is *not* logical is to continue a model by specialization (emotional disability [ED], learning disability [LD], at-risk, ELL, Title I, etc.) in a school that is structured by grades, houses, academies, or some other configuration. For example, support should not be configured such that particular teachers are responsible for groups of labeled students across grades; that is, support should not be configured such that one teacher is responsible for all students with the ED label across three or four grades or more. This practice disconnects teacher specializations and the graded structures of schools, resulting in fragmentation and failure-based programs.

One of the primary responsibilities of the Grade-Level Design Teams is to assign students and staff in ways that support ICS principles. Therefore, the School Planning Team completes the ICS formative analysis, but the School Service Delivery Team and the Grade-Level Design Teams develop, implement, and evaluate the service delivery design. These latter two teams are the ones who bring the vision to life. In so doing, the School Service Delivery Team suggests to the Grade-Level Design Teams some possibilities of how students can be supported. The Grade-Level Design Teams are then responsible for the actual implementation. These Grade-Level Design Teams make big schools into small and large numbers of students into individuals, and they minimize bureaucratic measures such as programming students en masse or clustering students by label or by statutory regulations.

Membership

Membership on the Grade-Level Design Teams should include all individuals assigned to or volunteering at the specific grade level to service students with disabilities, ESL students, students determined to be at-risk, and other similarly situated individuals. Each Grade-Level Design Team must include the general educators, special educators, at-risk teachers, ESL teachers, and any other teacher assigned to the grade-level team by the School Service Delivery Team. In addition, school social workers, guidance counselors, the school psychologist, gifted and talented teachers, speech and language pathologists, or other support people may be asked to focus on a particular grade level(s) for a variety of reasons. For example, guidance counselors may become part of the Grade-Level Design Team and service only those students at that particular grade level, or a speech and language clinician might be assigned to a kindergarten/first-grade cluster as the language needs are high in those two grades. Their roles would be specified by the Grade-Level Design team, but should include direct support to students in heterogeneous groups. Finally, a representative of the School Service Delivery Team should serve on each Grade-Level Design Team to provide a conduit between the two teams.

Goals

The goals of the Grade-Level Design Teams are to meet the individual needs of each learner, from the student with a mild learning disability or a third-year ESL student to a student with severe and profound cognitive disabilities or extreme behavioral challenges due to mental illness. To meet such diverse needs, the teams strategically assign staff to courses and classrooms and strategically place students in courses and classes to ensure students are not segregated and to maximize student learning.

Three additional functions comprise the work of the Grade-Level Design Teams. First, they must determine what professional development may be necessary to help teachers build their capacity to teach to a range of learners in their classrooms. Second, they must help staff incorporate planning time into their days and work weeks to enable staff to collaborate to meet student needs. Third, they must help secure the resources to carry these first two functions to fruition. A representative of each Grade-Level Design Team then takes the professional development, planning time, and resource needs to the School Service Delivery Team. The latter team then can coordinate professional development and planning time, and obtain resources for these needs in collaboration with the School Planning Team.

As we did with the School Service Delivery Teams, we now outline 10 specific steps for the Grade-Level Design Teams to meet their goals. First, the School Service Delivery Team needs to determine membership on each Grade-Level Design Team. For example, if all first-grade teachers in a school comprise the First Grade-Level Design Team, then the School Service Delivery Team may suggest assigning a special education teacher to the team to serve all first-grade students, and may also assign a bilingual specialist to this team. As the planning process continues, team membership may change depending on how the new service delivery is reconfigured.

Second, the Grade-Level Design Team lists the students within each particular grade level who struggle (see Figure 5.2). The students would include those eligible for special education, Title I, at-risk, English language learners, and other students who are struggling but have not met eligibility for a program. The team determines the natural supports that are available to these students (e.g., student peers), additional needed supports, and grade-level staff, and identifies the staff's specific areas of expertise (again, see Figure 5.2).

Third, all students who are eligible for special education must have an individualized education plan (IEP). For each of the struggling students who is not eligible for special education, the Grade-Level Design Team should create an individualized service plan (see Appendix E for a template; described in more detail in Capper et al., 2000) to assist the team in determining needs and appropriate percentage of individual, small-group, and large-group support.

Fourth, the Grade-Level Design Team strategically assigns students to particular classes or courses (see Table 5.2). Often, grade-level team members divide the group of students into smaller "caseloads" for each staff person to better determine specific needs. Most staff find it logical to place students with a teacher whose expertise matches their needs, or the staff member is familiar with the students and would be happy to continue working with them. However, the team must make sure students are naturally proportioned in integrated classrooms and that caseloads are balanced. For example, it is not logical to place all students with high behavioral needs with one teacher because the teacher will never be able to proactively support ten or more students with significant high needs in two or three different classrooms. However, it does make sound sense to place one or two students with high behavioral needs on one teacher's caseload along with eight other students who have fewer needs.

The concept of natural proportions should guide all decisions about student placement in classrooms. For example, if 12% of students in the school have disabilities, then no single classroom should enroll more than 12% of students with disabilities. If English language learners comprise 10% of the school population, then no single classroom or course should have more than 10% of its students be English language learners. Students with needs should be balanced across classrooms in the same proportion that they are in the school.

In addition, student placement decisions need to be guided by the premise of a continuum of support. That is, not all students who require support need direct support from a specialist. Some students will need the support of a team-taught classroom where a general education teacher and a support teacher (e.g., special education teacher or bilingual teacher) teach the course together. (The goal of such classrooms should be to build the teaching capacity of the general teacher such that, ultimately, team-taught support is not necessary.) Some students may require direct

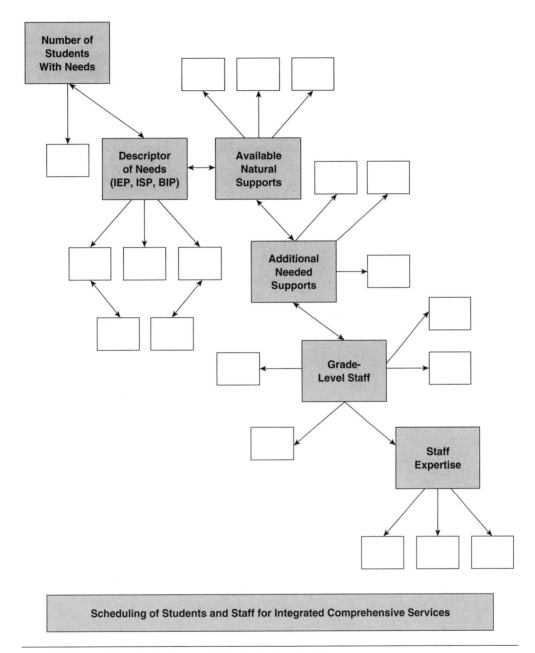

Figure 5.2   ICS Planning by Grade-Level Design Teams

instruction from a support teacher in the general education classroom for part of the school day. Others may benefit equally from the support of a teaching assistant or school volunteer for part of the school day. Still other students may require only a support teacher to check in with the general education teacher on a regular basis for feedback and assistance, or "on-call" support. Some students receive quality support from their peers in

Table 5.2   Scheduling of Staff and Students for ICS

Time	Staff Assignment	Student Placement in Flexible Groups	Academic/ Subject Area	Student Goals/ Objectives	Meeting Days	Compromises
8:00–9:00	Name Name Name		Literature Literature Literature			
9:00–10:00						
10:00–11:00						
11:00–12:00						
12:00–1:00						

collaborative learning classrooms. The students should not be placed in particular classrooms with the assumption that they all need direct support from a specialist. Also keep in mind that the primary purpose of support teachers is to build the capacity of general educators to teach to a range of student needs in their classrooms.

At the same time, within these guidelines, students should not be placed among different classrooms that do not allow them to receive the support they may need. For example, in one middle school we studied, English language learners were placed in three of five eighth-grade classrooms, rather than being placed across all of them. At the same time, their proportion in these classrooms did not exceed their proportion in the school. Similarly, if there are six sections of third grade, maybe a support teacher serves three of the six classrooms and two of these more frequently than the third. However, the students who need support in these classrooms represent their natural proportion in the school. In this manner, both support teachers and general educators are better able to build their curriculum from the ground up around each learner (see Table 5.2).

Fifth, after determining the primary areas of need and the necessary support, the team determines the student schedule for each student, based on the typical learner's schedule at that grade level. For each student schedule, the team identifies those areas where the student is receiving individual, small-group, and large-group instruction with or without support. As we stated in Chapter 1, based on our work in schools, students with the most needs often have the most transitions—including and most frustrating the number of schedule changes in the month of September. Therefore, at the middle and high school level, schedules for students with specific needs should be written before the mass scheduling by grade level and subjects begins. This alleviates many problems on the other end and allows students to begin their year with a schedule that is much more likely to remain unchanged.

Sixth, once the schedules are determined for each student, the team drafts a schedule of when and where teachers need to be to provide appropriate support (Table 5.2). Where there are conflicts, the team members determine how they can work together to support and resolve them proactively.

For the seventh step in the process, once support staff have identified their caseloads and schedules for students and staff are outlined, then the real work begins. Both support teachers and general educators need to determine exactly how their work together will look, i.e., when they will team teach, when the support teacher will be in the room for support only, and when the support teacher will assist with flexible groupings, among other considerations (see Chapter 11, under Professional Development via

Teacher Collaboration, for teaming details). Next, once the teaming schedule is organized, the curriculum and assessment must be developed for each section of the day (see Chapter 8 for curriculum and assessment information details).

Finally, the Grade-Level Design Teams should meet at least weekly to evaluate their efforts, such as determining how the support is working and where more support may be necessary, among other considerations. Teams at one grade level may need to meet with teams at other grade levels if they cannot work out the necessary small-group or individual support within their grade level. In this sense, students are fully supported across their grade levels, horizontally, and throughout all the grades, vertically.

If the School Service Delivery Team has recommended that Grade-Level Design Teams follow their students to the next grade and return back to their original grade in year three (known as looping), then early in February the teams should begin planning for the following school year using the steps outlined above and the feedback obtained from the ICS formative analysis. A thorough review of the ICS formative analysis should occur at least every two years.

Evaluation

The Grade-Level Design teams will frequently collect student achievement data as a prime determinant of their success. They will also work with the School Service Delivery Team to (a) receive feedback regarding how parents, students, and staff experience the evolutional changes of the service delivery structure for all learners, and to (b) update the School Service Delivery Team on their progress and any concerns that should be taken to the School Planning Team.

DISTRICTWIDE SERVICE DELIVERY TEAM

Often, students may receive services in an elementary school that meets their individual needs (such as time in the day for sensory integration, or being included with their peers for the majority of their day), only to advance to the next grade level or school where their ISP or IEP is changed because the staff have designed a model where such individual needs cannot be met. Without reservation, educators at every school must be responsible for developing a service delivery model that meets the needs of each and every student who could possibly walk in the door. For that reason, when implementing ICS, districts should institute a Districtwide Service Delivery Team to work through issues that may affect the district as a whole.

Membership

The membership of the Districtwide Service Delivery Team should include a representative from each School Service Delivery Team throughout the district. In addition, the district director of special education or student services and the district director of instruction should also be team members.

Goals

The goals of the Districtwide Service Delivery Team are to "take care of the whole." That is, the districtwide team is responsible for clarifying differences across School Service Delivery Teams and working toward the development of a continuous model of PreK–12 throughout the district. In this manner, students are not required to fit into whatever model is developed at each school.

The Districtwide Service Delivery Team typically meets four times per year to update and determine areas of need. Once areas of need or concern are clarified, the team sets an agenda and moves forward. At times, staff or administrators may be asked to join the team to provide more detailed information regarding a specific concern, such as if a sensory room (a room all learners can access that has a range of different stimuli for a student's senses) is used at the elementary school and the team wonders how it might work at the middle school, among other concerns.

Evaluation

The Districtwide Service Delivery Team monitors the status of service delivery at each of the schools. Team members use the ICS formative evaluations to ascertain their progress toward ICS.

In sum, educators need to be quite intentional and deliberate about decision making and team structures if ICS is to become a reality in schools. In this sense, ICS moves far beyond typical team structures, such as general education–based grade-level teams, or department teams, or strategic planning teams. In addition, team structures that support ICS also move beyond typical special education teams, such as prereferral intervention teams and special education evaluation teams. The simple structure and function of these three school-based teams and the district-level service delivery team described in this chapter will transform how decisions are made, who is involved in the decisions, how school resources are used, how teachers are assigned, and how students are served in ways that move far beyond compliance, to a high-quality education for every single student in the school.

Table 5.3   Chapter 5. Teams for Shared Decision Making, Staff Design, and Student Support

Focus Area	Focus Area Inquiry	Comments: What We Have	Phase of Application
Part A	**General Questions**		
1.	Describe the current team structure in your school—number of teams, names of the teams, membership, goals, and evaluation. Assess the effectiveness of each team. Which teams could be transformed into one or more of the four suggested ICS shared decision-making teams?		
2.	Membership on all teams includes proportionate representation of individuals of color, language-diverse individuals, and low-income individuals as compared to the percentage of students of color, ESL students, and low-income students in the school/district.		
3.	Membership on all teams includes the array of professionals who serve students who typically struggle in school.		
4.	All our teams set ground rules for discussion and decision making.		
5.	All our teams have established a communication process with the other teams and with other school community members.		
Part B	**Questions About the School Planning Team**		
6.	We have a School Planning Team.		
7.	The School Planning Team has completed all 15 sections of the ICS formative analysis.		
8.	The School Planning Team is beginning to set goals based on the focus areas of each of the four cornerstones of ICS.		

Focus Area	Focus Area Inquiry	Comments: What We Have	Phase of Application
Part C	**Questions About the School Service Delivery Team**		
9.	Our school has a Service Delivery Team.		
10.	Membership on the team does not exceed 10 to 12 individuals and membership meets the criteria in this chapter.		
11.	Team members have discussed ICS and are in general agreement about its philosophy.		
12.	The team has completed the "All Learners Learn Best When . . ." activity.		
13.	The team has drawn a detailed diagram of the current service delivery model at the school, in response to the question, What programs/practices are currently in place for students who struggle in the school?		
14.	The team has developed a list of discrepancies between current services and best practices (future vision).		
15.	The team has drawn its vision of a future service delivery model in the school based on ICS principles.		
16.	The team has delineated action items and drawn a strategic plan to move from a program-driven model to an ICS model.		
17.	The team has initiated and continuously evaluates the school service delivery model based on the school mission and ICS.		
18.	Based on feedback from Grade-Level Design Teams, the team has assigned staff at grade levels to meet student needs.		

(Continued)

Table 5.3 (Continued)

Focus Area	Focus Area Inquiry	Comments: What We Have	Phase of Application
Part C (cont.)			
19.	Based on feedback from Grade-Level Design Teams, the team has determined the necessary staff development plan to build teacher capacity to teach to a wide range of learners.		
20.	Based on feedback from the Grade-Level Design Teams, the team has determined appropriate planning time for grade-level teams of teachers on a daily, weekly, semester, and annual basis.		
21.	Based on feedback from the Grade-Level Design Teams, the team has determined appropriate resources needed to support staff development and planning time.		
Part D	**Questions About Grade-Level Design Teams**		
22.	We have Grade-Level Design Teams at all grade levels in our school.		
23.	The purpose of these teams includes assigning students and staff to classrooms and courses in ways that support ICS principles.		
24.	The team has listed all students at that grade level who struggle.		
25.	The team has ensured all these students have IEPs or ISPs.		
26.	The teams assign students to classes or courses based on the concept of natural proportions in the school.		
27.	The teams assign students to classes or courses based on the concept of a continuum of support.		
28.	These teams assign students with the most severe learning, physical, and emotional needs to heterogeneous, integrated settings.		

Focus Area	Focus Area Inquiry	Comments: What We Have	Phase of Application
29.	The teams have determined the appropriate schedules for each student.		
30.	The teams have determined teacher schedules based on student and teacher needs.		
31.	The teams have determined exactly how teachers will work together and in what ways to build teacher capacity and support students.		
32.	The teams meet regularly to evaluate their efforts using student achievement data, and the ICS formative analysis.		
33.	The teams meet with other Grade-Level Design Teams as needed.		
Part E	**Questions About Districtwide Service Delivery Team**		
34.	We have a Districtwide Service Delivery Team to assist in cohesive services across PreK–12.		
35.	The students in our district experience a seamless transition of services between grades, and between elementary, middle, and high school.		
Reflective Question:			
Given this formative evaluation, what areas should be priority?			

Creating a School Climate That Supports Students With Challenging Behaviors

Many researchers have written about the components necessary to create a positive professional environment where change and progress can be embraced and advanced (Quinn, 2004). We have a combined experience of over 50 years of being involved in public schools as teachers, administrators, consultants, and researchers, and we know when we walk into a school what kind of culture is dominant. We can tell if it is a culture of "doers" versus procrastinators, or a culture of respect versus backbiting. We can tell if it is a culture that has a shared vision; a culture of believers and advocates; or sadly, a culture of tired, worn out, use-to-be-believers and now complainers. We believe that when the adult behavior within an environment is positive, it will positively affect system behavior, which in turn will positively affect student behavior (therefore, we intentionally have *not* devoted a separate chapter to students with severe emotional behavior disorders). As such, we have a choice to create school cultures that are cohesive rather than fragmented, holistic rather than self-serving, ethical rather than unethical, and where equity *means* equity.

Building on Chapter 2, which addressed leadership for ICS and social justice, in this chapter we discuss the importance of adult behavior and how it can positively or negatively energize system behavior, and in turn impact student behavior. Students with challenging behaviors are especially sensitive to adult behavior, and how adults behave can go a long way in transforming the behavior of students with behavioral challenges. Thus, we conclude the chapter with a discussion of this interaction. We argue that as individuals and as a system of individuals, we have the ability to impact student behavior—but we must believe we have this ability and more important, this responsibility. Far too often we hear administrators, administrative students in our certification courses, and teachers tell us that of course they believe and understand the principles of Integrated Comprehensive Services, but there are just some children who do not belong in school. We typically respond with, "Who gets to draw the line for belonging?" We must function within our schools from a principle that all children belong, and we have a responsibility to do everything in our power to assist and support such a sense of belonging for each and every learner. When we begin from this premise, individual adult behavior can change system behavior and in turn influence student behavior (see Figure 6.1).

The climate of the school often correlates with the leadership style of the principal (Fullan, 1999; Green, 2004; Hoy & Miskel, 2001). If the principal is autocratic, often teachers wait to be told what to do and shared vision and decision making do not occur. In addition, often in an autocratically led environment, teachers function in ways that are similar to the principal, and students are taught in a traditional "sit-and-get" manner through a prescribed body of knowledge. Conversely, when the principal functions in a shared leadership capacity, staff are better able to develop a common vision and to work cooperatively.

Frequently, when there are many different visions of how students—including students with challenging behaviors—should be served, it is up to the principal to unify the group. For example, some teachers may be disenchanted with a noncompliant behavior of a specific child and ask that the child be removed from their classroom and possibly the school. Other teachers may feel that the child should stay. Often such disagreements can cause disharmony and frustration among staff. If the principal has already created a school based on the ICS principles, her job is much easier—she must meet with the appropriate staff and determine proactive solutions to teach the desired behavior and protect students and staff in the process. If the principal has worked in an autocratic manner and does not have a unified vision, she is almost forced to go with the majority rule of the staff to keep the peace and remove the child. The problem with the latter resolution is that there is always another child to remove, and adults

Figure 6.1   Interconnectedness of Behavior

are often dissatisfied with the reactionary process or convene the Service Delivery Team in efforts to remove the child. In return, teachers function at a level of uncertainty and pass that same discipline procedure on to their students, who in return function at a level of uncertainty—resulting in an environment that does not feel safe and staff and students do not feel secure to celebrate and rejoice in everyday activities and successes. In contrast, in a climate of shared leadership in support of ICS, staff already know that their voice will be heard and they will have the opportunity to work through difficult situations in support of all learners. Based on these experiences and observations, we offer the following 10 strategies for cocreating a positive school climate that can nurture and support adult and student behavior, and in turn can also facilitate the implementation of ICS:

1. Communication: The principal must honor the communication process in place in the building at all times, in the absence of an emergency.

2. Time: All staff need time to process—when possible, a set amount of time should be arranged to allow staff to share their concerns and then provide proactive suggestions.

3. Desire: Staff must have the desire to adhere to the principles of ICS; once this is established, difficult questions become an opportunity for creative resolutions.

4. Objectivity: Time and a small amount of distance from a question or concern may be necessary to allow for individuals to make objective decisions.

5. Shared ownership: All staff are responsible for all students and the wellness of the school.

6. Professional respect: Respect for each other means listening and functioning from a positive frame.

7. Understanding: Seek to create and assume the least harmful scenario. Follow through to build trust and provide support and encouragement for adults to be successful.

8. Solve the puzzle: Think "out of the box" using the principles of ICS as the foundation.

9. Humor: Keep situations light and productive with laughter.

10. Dedication: Find the balance between the work toward social justice and self-care, but be dedicated to the children and the school.

When these 10 aspects of positive climate are modeled by the principal, it sets the stage for a school culture that can contribute to a healthy work and learning environment for everyone. This in turn can lead to a proactive systems climate and positive outcomes for students with challenging behaviors.

SYSTEM BEHAVIOR

When the school leader can support the principles of ICS and the 10 strategies for cocreating a positive school climate, he or she will find that staff will begin to build trust with each other and will model the same behavior. We find that adults are no different from children in this way—when they feel respected, encouraged, trusted, and supported, they function at their best. When adults feel belittled, disrespected, or undervalued, they function at their worst. The bottom line is this: when adults feel good about themselves and they feel positive about the situation they are working in, they pass that positive energy on to children—and negative student behavior decreases.

STUDENT BEHAVIOR

We believe that 85% of the students will function well in a healthy school climate and that 10% of those students may challenge it at times but can be appropriately redirected. Four percent of the student population may need a detailed behavior protocol to assist teachers and the student in finding more solid ground from which to work. Finally, 1% of our student population has a mental illness or significant behavioral needs. Continuous behavioral plans as well as outside medical and psychological support will be necessary. We encourage staff to keep these percentages in perspective and remember that 1 out of every 100 students needs more support and understanding due to extreme needs that are often not within the student's control. If all other structures are in place and a student is continuing to be challenged by the rules within a school (approximately 4% of the population as describe above), it is imperative that staff create an individualized behavior plan. In our last book, we described how to complete an appropriate behavior plan for the child for whom the school and class behavior expectations are not working (see Appendix I of this book). At the very least, such a plan gives staff continuity in their antecedent and responsive behavior. That is, the student knows that regardless of the environment he or she is in—whether it is the lunch room, the school bus, the hall, or a particular class—the adult response will be consistent across all these environments. In addition, the process of developing the plan will help the adults who come in contact with the student to have a shared understanding of the situations that trigger the student's behavior and the strategies that can help mitigate this behavior. In addition, a behavior plan also allows for a layer of objectivity, which will help elicit clearer, more consistent staff responses. Just as a point of reminder—behavior plans must be written individually for each student. We have been involved in schools where the entire class is on a behavior modification system—that is different from an individualized behavioral protocol and should not be substituted.

Sadly, there are many legal ways to deny students with challenging behaviors access to education, such as the 45-day rule, positive manifestation hearings, expulsions, and suspensions, to name a few. Often we hear administrators say, "How do I get this kid out of my school?" Now, we all know that the administrators asking the question are not "bad" people—most often they are trying to protect other students, teachers, and other administrators. What happens, nevertheless, is these administrators spend a significant amount of time and energy trying to document why the child should *not* be in school instead of spending energy working with staff and the child to determine how the child can *remain* in the school. Others have asked, "Should a student *ever* be removed?" The answer—absolutely, but not without a plan for reentry.

There are times that students do require psychiatric treatment that a school cannot provide. With ICS, when that child leaves for treatment, the team of educators wrapped around him are not relieved of their duty. They simply transfer their attention to his progress in treatment and working with the family and physicians on a proactive reentry. Sometimes the stimuli within a school are too much for a student to gain control of her behavior; in such cases, removing the child as part of a plan to "gain control" is appropriate. It is not necessary to establish a segregated classroom for students with emotional disabilities as a place for a child to gain control. Instead, the Grade-Level Design Team should determine how to free up the most appropriate teacher to work individually with the student and then begin her reentry.

Often when a student is dangerous and is hurting himself or others, he should be removed; however, the removal should not be permanent. It should be temporary, and when the student regains composure and resolution, he should return to his school day. If we do not allow students to return, we are teaching them to drop out. At other times, staff may request to shorten a student's day. This may be appropriate for cases of school phobia (in order to build positive time in school before adding time) or when a child has been out for an extended period of time and needs to transition to a different environment slowly. Most often, half days are used for students whose behavior can no longer be tolerated by staff and administrators. In our work in the schools, we have found shortened days to be rarely if ever successful for students who challenge what we do—again, we typically are teaching them how to drop out. Shortened days are not any more of an intervention than retaining a child who is having trouble learning.

These suggestions provide a general guide for when and why a child might be removed temporarily from our care. We realize this is a controversial position—but we also are keenly aware of how drastically negative behavior can turn positive when children belong and feel supported.

Supporting a student with high behavior needs is never easy. It is important that the school climate is one of support, that the Grade-Level Design Team works together with the behavior plan developed by those individuals who are directly involved with the students, and that we never give up. We must approach every situation believing that we can prevail. Often the students recommended for removal are the same students who so badly want to belong.

When staff are successful with a student whom they would have typically removed, they will become more successful with other students over time. On the other hand, when a child is removed, it only promotes the removal of challenging students in the future. In such a case, teacher capacity does not grow but is inhibited. There is no choice but for staff and students to grow through each other if we want to keep our children in school. Cocreating a positive school climate where adults are respected and where this respect is in turn passed on to the students creates a context in which students with behavioral challenges can have the most hope for success. The success of students with behavioral challenges begins with adult behavior in the school.

Table 6.1   Chapter 6. Creating a School Climate That Supports Students With Challenging
Behaviors

Focus Area	Focus Area Inquiry	Comments: What We Have	Phase of Application
1.	We believe that all children should feel a sense of belonging in school, and we have the responsibility to support this with literally every student in the school.		
2.	We believe that adult behavior directly impacts students with behavioral challenges.		
3.	The climate in our school is one where all staff feel supported.		
4.	Staff behavior is positive and of a problem-solving nature.		
5.	Staff are aware of the proactive teams in place to help resolve issues and access them willingly (e.g., Grade-Level Design Team, School Service Delivery Team, etc.).		
6.	Staff are aware of the proactive systems in place to support students with behavioral needs (e.g., student mentoring, mediation team, counselors, support groups, etc.).		
7.	Staff use potentially reactionary issues as an opportunity to develop proactive response systems and supports for both students and staff.		
8.	Negative staff behavior does not set the tone/climate in the school, as the school leaders are able to work with staff in need and provide positive proactive supports to redirect negative behavior.		
9.	Negative student behavior does not set the tone/climate in the school because there are proactive school discipline procedures in place, proactive instructional mechanisms in all classrooms, and individualized behavior plans for those students who experience more chronic needs for unified support.		

Focus Area	Focus Area Inquiry	Comments: What We Have	Phase of Application
10.	Climate surveys have been developed; distributed to students, staff, and families; and analyzed by gender, race, disability, social class, sexual orientation, and language diversity. Action has been taken as a result of these surveys.		
11.	All students with severe challenging behaviors have individualized behavior plans that have been team developed, and all adults in the school who are in contact with these students follow through on the behavior plan.		
12.	Children receiving psychiatric care outside the school continue to be supported by school staff, and these staff work collaboratively with outside agencies, to plan for the students' reentry.		
13.	If a child is removed to help him or her gain control, the Grade-Level Design Team is able to free a teacher to work with this student and begin his or her reentry.		
14.	We do not use a shortened day as a behavior intervention.		
15.	We do not give up on students, but keep working toward positive solutions no matter what.		

Reflective Questions:

1. Describe the service delivery model for students with challenging behaviors. How many students in your setting would you consider in the 1% category as described in the chapter, and how are these students being served? To what extent does how they are being served match ICS principles, and what ideas do you have for making changes?

2. Given your phase of application, what goals will you set to build a positive climate in support of ICS?

School Involvement With Families

7

From one perspective, a chapter on school involvement with families in this book that focuses on Integrated Comprehensive Services is not necessary because we have learned from our experiences and research that students can achieve at high levels without typical school-family connections. For example, in one of the urban elementary schools we studied, a vast majority of the children lived in homes with parents who worked the night shift or who otherwise were often not available at home. Many of these young kindergarten, first, and second graders would arrive home from school with no adults in the home, feed themselves, put themselves to bed, get themselves up in the morning, and get themselves off to school on time. The principal, aware of this situation, spoke to all the students in the school, as a group, and told them that no matter what was happening in their families, that when they came to school, they would be safe, meals would be served, and all the staff in the school would do everything in their power to ensure they achieved the highest academic success. The reality of the home situation did not prevent this principal from reaching out to the families and over time, the vast majority of the school staff became quite involved with nearly all the families in a variety of different ways. However, this principal did not use the lack of traditional family involvement in school, or the lack of a traditional, middle-class family life as excuses for herself or her staff to not raise the achievement of these students to the highest academic levels. In this school, staff never complained about the lack of family involvement, and never blamed families or the family situations for the level of student achievement at the school.

In another example, again an urban elementary school, the principal knew that many of the children were exposed to harsh, sometimes violent situations in their inner-city homes. This principal collaborated with local medical professionals to ensure that all his students received basic medical care at school, and even secured the services of a dentist to work at the school to meet student dental needs. Like the first example, however, this principal never blamed the families, the neighborhood, or the community for the lack of achievement of the students in his school. Like the first principal, he diligently reached out to these families, but was firm in his belief that he and his staff could dramatically raise the academic achievement of the students in his school, with or without traditional family involvement—and he did so.

These two examples show how students can achieve at the highest level possible without traditional family involvement in schools; they also are examples of how engaging with families on their own terms over time created learning conditions for the students that made their high achievement even more probable. This chapter leads into the following chapter, Chapter 8, which focuses on Teaching within ICS and for Social Justice. Schools that are engaged with families in proactive ways, meaning that the educators in these schools develop meaningful relationships with their students' families, can radically inform classroom curriculum and instruction that is constructed from the students' and families' funds of knowledge. Culturally relevant teaching takes on a whole new meaning when the teachers and the principals actually learn about and are engaged with the culture of their students and their families.

For too long, we have heard educators complain about the "lack of family involvement" in their schools, and we have seen this lack of involvement used as the number one excuse for why particular students are not doing well in their schools. In fact, research has shown that when educators are asked, "Why are the students of color in your school and others performing at lower levels than their white counterparts?" the primary reason given by educators pertains, not to the school, but to the families (McKenzie & Scheurich, 2004). If a student is doing well, they point to the strong support of the student's family. If the student is not achieving up to par, they are quick to blame the family or the student's home life. In this way, educators take a deficit view of families (Valencia, 1997). Thus, families that do not ascribe to the white, middle-class cultural norm are viewed as deficient. Taking a deficit view of these families includes believing that the parents do not value education, that they do not want to be involved in their child's education, that they refuse to engage in activities with their children that will help them learn, that they do not care about their children or do not want their children to succeed, that children from these families come to school "unprepared to learn," that these families are "deprived" or "disadvantaged," or that the parents' values are different from those of the school. Thus, the students from these families hold values and engage in behaviors that are not congruent with school norms. These same educators often list the ways they have tried to get the family involved, or complain that the family does not attend parent-teacher conferences, or does not help the student with homework, or does not send back to school required papers and assignments, or does not provide the student with good meals or good sleep or clean clothes, or exposes the student to too much violence or television.

We have also witnessed well-meaning educators who take up the pity, sympathy, or charity perspective of families who do not align with the white, middle-class norm. These educators feel sorry for students who do not have two, opposite-gender parents living at home, or who live in poverty. They are not critical of these families and students, but instead, feel sorry for and pity them and wish there was something they could do to help. Along with this pity come lower expectations for student learning and achievement because of the family situation. We believe this pity, sympathy, or charity perspective of families is as damaging, disrespectful, degrading, and unproductive as being outright critical of families who do not match our white, middle-class norm of how families are supposed to be "involved with the school."

Frankly, we are shocked by the pervasiveness of this deficit view of families that persists even among well-meaning teachers and school leaders, among educators who have received some training in white privilege or poverty, and among educators who consider themselves leaders or advocates of social justice. We are also amazed by the unwillingness of these educators to engage with families of poverty, families of color, or families with same-gender parents, on these families' terms. They are reluctant to spend time getting to know these families, including what their values are, and to seek to help meet these families' needs. Instead, even though some of these educators do spend time with families in low-income neighborhoods conducting school business, they continue to wear the lens of white, middle-class privilege throughout the encounter and afterward. Thus, even after spending time with these families, these educators come away with their stereotypes and judgments not disrupted, but deepened. We find this fact quite troublesome, and with this perspective, traditionally marginalized students can expect to make little progress in this education system—when that happens, ironically, they and their families will be blamed.

Typically, educators expect families to be involved in the school based on white, middle-class definitions of parent involvement. Educators use white norms as the criteria to measure family involvement in schools, such as attending PTO meetings, attending parent-student conferences, volunteering at the school, helping the child with homework, reading to the child, serving on committees, chaperoning school events, or sending treats and snacks to school among other possibilities. In short, schools tend to limit family involvement practices to traditional activities that ignore perspectives of families of color or low-income families (Lopez, 2001; Lopez, Scribner, & Mahitivanichcha, 2001).

Most often, educators do not stop to think about why it may be difficult for families to be involved with schools in traditional ways. First, perhaps families may have had negative experiences with schools themselves; in some cases, the children in these families attended the same school as their parents when they were young. If family members have had negative experiences at school, they are less likely to want to reenter the school and engage with educators there. Just reentering the school may feel intimidating, shaming, and bring forth feelings of inadequacies of their own achievements as students and in their parenting. Other parents may be suspicious and angry about the school having treated them unfairly when they themselves were students (Friend & Bursuck, 2002).

Second, many parents are working long hours, sometimes at more than one job, to make ends meet. If there are other children in the family, there may just not be enough hours in the day for families to participate in traditional school-parent activities (Dwyer & Hecht, 1992). The same can be said for families with only one adult who is fully responsible for all the children in the home, with little outside help or assistance. In fact, most family members who are involved in schools in traditional ways, such as volunteering in classrooms, or participating in leadership of the parent organization to name a few possibilities, are often those who have much more discretionary time in their day than members of other families—that is, these family members may not be working full time, or may not be the main income earner in their families, and thus have the time to devote to in-school activities. In addition, some of these parents work in white collar careers that allow them time flexibility with their jobs to participate in school activities. If these family members take time off to visit the school, they are still getting paid. In contrast, a parent who is employed in a working-class or blue collar job may not have the flexibility to be able to leave to attend a school meeting, and when doing so, may not get paid or will have to use vacation or personal leave time—something that many families cannot afford to do.

A third possible reason why some families are not involved in schools in traditional ways, particularly related to homework, is that the student work outpaces what the parent knows (Dwyer & Hecht, 1992). For example, if a child brings home algebra for homework, some families do not have members with the educational background to be able to help this child with algebra.

Fourth, some schools clearly do not want parents involved and resist even legitimate family connections, such as parents wanting to visit classrooms to decide if their child should attend that school, and then set up rigid boundaries around when parents may visit and under what circumstances. Parents can clearly perceive the school as sending the message, "hands off." Not surprisingly, in these cases, parents feel disconnected from the real decisions within a school and feel too intimidated to break through this barrier (Littky & Grabelle, 2004).

Finally, some families may experience cultural and language barriers (Friend & Bursuck, 2002) with the school, while in other situations, ugly racial histories in many communities make some parents of color reticent to be a visible presence in some schools (Oakes & Lipton, 1999). Low-income parents may lack the powerful social networks that bring information to more advantaged parents (Oakes & Lipton, 1999), enabling the more advantaged parents to be more traditionally involved with the school.

Because of all these reasons many families are not involved in traditional ways with schools, in this chapter, we intentionally use the phrase "school involvement with families" rather than "family involvement in schools" (Lopez, 2001; Lopez et al., 2001). That is, within ICS, rather than attempting to get families involved in schools, we advocate for schools working harder to become involved in the lives of families. In this way, we can move beyond the deficit view that is unconsciously taken even in the "family involvement" literature. Fortunately, we are in a day and time where a new generation of scholars are rewriting the literature and story on families and schools. For example, Lopez (2001) and associates (Lopez et al., 2001) have extensively researched migrant, Latino families.

In this new literature, instead of taking a deficit view of families, educators focus on *asset* thinking about families (Lopez, 2001; Lopez et al., 2001). An assets perspective means believing that all families have strengths and gifts, that all families are doing the best they can at the time, that all families care about their children, and that all families are involved in their children's lives to some extent. According to Lopez (2001; Lopez et al., 2001), educators must always view families positively:

> If parents are viewed in nonfavorable terms, then the expectation placed on them is minimal; relegating them to marginal players in the schooling process. However, if parents are viewed as central to education's goal—and as essential players in their child's education—then parents will feel as though their input is highly

valued and respected. In these effective contexts, high expectations are placed on parents, and parents, in turn, feel empowered to get involved in their children's education in new and fundamentally different ways. (p. 270)

This assets view of families requires a rethinking of family involvement in at least three ways. First, Lopez (2001) contends that, "instead of trying to get marginalized parents involved in specific ways at school, schools should begin to identify the unique ways that marginalized parents are already involved in their children's education and search for creative ways to capitalize on these and other . . . forms of involvement" (p. 434). For example, there may be many ways that the family is involved in their child's life and is supportive at home, but these ways are not recognized by the school. In the next section, we will discuss the importance of getting to know families, and in so doing, become much more attuned to the unique ways that families are already involved in their child's education.

Second, rather than trying to get families involved within the school, educators should focus on supporting families' social, physical, or economic needs on a daily and ongoing basis (Lopez, 2001; Lopez et al., 2001). Third, educators need to place their priorities on families and to develop relationships with families that demonstrate a heightened level of commitment to them.

Educators in schools that focus on school involvement with families hold an unwavering commitment to make meeting parental needs the most important task with families, above all other involvement considerations (Lopez, 2001; Lopez et al., 2001). These educators hold themselves accountable to meet the multiple needs of parents on a daily and ongoing basis.

To meet family needs, educators must first generate an awareness about family needs, and second, mobilize school and community agencies to facilitate the involvement process. In schools that focus on school involvement with families and seeking to meet family needs, the educators make home visits a top priority. All staff in the school become involved in these home visits, including the school counselors, librarian, clerks, paraprofessionals, and all the other teaching staff. In these schools, all students' homes are visited at least once a year by someone in the school in a positive fashion. At these visits, they communicate with the families this message: "We want you to know that we care about your daughter or son and we want to know where you live and if we can help you in any way, we are here to serve you" (Lopez et al., 2001, p. 264).

Not only is each family visited at least once each school year with a positive message, but educators also ensure that this family contact continues throughout the academic year. In this way, educators get to know families for an extended period of time and are able to foster genuine relationships (Lopez, 2001; Lopez et al., 2001).

Similarly, to counter deficit views of families, McKenzie and Scheurich (2004) advocate for meeting with families in their homes and neighborhoods by conducting neighborhood walks. Some leaders require all their staff to conduct these home visits and walks in the families' neighborhoods as a way to spend time with each and every family in their classroom. These walks can occur at the beginning of the school year as a way for the teacher to introduce him- or herself to the family and to get to know them. This begins to build relationships with the families and helps families to see this interest from the start.

These home visits and the continuous contact with families help educators to become sensitive about a family's situation without judging the family or child's ability to succeed. These visits also allow educators to get to know a family's life history and gain knowledge of family needs, which can help educators to treat these families with respect and dignity regardless of family circumstances. Such family connections can also result in educators holding compassion and empathy for the families without pity or judgment. In so doing, these educators become willing to do whatever it takes to connect with the family.

By focusing on meeting family needs, parents feel less alone when facing hardships, and this helps prevent and alleviate family stress. Getting some relief—however minor—helps parents focus on the children's education; encourages further involvement in their children's lives; teaches parents that educational success depends on interactions with their children; reminds parents that children's needs extend beyond the economic or physical realm; helps families focus more on becoming formally involved in school settings; and most important, enables them to feel as though they have "ownership" over the involvement process (Lopez, 2001; Lopez et al., 2001). These visits also convey to the family that small actions with their children can be important for their education, such as checking in and talking to the child and finding out what's going on, as well as the successes or problems they are having (Lopez, 2001; Lopez et al., 2001).

Unfortunately, most parents are only contacted by educators when their child is having problems in school. For example, educators have shared with us that their discipline system requires students to call their parents after a certain level of infraction is reached. In another example, some educators visit only the families of students who have a particular number of unexcused absences, or parents receive calls when their child's homework is not completed. This negative contact only serves to further remove the family from the school and also lessens the possibility that the family will become more involved with the school. This can be especially true if the parent is struggling with the child, and negative contact from the school only serves to reinforce the parent's possible feelings of inadequacy with the child and with the school.

In addition to visiting families, three-way conferences between a family member, the student, and the teacher provide a second way to become involved with families (McKenzie & Scheurich, 2004). This idea, first developed by the FAST program (Families and Schools Together, 2004) in Wisconsin, can be implemented at the kindergarten through senior level of high school. These conferences can take place in the family's home or at a place the family is comfortable. The purpose of these conferences can be to set goals for the year and to review how the student is doing in school. Over time, the student can lead these conferences—the student presents examples from his or her portfolio to share with the family and teacher. At the fifth- and sixth-grade level, the conferences can include career planning with families. Specifically, the meetings can require the teacher, student, and family member to review the student's achievement to date, discuss career goals and possibilities, and then plan the middle school and high school course schedule in a way that these career goals can be realized. Educators can engage in these three-way conferences on an annual basis to update career goals and course planning.

A third method for educators to become involved with families is through structuring academic assignments with students in ways that involve their families. For example, some schools have found great success in having their students conduct oral histories with family members (McKenzie & Scheurich, 2004). One of the first examples of using family and community oral histories in education occurred in the Foxfire book series, where students in the Appalachian region interviewed family and community members not only about their life histories, but also about how they accomplished particular tasks, such as quilting, building a cabin, and making a candle (Wigginton, 1977; Wigginton & Bennett, 1986). Students then took photos of these tasks and assembled the histories and explanations for various activities into an entire set of commercially published books. Family and community oral histories can be conducted at any grade level, and the students may interview and record autobiographical histories of any family member, be it a parent, grandparent, aunt, uncle, or whomever. Students then bring these oral histories back to school to share with the class, and various projects can be developed from them. In addition, family and community members can be invited to the school to share their skills, talents, perspectives, and culture with the class or school.

Some schools reach out proactively and positively with parents in other ways. For example, in one school, parents receive attendance awards when their children receive such awards. Other leaders have required their teachers to make four positive phone calls home each week to families of the students in their class or courses as a way to build positive, proactive relationships with families.

In addition to school involvement with families, educators still must ensure that parent involvement at the school includes proportional representation of families of color and low-income families. For example, on any school committee that includes families, educators need to ensure that families of color, low-income families, and families of students with disabilities are proportionally represented. Likewise, the parent-teacher organization also needs to reach out to marginalized families and ensure that any parent group at the school includes a proportional representation of all families. Equity data should be routinely collected and analyzed about which families participate in in-school activities. It should go without saying that the school should always provide transportation, interpreters if needed, and child care if they wish families to participate in these kinds of school activities. In addition, many schools have had great success with conducting parent conferences in the parent's home, workplace, community center, church, or other settings where the family feels most comfortable.

In the successful schools we have been involved in, school leaders and the other educators go out of their way to greet families at the door and to treat them with the utmost courtesy and respect. Similar to the discussion you will find in Chapter 8 on culturally relevant pedagogy, when families enter these schools, they find themselves reflected back in the art on the walls, in the language used in the signage around and within the school, and in the books and information available to families. In schools that include students for whom English is not their first language, all school information is translated and readily available for these families, and the taped phone voice greeting that families receive when the office is closed is always given in languages that reflect the culture of the school. In the early elementary grades when a unit on "families" is traditionally included in the curriculum, educators should ensure that however students wish to depict their families or whomever they identify as "family" should always be respected, appreciated, and honored. For example, in some cultures, students' families include grandparents, uncles, neighbors, and other influential individuals in their lives. Toward this end, we highly recommend the video, *That's a Family* (Chasnoff, Ben-Dov, & Yacker, 2000). Appropriate for use for at least the K–8 level, the video is geared toward students and depicts the wide range of individuals in students' lives whom they consider family.

We need also to welcome those families with the social and cultural capital, time, and resources who wish to participate in schools in traditional ways. Some family members see their involvement solely as that of an advocate, some think of it as a way to give back to the school, others are involved because they know how hard it is for teachers to juggle everything, and then there are those who want to be in the know. In still other cases, there are those families who have a variety of issues with the school. Regardless of the rationale for families to be involved in their children's school, educators must accept that families are involved for a variety of different reasons and must respect whatever level of involvement they can have and for whatever purpose.

While some of the contemporary research on families and schools emphasizes proactive, positive connections with families, particularly for families of color and those of low income, this literature does not address the unique needs of families of students with disabilities. We discuss this area next.

FAMILIES OF STUDENTS WITH DISABILITIES

We have witnessed a variety of ways that educators distance themselves from families of students with disabilities. First, many educators make assumptions about these families, including blaming the family for the child's disability, seeing it as a result of poor parenting or some other family factor. For example, we have heard educators comment that "the apple does not fall far from the tree." Blaming parents for their child's disability most often happens with parents of students with challenging behaviors or students whose disability lies along the autism spectrum. Educators often expect the parents to change their child's behavior. Holding parents responsible for their child's behavior is illogical, and it in no way furthers the cause of educating all students. Instead, we all must share in the responsibility and accountability for student behavior; educate ourselves and the parents, if needed; and provide as much support to the parents as possible.

A second assumption that many educators make about families of students with disabilities is that these families have not accepted their child's disability, that this family is somehow "stuck" in the grief process with their child. Educators typically assign this assumption to families who are quite involved in their child's education, who want to meet often with educators and educational leaders about their child's education, and who make particular educational demands for their child.

It is critical that educators never make either of these assumptions about families of students with disabilities. First, as educators, we have no idea how we would respond to having a child, 24 hours a day, with a disability (see Philpott, 2003), or having a child with challenging behaviors who did not respond to typical parenting. Further, given the outcomes of special education that we described in Chapter 1 of this book, parents of students with disabilities have plenty of good reasons to be upset with educators. Thus, in schools that are implementing ICS, educators' negative, pedantic, unprofessional views of families of students with disabilities must stop. As discussed in the previous section, instead, educators should seek out these families, spend time with them, develop meaningful relationships with them, and find out what their needs are and if there are ways that the school can alleviate some of those needs. In so doing, educators can learn from these families and treat them in respectful and professional ways.

Toward this end, we believe it is poor practice to discuss children in a teacher team meeting without first informing the parent. If a child is of enough concern that a team of teachers or staff has assembled to discuss this child, then the parent should be informed and invited to the meeting as well. We are amazed at how many of these meetings about children occur without informing the parent. Yet, if we knew a team of professionals were meeting about our own child because of their concerns, we most certainly would want to know about it.

Likewise, the practice of assembling a team of professionals, inviting the parent, and then proceeding to inform that parent about everything possible that is wrong or deficient in their child, we believe constitutes educational abuse of that parent/family and of the child. These meetings most often occur as part of the special education identification and placement process. Typically, if the focus of the meeting is to share evaluation information about the child, the meeting is full of professional jargon all cast in negative terms about the child. Again, imagine how we would feel if we were called to a meeting of professionals around a table, in which the number of professionals far outnumbered us, and then this team, after a few perfunctory polite remarks, launches into every deficit imaginable about our child. Federal or state law does not require this type of meeting. To be sure, evaluation information must be shared with parents as well as other information about the child, but we suggest adopting aspects of the MAPS process (Vandercook & York, 1989) as one way to rethink and recast these meetings. The MAPS process includes encouraging parents to invite others to school meetings, including the student, siblings, and peers. Here, parents play the lead role, sharing their history of the student, and their dreams, hopes, and fears. The team, beginning with the parent and others the parent has invited to the process, identifies the student's strengths and only then are needs identified. Thus, in this process, the traditional power dynamics of a typical special education meeting are shifted so that the family has an equal voice in the process.

Importantly, if educators in the school have developed a meaningful, ongoing relationship with literally all families in the school, including families of students with disabilities, then it will be less difficult to see these families as partners in their child's education, to see these families' strengths and their needs, to endeavor to help meet these families' needs instead of blaming them, and then to not be put off by their requests about their child's education. To be sure, not all family requests for their children are in the best interests of their own child. But in the context of a meaningful relationship with these families, we can share our best insights into the situation and work toward an amicable solution.

DEVELOPING FAMILY CAPACITY

While some educators resist families who advocate for their own children, in schools that are implementing ICS principles and practices, educators seek to develop the leadership capacity of families. For example, in one school, the educators reached out to the Latino families of their students. Their efforts included hiring a Spanish-speaking, Latino community member to serve as a bilingual resource person in the school. Though this person was not certified to teach, he supported teachers and students in the classroom, assisted with language interpretation, and served as a liaison between the school and the Latino community. In addition, the Latino parents wished to form their own parent group, which the principal supported. Within this group, the principal and other educators taught the family members about the U.S. education system—not only how it works, but also how to work the system. That is, the educators at this school made explicit the informal and formal knowledge about schooling that white, middle-class families already have and know how to use for the benefit of their own children. At another school, the principal offered evening sessions where interested parents could learn the function of meetings and how to participate in and lead successful meetings. This principal also invited families to all the professional development activities offered at the school at no cost to the families.

While ideally, we would want a parent organization that reflects the diversity of the school, in some schools, educators have learned that some families of color prefer to meet with their own ethnic group as a safe way to connect with and support each other in the school system. For example, at one school, though the parent organization was quite active, the school also supported, at the families' request, separate African American and Latino parent groups. Perhaps if educators reach out and engage these families in positive and proactive ways from the beginning of the school year, there might be less of a need for these families to meet as an ethnic group—or perhaps not. The schools that have supported, at the families' request, separate ethnic parent groups, typically have been located in predominantly white, middle- to upper-class communities and neighborhoods. Thus, perhaps in this context, families of color feel a stronger need to connect with each other in such a group. Having said that, we do not think it is wise to purposely establish a separate group for families of students with disabilities. Perhaps a parent might request such a group, but educators should not intentionally establish it, because such a group further separates general and special education—and works in opposition to moving beyond with ICS. The knowledge and wisdom of these families deserves to be shared with other families—all families can find their similarities and differences of experience, whether or not they have a child with a disability. Instead, these families should be encouraged to become involved in the parent-teacher organization or other aspects of the school where their perspectives would be quite valuable for all families and educators.

PARENT RESISTANCE TO ICS AND SOCIAL JUSTICE

Unfortunately, families of students who historically have benefited most from segregated programs and tracking may be the most fierce opponents to moving toward ICS. Oakes and Lipton (1999) explain it this way:

> Teachers who are entertaining socio-cultural conceptions of learning and intelligence and principles of social justice must withstand the scrutiny of skeptical parents who fear they have much to lose if traditional practices are altered. Parents who did well with traditional instruction can become apprehensive if their children experience nontraditional classrooms. Pressures around grades, test scores, and traditional indicators of success (such as scores on weekly spelling tests) emerge even in the earliest grades. In tracked schools or those with pullout programs for gifted students, savvy parents invariably (and understandably) want their children enrolled in the "best" classes. Because so many schools operate competitive systems, permitting only a small percentage of student slots in high-track classes, these parents have had few options but to push to have their children better educated than others. Because schools need political support—not only for funding and physical resources, but also for credibility—they often respond to parental resistance by reining in the reform, and they sometimes suspend their efforts out of frustration. (p. 357)

Hence, some of the most vociferous voices against the implementation of ICS may be from white, middle- or upper-class families whose children have benefited from the current segregated programs by allowing their children easy access to advanced courses and opportunities. Leaders should be prepared for possible conflicts from families who want to maintain their current existence. Theoharis (2004) found that in schools whose leaders were oriented toward justice, some parents threatened the principal's job by insisting that if their demands were not met for their own children, they would see to it that the principal would be removed. These parents may also complain to the school board and superintendent, write vicious editorials in the local paper, circulate petitions against the principal, and even pressure other parents to remove their "problem" child from particular courses and classrooms.

Surprisingly, research has also suggested that even families who consider themselves liberal may strongly resist school practices that are similar to ICS. For example, Brantlinger, Majd-Jabbari, and Guskin (1996) studied white, liberal, female parents and found that though these women considered themselves liberal, in the end, they primarily sought advantages for their own child that at the same time did not promote equity for all students in the school. Theoharis (2004), in his study of social justice leaders, surfaced similar findings from parents who would begin their complaints to the principal with the phrase, "Now, I'm not racist, but . . ." and then go on to complain about the students of color in the school. These same white, liberal, middle-class families often viewed traditionally marginalized students and families from a charity perspective, not an equity perspective.

The best response to any resistance is continued communication and education. School leaders must always remember that, though they are in a formal position of authority, they are teachers first and foremost. Great leaders have always been great teachers. Thus, leaders will need to patiently communicate and continue to educate parents who seemingly have plenty of education. For example, in one new bilingual school, the principal hosted a parent meeting where the families of the students learned about the progress of the school and their children. The school was almost exactly half Caucasian and half Latino (and most of the Caucasian students were from middle- to upper-class families). When the white parents arrived at the meeting, they noticed the translator headsets on the desks and assumed these were going to be for the Latino families. To their surprise, however, the bilingual principal conducted the entire meeting in Spanish. Thus, the white parents were required to wear headsets that enabled them to hear an interpreter translate what the principal was saying into English. This is a powerful example of how the principal sought to educate his students' families. In an informal, natural way, he taught the white, middle- and upper-class families at this meeting what it is like to be in a room and not be able to understand the language that is being spoken. Likewise, he also taught these families what it might feel like to not be the dominant group. He also taught the Latino families respect for their language and culture and demonstrated his value of their language and culture—in this meeting, they were not a devalued, second-class group.

In addition, some families of students with disabilities may also oppose ICS if they feel their child has been successful in a segregated setting and will not be as successful in integrated environments. When educators face this opposition, it is important to remember that these families have learned their lesson well. That is, up to now, we have educated these families into believing that their child will not be successful in integrated environments and that the best option is to segregate their child, not only for academic purposes, but to provide safe havens apart from the swirling dysfunction of public education. However, if, in the past, many families have learned from educators that segregated options are the best, educators now have the responsibility to educate parents about the benefits of ICS principles. Chapter 1 of this book provides plenty of information to be shared with parents toward this end.

Families of English language learners may also oppose ICS principles and practices. If their child has been served in a pullout bilingual program, and now their child will receive these services within a general education classroom, they may feel as if bilingual programs are being eliminated. If white educators and leaders are the ones implementing ICS, then they may be considered racist and discriminatory toward English language learners. Similar to the families of students with disabilities, this situation calls for educators to clearly communicate their intentions with ICS and to reassure these families that their children will indeed benefit most from an ICS instructional arrangement. Frequent and clear communication with these families will be quite essential. Again, if educators have established meaningful relationships with these families to begin with, then communication about ICS will be facilitated by these relationships.

In sum, this chapter has suggested that, while family involvement in schools is not necessary for student achievement, school involvement with families can result in meaningful, long-term relationships, and these relationships in turn can inform the curriculum and instruction at the school and create conditions that will foster student achievement in the long run. School involvement with families can include acknowledging the ways that parents are already involved in their child's life in typical and untypical ways—but ways that often go unrecognized or are judged by the school. Home visits, three-way conferences, and academic projects that involve the family and community are all critical strategies for developing meaningful relationships. By employing these strategies, the school can reach out and support families, making such ongoing support and connection a primary focus and commitment of the school.

Families of students with disabilities have a different kind of history with the schools, and schools have largely responded by making assumptions about these families, being judgmental and critical about their approaches, and feeling threatened by these families. The traditional ways the schools interact with these families and the formal special education processes that devalue these families need to be discarded in favor of more proactive, positive relationships.

Finally, leaders who wish to implement ICS principles and practices can expect parent resistance in a multitude of forms across the spectrum of parent beliefs and values. However, circling back to the beginning of the chapter, seeking to reach out and develop ongoing, meaningful relationships with families can mitigate parental backlash against the ICS efforts.

Families within ICS are not just welcomed or tolerated, they are needed to build the community of learning that is important for the success of all students. Families can and will be involved differently in schools, and it will not and should not look the same for all families. Educators within ICS need to hold the least harmful assumption about families and assume that all families are doing the best they can at that moment in time. When this occurs, there tends to be a different culture within the school that allows for a more accepting ebb and flow of relationships with families.

In schools where Integrated Comprehensive Services are prospering, all educators believe that all families love their children, and they are all involved in their child's lives in a variety of different ways. If we lead with care and compassion, we can assist more families in belonging and provide the opportunity for mutually trusting and supporting relationships to flourish. Schools and students need their families and their teachers to be wrapped around them differently, that is, in a way that is nonjudgmental, which will lead to better student performance all around—emotionally, socially, and academically.

Table 7.1   Chapter 7. School Involvement With Families

Focus Area	Focus Area Inquiry	Comments: What We Have	Phase of Application
1.	We never blame families for the level of achievement at our school.		
2.	We never complain about the lack of parent involvement.		
3.	We do not take a deficit view of families.		
4.	We believe that all parents value education—they care about their children and want them to succeed.		
5.	We do not consider any families "deprived" or "disadvantaged."		
6.	We do not take a sympathy or charity perspective of families who do not align with the white, middle-class norm.		
7.	We understand there are a variety of reasons why families may not participate in schools in traditional ways.		
8.	In our school, we emphasize school involvement with families, rather than family involvement in schools.		
9.	We take an assets view of families, that all families have strengths and gifts, all families are doing the best they can at the time, and all are involved in their children's lives.		
10.	We have identified the unique ways that marginalized families are already involved in their children's education.		
11.	We are committed to supporting families' social, physical, and economic needs on an ongoing basis.		

(Continued)

Table 7.1 (Continued)

Focus Area	Focus Area Inquiry	Comments: What We Have	Phase of Application
12.	All staff in our school are involved in positive, proactive home visits with every family in the school. All families are visited at the beginning of the school year, and ongoing communication continues with each family.		
13.	We hold at least annual three-way conferences with each student, a family member, and a staff member.		
14.	Academic assignments are structured that involve students gathering oral histories and other information from their families and communities.		
15.	We have identified all the ways that we positively and proactively connect with families.		
16.	Families of color, of low income, and of language diversity; same-gender families; and families with students with disabilities are proportionally represented on all school committees that include parental members. We routinely collect and analyze equity data on this fact.		
17.	The school always willingly provides transportation, child care, and interpreters if needed to help families participate in school activities.		
18.	We conduct all parent meetings/conferences at a time and place that is convenient for the parent.		
19.	All staff share responsibility for genuinely welcoming all families into the school.		
20.	When families enter our school, they see themselves reflected back in the		

Focus Area	Focus Area Inquiry	Comments: What We Have	Phase of Application
	art, the language used in the signage, and the books and information available.		
21.	Even if we only have a small number of students for whom English is a second language, we provide all family information in the language of the students' families.		
22.	We have conducted an equity audit on the ways that the "family" unit is taught in the early elementary grades, the materials used, and the books and resources available in the classrooms and media center that depict the wide variety of families.		
23.	We never blame families for their children's disabilities.		
24.	We never assume a family's relationship with the school is a result of unsolved grief about their child with a disability.		
25.	We involve families in all meetings regarding their child.		
26.	We have consciously revamped all parent meetings that are part of the special education process in ways that provide space for families to be equal members of the team.		
27.	We are developing the leadership capacity of families.		
28.	We expect some parent resistance to ICS and respond with continued communication and education.		
29.	Families know each and every specialist who works with their child and what they do.		

(Continued)

Table 7.1 (Continued)

Focus Area	Focus Area Inquiry	Comments: What We Have	Phase of Application
30.	Families know that when staff does not agree with their request, it is based on the best interest of their child—not a blanket comment because of who the family is or a uniform policy.		
31.	Families know that their child's teacher thinks that their child is special and worth their time and energy to support.		

Reflective Questions:

1. How are typically marginalized families at your school already involved in their children's education in untypical ways?

2. List all the assets (positive qualities) of the families who you believe have not been involved in traditional ways with the school.

CORNERSTONE 3

Providing Access to High-Quality Teaching and Learning: Building Teacher Capacity and Curriculum and Instruction

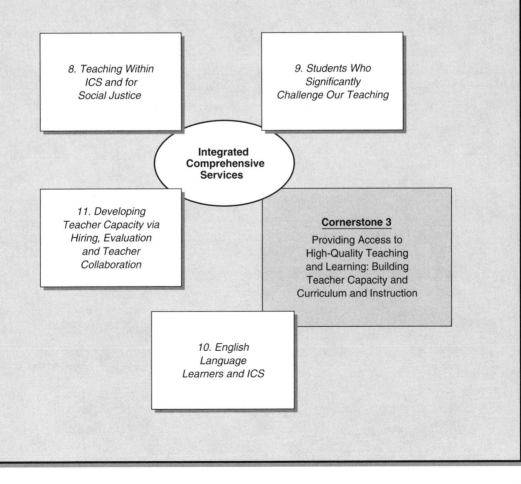

8. Teaching Within ICS and for Social Justice

9. Students Who Significantly Challenge Our Teaching

Integrated Comprehensive Services

11. Developing Teacher Capacity via Hiring, Evaluation and Teacher Collaboration

Cornerstone 3

Providing Access to High-Quality Teaching and Learning: Building Teacher Capacity and Curriculum and Instruction

10. English Language Learners and ICS

Teaching Within ICS and for Social Justice

We are at a crucial time in the history of education in which educators have a choice to cast a wide net that could bring about increases in student achievement or follow a distinct course of action that would minimize and discard a large percentage of our student population to the educational sidelines, continuing to perpetuate an educational and societal caste system—all as a result of how we choose to teach. We want our students to embrace learning as a process of knowing and understanding—not rote memorization. We want all our students to have opportunities for inquiry—to problem solve, hypothesize, and in the end, come to their own understanding that they may then have the opportunity to apply and evaluate. Educators must apply these same ideas to their understanding of pedagogy and standards.

If, in fact, we use the standards as a general guide of appropriate knowledge by grade level, how we teach students to obtain that knowledge must be conducted in a manner in which students learn how to learn. All children must have such opportunities, not just our children who have privileged access to accelerated classes. The irony of cross-content, problem-based learning that often occurs in accelerated classes or gifted programs is that this same kind of teaching and learning would be quite beneficial to learners who have a difficult time retaining, recouping, and generalizing information. For these learners, the curriculum and instruction that often occurs in advanced classes would be a much better fit than forced rote memorization of useless facts that do not apply to any aspect of their lives. As Oakes and Lipton (1999) state, "If good teaching and rigorous academic achievement do not reach every student in every class, we block our possibility of both social justice and excellence, even for a few. We know that 'excellent teaching' requires social justice" (p. xviii).

In this chapter, we first discuss four key considerations for teaching within ICS and for social justice. Next, we discuss the standards and accountability movement and considerations for students who struggle in relation to standards. We end the chapter with practical examples of teaching within ICS and social justice in action. In so doing, we first discuss the importance of staff assignment on teaching within ICS and for social justice, and provide a middle school example of how staff can be assigned so as to enable all students to benefit from high-quality teaching and learning. Then, we discuss differentiated and culturally relevant curriculum and instruction and provide a differentiated lesson plan for a fourth-grade science unit to demonstrate how a variety of learner needs can be met within the ICS model. Finally, we briefly address student assessment and provide an example of a student individualized service plan and describe its use. Though this chapter focuses on the curriculum and instruction within ICS and for social justice, we also refer readers to Chapter 9, which includes additional curriculum and instruction considerations for students with significant disabilities, and Chapter 10, which includes teaching strategies for English language learners.

FOUR KEY CONSIDERATIONS FOR TEACHING WITHIN ICS AND FOR SOCIAL JUSTICE

A first consideration for teaching within ICS and for social justice relates to hiring. As we discuss in Chapter 11, effective teaching within ICS and for social justice begins at initial staff employment. Leaders must only hire staff who are willing and able to teach across a range of students' needs. This fact of the prospective teaching assignment needs to be made crystal clear in the educator recruitment and hiring process, and the potential candidate should be able to demonstrate his or her competency in teaching across this range. Ideally, prospective candidates will hold dual certifications across student differences, such as combined degrees in general education, special education, bilingual education, English as a second language, and reading, to name a few.

A second key factor in teaching within ICS and for social justice is the understanding that nothing magic has ever happened behind the doors of a special education classroom, or a reading resource room, or an ESL room, or a gifted and talented resource room. That is, the curriculum and instruction that has been successful in those settings is nothing magical, mysterious, and esoteric that only a few highly gifted individuals in the world can learn how to teach. Put another way, if magical teaching and learning have occurred behind those doors, we are arguing that any teacher, in any classroom, at any time, can easily learn this same magic in working with all the students in his or her classroom. We agree with Ladson-Billings (1995) that when white teachers or teachers of color are successful with students of color, the transaction taking place is nothing more than "good teaching." Ladson-Billings suggests that we need to reconceptualize good teaching to mean teaching that is composed of culturally relevant instruction and instruction that is differentiated to various student learning needs. There is nothing magic or mysterious about culturally relevant instruction—it is just good teaching.

Thus, teaching within ICS and for social justice begins with all educators believing that they each possess the knowledge and skills to teach to a range of student needs in their classrooms—that they are competent or can become competent to do so. These educators come to believe that they themselves are the experts on the needs of diverse students. They no longer concede or defer their power or expertise to so-called "experts" down the hall, at another school, or in another district.

ICS requires these "expert" educators (e.g., special education, bilingual, or reading teachers to name a few) to no longer view themselves as responsible for meeting the needs of only particular students or subject areas. Instead, these educators must view their primary roles as developing the capacity of each other to teach to a range of students in the classroom. In that sense, though they may work with individual students in particular classrooms, in every single teaching situation, their primary focus shifts to sharing expertise. Again, when teachers are hired into the school or district, they must be willing to view their role in this way and be willing to learn the collaborative and development skills necessary to extend the teaching skills of all staff with whom they work.

A third consideration for teaching and learning within ICS and for social justice emphasizes that teaching and learning must become the central focus of all school activities. Leaders need to protect the "sacredness" of learning time and eliminate as many distractions as possible. The most direct way to increase learning time is located in a central feature of ICS—that of eliminating segregated pullout programs. When particular students no longer need to wander down the hall several times each day to receive services elsewhere, their learning time can significantly increase. In addition, moving to a block schedule is another way to eliminate wasted time between courses and facilitates a focus on teaching and learning. For example, at the elementary school level, some principals schedule literacy blocks where all classrooms focus on literacy for an extended period of time each day. Some principals take this a step further and assign all staff, such as allied arts teachers, librarians, and custodial staff, to work directly with groups of students during the literacy block.

Relatedly, to raise student academic achievement, leaders must target and focus their efforts on activities and processes that would raise that achievement. We have often witnessed that when achievement lags, well-intentioned educators will implement any number of "initiatives" and activities, nearly all of which fail to directly target the academic areas of concern. We compare this educational strategy to trying to douse a fire by taking a fire hose and indiscriminately spraying in every which direction with our eyes shut, pausing, and hoping that somehow, some way, we put the fire out. These general initiatives can include, for example, reaching out to families, initiating a "power of positive thinking" program with students, increasing teacher collaboration, instituting a morning book club for staff, and providing a vast array of professional development opportunities. While well intentioned, educators could engage in all these initiatives, and yet these initiatives may not impact achievement at all.

Instead, to increase achievement, leaders need to focus specifically on practices that will have the most direct impact on achievement. An important way to focus on achievement is to help classroom teachers become data consumers on their own students. In turn, these teachers can teach their own students to become data consumers about their own learning. Educators need to learn how to regularly measure achievement in specific ways. They then need to learn how to analyze and interpret these data on an ongoing, almost daily basis for each student they teach, and acquire a thorough knowledge of the achievement levels of every student, not only by subject, but by specific skills within the subject area. For example, they need to know, not just that their class needs work on language arts, but that these four specific students need additional work on synonyms. Next, they need to know how to use these data to inform changes in their teaching. To do so, they must have access to a plethora of resources and activities that can help students learn these specific skills in integrated and interesting ways. To facilitate this, leaders need to provide an abundance of teaching resources at graded levels for teachers to draw from for their teaching. Many schools have established book rooms or resource rooms whose sole function is to be a laboratory of leveled (by grades/ages) resources that teachers can readily access to target specific skill needs with students (see Chapter 4 for additional specific suggestions in working with data).

A fourth consideration for teaching within ICS and for social justice addresses class size. If teachers are to teach to a range of students in their classrooms, then class size must be controlled as much as possible. We offer four possible suggestions for reducing class size. First, reduction in class size is a natural outcome of reallocating resources and staff (see Chapter 12). That is, when special services and other staff are reallocated to support teachers in general education classrooms, the student-teacher ratio is automatically reduced. Second, when implementing ICS, special services staff who are dually certified for general education may at times move from being a pullout program teacher to a general education classroom teacher. These additional general education teachers spread among the established student enrollment effectively reduce class size. Third, accepting the assistance of student teachers and teacher interns is a way to reduce class size. This requires leaders to extensively and creatively collaborate with local colleges and universities. Fourth, successful ICS leaders recruit and develop long-term community volunteers. For example, they may draw from students' families, local senior centers, tribal councils, corporations, nonprofits, and service clubs seeking volunteer avenues for their members. Importantly, the primary focus of all these volunteers is student learning, and their energy is focused directly on particular student needs and interests. ICS leaders ensure that volunteer time is not wasted on jazzy bulletin board displays or other classroom activities that are not directly related to student achievement. In addition, when pullout programs are reduced and eliminated, this frees up more space in the school for integrated small-group instruction and for additional, smaller classes.

At the same time, an increase in class size is never a reason or excuse to abandon ICS. We have worked with schools who have implemented "conditional" ICS. That is, teachers agreed to work with a range of needs as long as particular criteria were met, one being reductions in class size. While a smaller class size certainly can facilitate ICS, smaller classes are not a prerequisite for ICS success. Again, if ICS is fully implemented, smaller class sizes are typically a natural byproduct.

In addition to these four considerations, teaching within ICS and for social justice requires consideration of federal and state curriculum standards, which we address next.

TEACHING WITHIN ICS AND FOR SOCIAL JUSTICE AND THE STANDARDS

The No Child Left Behind Act requires that all students, regardless of race, ethnicity, language, disability, or income, meet grade-level standards as measured by standardized achievement tests. For example, a student in the fourth grade, regardless of race, ethnicity, language, disability, or income, is expected to read, compute, and achieve in academic tasks at the fourth-grade level. Students who do not reach grade-level proficiency at certain grades (i.e., fourth grade and eighth grade) are required to be retained in that grade until they achieve their grade-level standards. We have a choice with NCLB. We can follow the high-accountability, standardized reform efforts without question or attempt to circumvent the requirements, or we can take what we know of student learning and comingle our efforts with a high level of educational accountability. We are well aware of the arguments for and against NCLB, and in this book, we do not wish to regurgitate them. However, we present the example below to illustrate a concern and to offer a positive approach.

Suppose a school has enrolled a student in the fourth grade who is considered to have a label of severe disabilities (we describe students with this label in Chapter 9). Let's say that this student has a mental age of six months. We know that no matter how long we teach this student, the student will never be able to achieve at the fourth-grade level in any subject area.

The spirit of NCLB, however, requires us to ramp up our expectations of this student. Though most educators are well intentioned, and many are excellent educators with students with severe disabilities, our experience is that teaching children with severe disabilities with evidence-based teaching strategies in the general classroom is the exception, not the rule. Usually, these students are segregated for nearly their entire school day. Their daily education experience does not meet the curriculum and instruction criteria we set forth in Chapter 9, by any stretch of the imagination. Even the social justice literature rarely mentions students with severe disabilities.

One possibility concerning the standards is to consider them as "progress toward and beyond grade-level standards." Thus, though the student with severe disabilities in this case example will not achieve fourth-grade level standards by fourth grade, the student is not a failure, nor are the teachers or the school that is educating this student, as long as these educators are adhering to the curriculum and instructional criteria we describe in Chapter 9. Though we know we will never raise the achievement of this student to fourth-grade level standards, we can use NCLB as policy leverage to raise our expectations and to implement best practices when teaching this student. We can expect this student to continue to make real, concrete progress toward functional IEP goals with the ultimate goal of this student being a productive and happy citizen in our community.

Let's take a second example. In this case, the student is labeled with a moderate disability (mentally handicapped or educable mentally handicapped). This student, also in fourth grade, is reading at a first-grade level. We cannot stereotype or generalize across labels. It might be possible for some students with this label to read at the fourth-grade level, while for other students with this label, no matter how long we teach them, they may never achieve at fourth-grade level standards. Again, the spirit of NCLB requires educators to work with positive determination, hold the highest of expectations, provide this student with the best reading instruction possible in heterogeneous environments, and carefully measure the student's progress toward this end. Thus, holding students to grade level may be appropriate or not, depending on the student. Regardless, we hold the highest expectations for these students and push their achievement level as high as possible.

As a third example, we consider a student who is already achieving at the fourth-grade level in the third grade. When the student reaches the fourth grade, it would not be appropriate to hold the student accountable to only fourth-grade level standards. Again, the spirit of NCLB requires us as educators to hold the highest expectations for this student, and provide the highest level of instruction to move this student beyond the grade-level standards in fourth grade.

As previously mentioned, some argue that our educational goal should be that of students "moving toward grade-level standards" as the indicator for success instead of the grade-level standards themselves. That is, we need to celebrate student progress toward grade-level standards, even if the student falls short of these standards. Of course, students should always be praised for achievement progress. Praising students for achievement progress does not negate the ultimate end goal of grade-level standards. Our concern about using "moving toward grade-level standards" as an indicator of educator and student success is that, unfortunately, this is the standard many of us have used over the past years for many students. As long as students were making some sort of progress, we were satisfied. This was particularly true for low-income students, students of color, ESL students, and students with disabilities. However, for many of these students, this standard of making progress toward a goal was too low. It is a standard that most middle- to upper-class white families probably would not accept for their own children.

Thus, when the federal law required that all students meet particular grade-level standards, the law did not address some students with moderate to severe disability labels who would never meet a particular grade-level standard. For some of these students, determined on an individual basis, perhaps the goal of "progress toward grade-level standards" in the context of high expectations and state-of-the-art instruction is appropriate.

While the goal of "progress toward grade-level standards" would merit praise and support for students and teachers moving in this direction, the ultimate goal still must be grade-level standards, or beyond as the case might be. Otherwise, progress *toward* the standards, if used as the ultimate goal by educators, may be an excuse for low expectations, poor teaching, and ineffective instructional arrangements (i.e., pullout, segregated programs). The goal of "progress toward grade-level standards" will let too many educators off the hook and provide an excuse not to push to the next level of achievement. We now have in our hands too much empirical research about the damaging effects of inequities and about how to raise student achievement to do otherwise.

For example, we now have empirical data that show that no matter how low the income of students and their families, no matter their race or ethnicity, regardless of their language ability or disability label, these students can achieve at high levels. If a low-income student of color, for whom English is not her first language, can achieve at grade level in District A, then there is absolutely no excuse why this same student cannot achieve at grade level in any school or district in the entire country.

Thus, while there may be individual students with a severe disability label who may never achieve grade-level standards, and there will be students who can achieve above their grade level, the standard for all other students should remain focused on grade-level standards. We should also celebrate the success of moving toward those standards, but never forget our ultimate goal, and never stop in our quest to push toward grade-level standards for all students.

STAFF DESIGN AND TEACHING FOR ICS AND SOCIAL JUSTICE

As we discussed in Chapter 5 regarding decision-making teams, it is imperative that schools structurally redesign their model of how students receive services if we are to establish communities of learners who have access to equal learning opportunities. Before teachers and students can engage in proactive teaching for ICS and social justice, staff must be assigned in ways that allow for all learners to experience small-group, large-group, and one-on-one integrated instruction in the school or community and that honor the principles of ICS. Staff must be assigned based on teacher skills being matched to student need (see Appendix F).

Teaching within ICS and for social justice first requires that students with labels are placed in heterogeneous classrooms and courses. Hence, teaching begins with the student and teacher schedule. Appendix B depicts one such schedule for students with disability labels in the seventh grade. This particular middle school enrolls 660 students, or about 220 students per grade. This school is structured on the house system where students and teachers in each grade are grouped into smaller houses. The teachers at each grade level can decide how many houses to divide the grade into. Some teachers prefer to divide the students into two houses while teachers at other grades prefer three houses. Other ways grades can be structured is to have two houses with three teachers in each, or one house with two teachers and a second house with four teachers. In Appendix F, we show the staff assignment for the seventh grade, which has been divided into two houses of 110 students per house, and four teachers are responsible for each house. Students with disabilities at each grade level are assigned evenly throughout the houses, and are assigned to houses in the same way students without disability labels are assigned—based on learning styles; transition skills (that is, a particular student may be better off in a smaller house that has fewer teachers and allows for more time with one teacher); and a balance of boys, girls, race, ethnicity, age range, and needs.

In this example, out of 110 seventh-grade students in one house, 17 students have special needs, and 15 of these have disability labels. This house is staffed with four general education teachers, one special education teacher, and one special education assistant, and the house also has access to support from a school psychologist, bilingual resource teacher, and reading resource teacher. In this scenario, rather than sending at-risk or other high-needs students out to other districts and paying for tuition and transportation, all these students are served in the school and district. The cost savings then allows funds for hiring a part-time integration support person who supports students with a range of needs, with or without a disability label, throughout the middle school grades.

The special education teacher in this case is responsible for all the students with disabilities in this house, and she is also responsible for working with the four general education teachers in building their capacity to teach to a wide range of student needs. Because there are four general education teachers, these 110 students are divided among four general education teacher classrooms. However, the general education teachers team teach with each other, and the special education teacher team teaches with the general education teachers throughout the day. Because of this teaching configuration, the special education teacher supports students in two to three different teaching environments (classrooms) in a day.

This middle school has adopted the block scheduling system, whereby subjects are paired and taught in a larger block of time. In the first row in the table of Appendix F, even though the two general education teachers have their own classroom, they team teach the entire school day, sharing responsibilities in the different subject areas. In addition, these two teachers are responsible for a student with high behavioral needs and a student with the label of autism who functions at a high academic level. With the exception of allied arts classes, these two students are with these general education teachers all day, while the special education teacher provides consulting support. Thus, during the first block of the day of math/science, the two teachers teach the two students with labels along with the rest of the class.

In the second block of the day, Family Education/Spanish, students receive this instruction from allied arts teachers, and this block is a planning time for the two general education teachers. During the first half of this block, the special education teacher consults with the two general education teachers in curriculum planning and providing behavioral support. During the second half, the two general education teachers continue to have planning time, while the special education teacher provides support to the two students with labels and to the Spanish teacher. Block 4, Language and History, functions the same as Block 1. During Block 5, Health and Physical Education, the general educators again team teach for Health, but during Physical Education, they have planning time, while the special education assistant supports students with labels and other students and also supports the physical education teacher.

In the second row in the table, the other two general education teachers are responsible for three students with learning disabilities (with curriculum support from the school psychologist and special education teacher). The remainder of their teaching blocks is similar to that of the first two general education teachers.

In the third row of the table, the special education teacher provides support during Math/Science, working with nine students—seven with LD, one at-risk, and one with behavioral challenges—across the two classrooms. These students receive large-group instruction during the first part of class. During the second part of the class, students are placed in flexible groupings based on learning styles (not disability). During the second block, the special education teacher spends the first half consulting with the general education teachers on curriculum design, while during the last half of the block she supports the students with autism and high behavioral challenges in Spanish. After having lunch in the third block, the special educator then works with the student with autism and a student requiring functional skill support, preparing for community instruction by developing a grocery list and a budget and checking out the bus route. During Block 4, Language and History, the special educator team teaches with both general education teachers. The curriculum is based on learning styles, and students are aligned in project groups to meet their individual needs. In the last block of the day, the special education teacher team teaches in the Health class with the general educators. During Physical Education, she provides small-group instruction for a range of different learners requiring lifelong physical skills such as swimming and aerobic exercises.

The special education assistant begins his day by meeting with a student with cognitive disabilities and a student with behavioral challenges in the school library to prepare for community instruction. The last half of this block is spent in the community, helping the two students meet individual functional goals (i.e., managing city transportation, grocery shopping, banking, etc.). During Block 2, the special education assistant lends support during the Family and Consumer Education class. After lunch, she lends support in the lunch room and other common student areas by facilitating friendships, addressing bullying concerns and other social relationship issues among students. During Block 4, she teaches vocational skills in the community with one student with a disability and one without—both of whom require functional and social skill development—at the local hardware store stocking shelves, at a computer store checking in equipment, or at the state office building delivering mail. In the last block of the day, she provides assistance and support to the physical education teacher and students.

The other support staff, including the bilingual resource assistant, school psychologist, guidance counselor, and reading resource teacher, all provide support at various times of the day. During the first block of the day, the school psychologist supervises/supports one of the students with cognitive disabilities who spends that block doing office work in the school office. The rest of the day, this student participates in Consumer Education, lunch, Vocational Education, and Physical Education. During Blocks 1 and 2, the other student with cognitive disabilities performs office work at the adjoining elementary school office where the student is supervised/supported by the elementary school guidance counselor. This student joins his classmates for lunch, Communication, Vocational Education, and Physical Education. During the last block of the day, the reading resource teacher works with a small group of students, including the student with autism and three students considered gifted, and also helps a student considered at-risk to complete a school project.

The Staff Design in Appendix F that was discussed in the preceding sections and the supporting narrative illuminate five critical aspects of ICS principles and practices. First, the table illustrates the importance of student placement and staff design as critical planning components of teaching within ICS and for social justice. Within ICS, staff and student assignment must precede any conversation about curriculum and instruction. Second, the table shows how support is intentionally configured across the day for all students—that students are not dumped into various classes without being supported, along with their teachers. Third, the table also shows the expectations that ICS places on general education staff and other staff to teach to a range of student needs and to increase their teaching capacity to do so. Fourth, the Staff Design table illustrates how ICS does *not* mean that students with labels are placed in a general education classroom for the entire day and only experience large-group instruction. Instead, the table shows how all students in the seventh grade experience a variety of small-group, individual, large-group, and whole-group instruction in integrated settings to meet their learning needs. Finally, the table counterbalances the limitations of all the literature and research on differentiated curriculum and social justice leadership and schools. That research spells out the importance of holding high academic expectations for students and differentiating the curriculum. However, as described in the preface to this book, the research says nothing at all about where or under what conditions this teaching should take place. Thus, a teacher in a segregated advanced placement math class could be modeling high teaching competency, but if students with a variety of learning needs and styles do not have access to this class, then the teaching does not reach all students. This is why ICS insists on the importance of changing the structure of education—that where and with whom students learn critically matters.

DIFFERENTIATED AND CULTURALLY RELEVANT CURRICULUM AND INSTRUCTION

After students and staff are assigned to classrooms and settings, the classroom instruction and curriculum must be addressed. This is why ICS must be seamlessly tied to and grounded in the core of curricular standards and instruction within the school. If students with a wide range of needs are to succeed together, then the curriculum and instruction will need to accommodate those needs. As we explained in Chapter 1, teachers need to design their curriculum and instruction to allow for universal access by all students (Bremer et al., 2002). That is, the curriculum and instruction are developed from the beginning with a range of different learning needs in mind. In so doing, all the students benefit from such a curriculum.

To further explain universal access, take the example of sidewalk curbs that are cut to allow wheelchairs to easily be wheeled down to the street and back up. It is much easier and less expensive to design a sidewalk with the smooth cut in place than to build the sidewalk with a curb, and then go back later and cut the curb to make the street accessible. Likewise, it is much easier to develop a differentiated curriculum at the beginning of lesson creation, rather than create lessons, and then go back and try to adjust them to meet a range of learning needs in the classroom. Moreover, in making the sidewalk accessible from the beginning, many individuals other than those who use wheelchairs benefit from the sloping sidewalk (e.g., people using walkers, children on bikes or skateboards, and families pushing strollers, to name a few). Likewise, differentiation benefits all classroom learners, not just students who typically struggle.

Importantly, educators now are able to choose from among a plethora of professional development opportunities and resources to increase their teaching capacity to teach to a range of learners in the classroom (e.g., The University of New Hampshire Institute on Disability, 1999; see also Tomlinson, 2001). To briefly review, these resources suggest the following successful tenets of differentiated instruction:

- Offer students challenging, interesting activities and rich materials for learning that foster thinking, creativity, and production.
- Make available a variety of pathways to learning that accommodate different intelligences and learning experiences.
- Use methods that engage students in hands-on learning.
- Focus instruction on reasoning and problem solving rather than only recall of facts.
- Foster peer collaboration and interaction between students and teachers.
- Stimulate internal rather than external motivation.
- Feature a variety of teaching techniques including demonstrations, small-group activities, peer tutoring, and individual work, in addition to occasional lectures.
- Support energetic and integrated learning aimed at exploring concepts and producing work that is guided by rigorous standards.

We do wish to reiterate that for teachers who are not accustomed to differentiating their curriculum, doing so may feel quite daunting. We agree with Tomlinson (2001) who suggests that teachers begin with one lesson for one subject area, and then build their differentiated curriculum from there. Otherwise, it is initially too overwhelming to differentiate every lesson in every subject area for the entire day. While that is the goal of differentiated instruction, perhaps differentiating one lesson plan a week, then one each day, and so on, is a good start. To that end, in Appendix G, we offer one example of an elementary science curriculum unit and how it could be differentiated for a wide variety of student learning needs based on the principle of universal access. (This lesson plan was developed by Mary Moroder, Verona Area School District, Verona, Wisconsin.)

The need to teach in ways that are culturally relevant for and with students seems so obvious to us that it hardly seems worth repeating. It must not be obvious, however, to most, given the lack of such instruction in schools. Much has been written on culturally relevant instruction, and we encourage readers to read further on this idea (we suggest Ladson-Billings, 1994, 1995, 2001). In a nutshell, culturally relevant instruction simply means considering a student's family and background culture within the curriculum, instruction, and culture of the classroom and school. It means providing a curriculum that depicts more than just traditional, white, middle-class ways of knowing and of life. All students need to see themselves reflected back in their classrooms, in the curriculum, and in other resources in the school. We encourage educators to imagine they are one of their nonwhite students, or a lower social class student, or a lesbian/gay/bisexual/ transgender student, or a student from a same-gender family in their classroom. When that student walks into the teacher's classroom, can the student see him- or herself, family, and life reflected back in the art on the walls, on the bulletin boards, in the library and media materials in the room, in the toys and choice activities, in the textbooks and handouts, in the stories that are read, in the assessments that are given, in the language that is used and in language used in the signs and informational materials from the school, in the volunteers and other adults who participate in the classroom, in the extracurricular activities that are provided, in the games that are played at recess, in the snacks, and in the classroom rituals and celebrations? Leaders and educators need to ask themselves this about every student in the school who is not white and middle class or is not from a traditional family—and to endeavor to create a school and every classroom within it that reflects back the personhood of each child in the school. A culturally relevant curriculum, instruction, and culture are not at odds with high student achievement. While federal and state assessments may be culturally biased (and that is no small issue), at the district, school, and classroom level we have no excuse not to create culturally relevant instruction, curriculum, and assessments for all learners—and in so doing, we can only positively affect student achievement.

ASSESSING STUDENT LEARNING

In our first book (Capper et al., 2000), we discussed in detail various ways to assess student learning, and we described the creation and use of electronic student portfolios. These portfolios can also serve as individualized service plans for all learners instead of or along with a grade report card. That is, the individualized service plan can delineate student learning goals based on the standards and also show student progress toward those goals. Alternative grading procedures such as these may be applied at the elementary level, though less so at the middle school level, and rarely if ever at the high school level. Given the constraints placed upon high schools from post-secondary entrance procedures and evaluation systems, at this point, we are not interested in tackling alternative grading methods at the secondary level. Nevertheless, this does not prohibit us from addressing ways to show student work and maintain student electronic portfolios that reflect work that is graded on a typical letter grade basis.

By using student-based electronic portfolios via the individualized service plan (see Appendix E for one example), educators have the opportunity to work collaboratively with students and their families to effectively show student knowledge gained and areas in which a student may focus his or her energies. A well-designed student-based portfolio will reflect the following information. It will

1. describe current academic function through standards;

2. display student work quarterly and for struggling learners biquarterly;

3. delineate assessment procedures used for individual students to enable them to show what they know in a manner that addresses their learning style and needs;

4. describe the instructional techniques used to motivate and assist the student to demonstrate his or her new knowledge;

5. describe curriculum used that was motivating and successful for the student.

CONCLUSION

In sum, teaching and learning within ICS and for social justice require leaders to hire educators who are willing and able to teach to a range of student learning needs. In the midst of all the educational distractions, educators must remember that teaching, learning, and student achievement are the focus of the day—that learning time is sacred time, and the school structure and daily schedule must be established to protect this time. Class size reductions are often a natural outcome of ICS, though reduced class size is not a prerequisite for ICS success. The standards movement can help us remember to always hold the highest academic and learning standards for every student in the school. ICS teaches us that student placement and staff design are critical prerequisites to developing a differentiated and culturally relevant curriculum for and with students. Finally, all students can benefit from an individualized service plan, and students and their families need access to user-friendly electronic student portfolios to help them track their success. In the next chapter, we extend these ideas further when we address students who significantly challenge our teaching.

Table 8.1   Chapter 8. Teaching Within ICS and for Social Justice

Focus Area	Focus Area Inquiry	Comments: What We Have	Phase of Application
1.	Staff are not hired unless they are willing and able to teach across a range of student needs.		
2.	What percentage of staff is willing to teach across a range of student needs?		
3.	What percentage of staff is able to teach across a range of student needs?		
4.	Student services educators are viewed as resources for building the capacity of general educators to meet the needs of all students.		
5.	Teaching, learning, and academic achievement are the central focus of all school activities.		
6.	Student learning time is viewed as sacred and distractions are minimized.		
7.	The academic schedule has been revised to focus on teaching and learning.		
8.	All school initiatives and activities are targeted toward specific areas of academic achievement.		
9.	What percentage of teachers regularly collects, analyzes, and uses student achievement data to make specific changes in their teaching for specific students?		
10.	Teachers have easy access to many resources and activities that are targeted to specific areas of student achievement.		

Focus Area	Focus Area Inquiry	Comments: What We Have	Phase of Application
11.	Reducing class size has been considered to effectively teach a range of students.		
12.	What percentage of school volunteers focuses all their efforts on student achievement?		
13.	What percentage of educators in the school uses NCLB requirements as a way to hold the highest expectations for student achievement for literally every student in the school?		
14.	All students are assigned to heterogeneous classrooms and courses as a prerequisite for curriculum and instruction considerations.		
15.	What percentage of teachers develops curriculum using the principle of universal access to differentiate the learning process for each student?		
16.	Staff design (assignment) to classes and students precedes curriculum and instruction considerations.		
17.	Students and staff are supported throughout the day as needed in heterogeneous settings.		
18.	All students, regardless of label, experience large-group, small-group, individual, and whole-group instruction throughout the day in heterogeneous settings.		
19.	What percentage of teachers engages in culturally relevant instruction with all their students?		

(Continued)

Table 8.1 (Continued)

Focus Area	Focus Area Inquiry	Comments: What We Have	Phase of Application
20.	Literally all students in the school can see themselves, their families, and their lives reflected back to them in all aspects of the school setting.		
21.	What percentage of students has electronic individualized service plans (ISP) to assist in appropriately targeting grade-level standards?		
22.	Teachers provide students with a range of differing assessment options to obtain performance levels and meet appropriate standards (performance based, normative, etc.).		

Reflective Question:

After gathering the necessary information, how will you begin to assist teachers in meeting the range of learner needs within their classroom in support of Integrated Comprehensive Services?

Students Who Significantly Challenge Our Teaching

We have found that students in our courses and educators with whom we work agree with the principles and practices of ICS, until our attention turns to students who significantly challenge our teaching such as those with severe physical and cognitive challenges. At that point, heads shake, utterances are mumbled out of our range of hearing, while others outright take us to task and argue that students who significantly challenge our teaching should not be part of the ICS conversation. Even educators who claim to work in so-called inclusive schools argue that their schools are inclusive, even though some of their students are segregated from their peers for the majority of the school day.

Durtschi's (2005) study of elementary school principals in one Midwestern state illustrates our point. These principals were positive about inclusion in general (86.3%), and 98.9% stated that they "support including students in general education classrooms." However, these same principals drew the line for students with severe disabilities. Nearly one-third (31%) of these principals supported separate schools or classrooms for students with severe/profound disabilities. More than half of the principals (56.6%) would oppose a law that required students with severe disabilities to be integrated with general education students. More than 10% (12.8%) believed that students with severe disabilities are too impaired to benefit from the activities of a regular school. In short, most educators agree with inclusive practices but only for particular students in particular ways—a clear contradiction to inclusion (Chin & Capper, 1999).

Who are these students with severe disabilities? We draw from Dr. Lou Brown throughout this chapter, as he was one of the first educators to assist families and school personnel in developing appropriate services for students with significant disabilities in integrated school and community environments. Since then, others have supported his concepts through universal access to curriculum, and "least harmful" assumptions (Donnellan, 1984). In 1988, Brown explained that students who comprise the lowest intellectually functioning 1% of a particular chronological age are referred to as significantly disabled. Often such measures of intellectual functioning are used to categorize people and make assumptions about their needs. The phrase "significant or severe disabilities" should signify particular direct instructional strategies for individual students. Instead, the label "severe disabilities" is used to isolate and categorize students into subgroups of people who are denied rights and privileges.

For the past 20 years, many educators have been involved in a shift to provide an integrated education for students with severe disabilities. If we define success by the number of students with a range of disabilities attending general education schools, we have been reasonably successful at 96% (U.S. Department of Education, 2002). What this statistic does not address, however, is that although more students with a range of disabilities are provided an education in public schools, students who significantly challenge our teaching continue to be placed in segregated environments or are not allowed to attend their neighborhood school or school of choice. In this chapter, we examine the current state of education for students with severe disabilities and principles in support of integrated education for these students.

CURRENT STATE OF EDUCATION FOR STUDENTS WITH SEVERE DISABILITIES

We know from research conducted over 20 years ago that students with severe disabilities need instruction in four domains (community, vocational, recreational, and domestic), and that this instruction should occur in the natural environment (the environment the activity naturally occurs within for individuals without disabilities) or setting (Brown, 1988). Though students with severe disabilities are included in public schools more often today, we see educators engage in five practices that severely diminish the potential of these students.

First, many educators continue to believe that these students need to be warehoused in the "special room" down the hall. Often, directors of student services and special education are actually relieved when they have enough students with a particular label—for example, autism—that they can then cluster these students in one classroom in a building with extra space, or better yet, in someone else's school.

Relatedly, educators point with pride at their special classrooms with a washing machine and other home furnishings constructed just for students with severe disabilities. We know, however, from research that students with severe disabilities cannot take skills learned in segregated environments, like these classrooms, and generalize these skills to other environments (Brown et al., 1983).

Third, schools continue to provide separate busses or transportation for students with severe disabilities and take these students in isolated groups on community field trips. When we place people with severe disabilities in groups with others who are only like themselves, we take away their individual identities and dignity and deprive students without disability labels the opportunity to learn with and develop friendships with students of all abilities.

Fourth, because it is sometimes difficult to plan individual employment opportunities for students with severe disabilities, schools are resorting to teaching vocational skills to these students as a clustered group within their buildings. We have heard educators claim they are engaged in inclusive practices while also explaining they are preparing these students for segregated vocational sites after high school. This practice again points to a contradiction in inclusion. Moreover, often these students are asked to complete vocational tasks that would be demeaning for a peer without a disability to complete. In so doing, we elicit pity for these students that in turn undermines their dignity and self-respect.

Finally, if a student with severe challenges is included in the general education classroom, he or she is often assigned an individual teaching assistant, and then the child's education becomes the responsibility of the teaching assistant and general education classroom teacher, neither of whom may have seen the child's individualized education plan, or may not be able to implement that plan. These ineffective, unethical practices are initiated and continue because they are administratively convenient or philosophically supported without regard for the quality of life of the individual student. None of these five practices aligns with the principles of ICS.

PRINCIPLES AND PRACTICE IN SUPPORT OF INTEGRATED EDUCATION FOR STUDENTS WITH SEVERE DISABILITIES

Research and practice has shown that it is possible to educate children with severe disabilities in the schools and classrooms they would attend if not disabled. Here we describe 11 principles and practices that educators must consider to support an integrated education for students with severe disabilities: neighborhood schools, integrated classrooms, age-appropriate placements and activities, nonschool and community environments, partial participation, natural proportions, functional skills, prioritization of skills to be learned, student/family preferences, opportunities for real work, and determining an appropriate education.

Neighborhood Schools

Years ago, we wrote that students should attend their home or neighborhood schools, or those schools that they would attend if not disabled (Brown et al., 1989) for three reasons. First, being able to attend one's home school is a basic civil right and is of benefit to all students. Students cannot learn to be comfortable with peers who may appear different from them if they do not interact with each other on a daily basis. Students will not learn compassion and the ability to make decisions that include all people if they are not in proximity to all people.

Second, in their neighborhood school, students with severe intellectual disabilities may receive community-based functional instruction in the environments where their families live. This will increase their opportunities for using these skills in their natural environments.

Third, when children with severe intellectual disabilities attend the school they would attend if not disabled, they have opportunities to interact with and form friendships with the same peers and families that they will interact with in their own neighborhoods. The students and their families become part of the larger school and neighborhood family network and the associated social activities. For example, if they play with and go to school with their neighborhood peers, it is more likely these peers will invite students with severe disabilities to birthday parties and other peer functions. Relatedly, attending their home school keeps families together. It is a travesty when one child in the family walks up the block to school, and the other child must wait for a little yellow school bus to be picked up and taken to a school away from his or her home.

Integrated Classrooms

Within their home schools, students with severe intellectual disabilities must be based or enrolled in regular education classrooms (Brown et al., 1989) with peers of similar age. This type of situation is not extreme or radical if the goals for the students with severe disabilities are clear, and if natural and artificial supports are clearly articulated and provided. We now know that such placements do not adversely affect nondisabled students (Peterson & Hittie, 2003) and can in fact benefit all students.

Age-Appropriate Placements and Activities

Students with significant disabilities also need to be placed in age-appropriate situations and activities for their learning (Brown et al., 1979). That is, if a student is 15 years old, but functioning at a 3-year-old level, this student needs to be placed with and engaged in similar activities to other 15-year-old students. Too often, we see high school–age students with severe disabilities placed in classrooms at the elementary or middle school level out of administrative convenience. Or, as another example, we have seen middle or elementary school–age students with severe disabilities placed at the high school level when school administrators attempt to group all students with severe disabilities in their school district together. These students are placed in this age-inappropiate settings out of administrative convenience, not student need. It is important for students with significant disabilities to be educated with their same-age peers for three reasons.

First, all students have a basic civil right, regardless of the severity of their disability, to be educated with same-age peers. Second, we can use the activities of same-age peers as a benchmark for teaching content for students with significant disabilities. For example, if 15-year-old students are using an iPod music device, then perhaps learning to use an iPod music device would become a means to achieve IEP goals for the 15-year-old with severe disabilities. As another example, if students from the high school forensics club raise funds by selling concessions at a basketball game, then a high school student with significant disabilities could participate as well, again completing tasks tied to his or her IEP goals. In contrast, having a group of high school students, all with disabilities, running the high school concession stand would not be in agreement with ICS principles, because this activity is not integrated with students with and without disabilities. In addition, the number of students with disabilities participating in this activity at one time (in this example, 100% of the students involved are labeled with a disability) is not a natural proportion of students with disabilities. The number of students with disabilities actually participating should not exceed the percentage of those same students in the entire school.

Third, being placed in age-appropriate environments can foster true friendships between students with and without disability labels. These friendships can be nurtured both within the school and in the students' neighborhoods.

Brown et al. (1979) discusses four interrelated hypotheses that often prevent instruction that is age appropriate. First, the mental age and chronological age discrepancy hypothesis—that is, educators presumably determine a child's mental age and then teach to that instead of the individual's chronological age. If, however, we teach the skills appropriate for a 3-year-old to a student who has a 3-year-old mental age, but who is 18 years old chronologically, we will deny that individual a lifetime of opportunities to belong because there will not be enough time for that student to "catch up" to an 18-year-old skill level.

A second hypothesis that prevents age-appropriate instruction is the earlier stage hypothesis—that is, educators believe that they must teach skills to students with severe disabilities at a slower pace and in a sequential order based on the developmental milestones of typical learners. Again, however, if educators teach an 18-year-old student with a mental age of 3, based on this hypothesis, it will take them over 60 years to teach this student, and the student may never proceed beyond the mental age of 5. Therefore, educators must target skills that students with intellectual disabilities need and teach them in a way that these students can acquire these skills within a reasonable time frame.

A third hypothesis that mitigates against age-appropriate teaching is the "Not ready for" hypothesis. This hypothesis assumes that we need to wait to teach particular skills until the student is mentally ready. However, if we wait to teach functional skills to a person with severe disabilities until we deem them capable by mental age standards, it will never happen.

Finally, the artificial approximation hypothesis suggests that educators teach approximations of a skill out of the context of the activity and the appropriate environment. For example, if we teach someone to cross a street in a classroom using artificial stop and go lights and then expect the student to be able to generalize the approximations to a four-lane automated walk signal in the real world, we are placing that individual in harm's way. Not only have we wasted the student's time, we have also denied him or her the opportunity to learn in the natural environment.

Nonschool and Community Environments

When educators understand that students with severe disabilities must be fully considered in the ICS process, they often assume we mean that these students must spend 100% of their day within the general education classroom, regardless of their age or needs. In fact, ICS does require that students with severe disabilities spend 100% of their day in integrated education environments, but these environments include both school and nonschool settings.

Brown et al. (1983) agree that serving students with significant disabilities in age-appropriate regular schools and classes they would attend if not disabled is necessary but not totally sufficient for an effective education. Their education must also include access to integrated vocational, domestic, recreation/leisure, and general community environments. Brown and colleagues contend that it is necessary to take into consideration the learning needs of the student to determine the balance between nonschool activities and instruction in the child's home school. As with all students, those with significant disabilities require direct, individualized, longitudinal, comprehensive, and systematic instruction in a wide variety of integrated environments.

Brown et al. (1991) delineate factors to consider when determining time spent in regular education classrooms and elsewhere. First, the number of environments in which a student with severe disabilities spends time should be similar to the number of environments in which a nondisabled peer spends time. These learning environments must provide a range of different learning opportunities and stimuli, increasing the probability for skill acquisition with minimal support.

Second, the chronological age of the student is important to determine how much time should be available for instruction, how much the student has to learn, and where are the most appropriate environments and subenvironments for the student to learn specific activities and skills. In general, the older the child, the more time the students should spend learning functional skills in the environments those skills actually are used such as in the community.

Hence, students with severe disabilities may learn in a general education classroom some of the time, but will learn in integrated environments with typical peers 100% of the time. Additional factors to consider when deciding how much learning should occur in school and nonschool environments are the skills a student can learn; the amount of time the student has to learn them; and the student's ability to generalize, recoup, and retain information. These factors will help determine specifically what skills, activities, and environments will maximize the student's independence.

Usually, concrete, practical skills can be taught more effectively in a nonschool environment than in a school environment. However, community-based instruction must not be confined to occasional field trips. When students with severe disabilities participate in a range of different field trips per week with little to no attention to particular skill learning, then these trips are not of value. Community-based instruction is an individually choreographed instructional technique to teach skills that are necessary for the student to be as independent as possible as an adult.

Therefore, educators need to provide a balanced school and community schedule for a student with significant disabilities. The older the individual, and the less they generalize, recoup, and transfer information, the more opportunities they must have to receive instruction in the environments in which those activities actually occur. That is, a student at the elementary level with a significant disability may spend a large part of their day in the general education classroom with instruction in the community included as part of the typical third-grade curriculum and its community service projects. As the student gets older, the student receives an increasing amount of instruction in the community—for example, during the last periods of the day, three days a week, with a student without disabilities, perhaps as part of a community service project.

To illustrate, we offer the case of Miguel, a high school student with severe disabilities. Miguel is on the ninth-grade support teacher's caseload. The grade-level support teacher and IEP team will examine the individual needs of Miguel, and determine the skills he must learn to be independent and what skills and activities are the most important for students in ninth grade to know. Given the age of Miguel and the amount of time he has remaining in school, after completing a functional assessment (see Appendix H), the staff may determine that Miguel will require community instruction in the areas of banking, food prep, shopping, housecleaning, and public transportation. Other information about Miguel includes the fact that he likes U.S. History, especially information on wars.

Therefore, Miguel's weekly schedule will include community instruction in the morning at an off-campus job site, completing food prep with one other student with whom he rides the city bus and then returns to school for lunch and U.S. History. During the morning community instruction time, on Mondays, Miguel receives instruction for shopping and banking. On Tuesdays, he receives instruction in housekeeping at his own house. On Wednesdays and Fridays, he will visit the local health club to exercise and learn new lifelong health habits with a nondisabled high school student involved in community service and one other student with mild disabilities.

During the time Miguel is in history class, the general educator and grade-level support staff will develop universal access to the curriculum—that is, the history curriculum will address the range of learner skills in the classroom. Then, if necessary, adaptations may be made to address Miguel's more specific needs. For example, the instructional arrangements, the lesson format, teaching strategies, curricular and social goals specific to the lesson, the instructional materials, the level of natural supports, the supervision arrangements, and the physical and social aspects of the classroom can all be designed to support the specific needs of Miguel (Udvari-Solner & Thousand, 1995).

Partial Participation

Sometimes, a student with a severe disability may not be able to fully participate in an activity with peers who do not have a disability label. For this reason, educators may exclude the student with severe disabilities from the activity. However, the principle of partial participation suggests that though a student with severe disabilities may not be able to fully participate in an activity, he or she may be able to partially participate, thus allowing the student to be included.

The ability to partially participate (Meyer, Peck, & Brown, 1991) in chronological age–appropriate environments and activities is educationally more advantageous than exclusion from such environments and activities. Students with severe disabilities, regardless of their degrees of dependence or levels of functioning, should be supported to partially participate in a wide range of school and nonschool environments and activities. The kinds and degrees of partial participation should be increased through direct and systematic instruction. Partial participation in school and nonschool environments and activities will result in a student learning more skills and thus gaining greater independence. Systematic, coordinated, and longitudinal efforts must be initiated at a young age to prepare students with severe disabilities for partial participation in as many environments and activities as possible with chronological age–appropriate, nondisabled peers.

Natural Proportions

As we defined the term in Chapter 1, "natural proportion" means that the numbers of students of a particular label or need in any school setting should reflect the numbers of such students in the overall school setting. Students with severe intellectual needs comprise about 1% of the school population (Brown et al., 1988). Therefore, we need to be cognizant of how many students with severe disabilities are clustered into one environment and ensure that no more than 1% of that setting is composed of students with severe disabilities. Typically, if students with severe disabilities are not railroaded into institutions or "clustered educational placements," the proportions of students with and without disabilities will maintain a natural balance. When such a natural balance occurs, people are treated, viewed, and respected as individuals and not as a group of people to be circumvented and denied privilege (Brown, Udvari-Solner, Long, Davis, & Jorgensen, 1990).

Functional Skills

It is reasonable to expect that students with intellectual disabilities will acquire fewer skills during an educational career than approximately 97% of their chronological-age peers. If such a relatively limited number of skills are to be learned, it seems prudent that a reasonable proportion of these should be "functional." Functional skills are those that someone else would have to do for the individual with a disability if he or she could not complete the activity on his or her own. For example, if a student with disabilities does not learn to open the door to the school, the chances are that someone else will need to assist. If a person with significant disabilities does not learn to wash the dishes, someone else will have to wash the dishes. However, if a person with significant disabilities does not learn the capitals of all the states, the chances are that no one else will have to learn the capitals for him or her. When considering what skills to teach, it is important to balance functional skills with the individual's interest, with the social importance of the skill, and with the preparation for adulthood, as well as the recreational significance of the skill. For example, if an individual does not swim, the chances are that no one else will have to swim for him or her; however, the individual with the disability will gain much from the physical activity of swimming for lifelong fitness.

Prioritization of Skills to Be Learned

Students with significant disabilities learn less than 99% of their peers, recoup less, retain less, and generalize less. Therefore, educators must consider three factors when deciding which skills to teach students with severe disabilities that will result in as much adult independence as possible. First, educators need to consider the number of skills that should be taught. Brown et al. (1983) state that there are thousands of skills that can be acquired by others that either cannot be acquired by students with severe intellectual disabilities or are extremely cost-inefficient when the return for educational investment is considered. Completing long-division worksheets and memorizing multiplication tables or the presidents of the United States are a few examples. Therefore, it is essential to look at the skills that will assist children with significant disabilities to be productive members of society and help them as they become young adults to be as independent as possible in the community, home, workplace, and when recreating. When teaching a child with severe disabilities, the complexity of such skills must be minimized to increase independence.

A second consideration for teaching skills is the number and kinds of opportunities a student will have to learn these skills. For example, making eggplant parmesan may be a wonderful skill to have, but if the individual does not know how to make a sandwich for lunch, the Teen Living class that teaches how to cook gourmet dishes may not be the most appropriate use of the student's time. However, if in fact the high school foods class is teaching survival cooking skills and the student has the opportunity to make everyday foods in an integrated class, during instruction in a domestic environment, and at home in the evening, the chances of acquiring the skills for those specific activities have now tripled in probability due to the increase in opportunities. Students with severe disabilities must be provided opportunities to repeatedly practice these skills in natural environments with meaningful performance criteria. Repeated practice is important, as a student might not recoup a skill that was learned if it is used infrequently.

Accordingly, Brown (1988) cautions teachers about "time-determined progressions" or unit instructional practices. That is, educators may decide, for example, that in February, student will learn grocery shopping skills. However, students with severe disabilities may need teaching related to grocery shopping to occur over a period of three to five years and at regular intervals throughout the year. This instruction can progress from the most basic shopping patterns (following a picture list), to higher-order experiences of developing a picture grocery list based on the items necessary for the projected meals for the week, to staying within a weekly budget based on the individual's earnings.

A third consideration involves practicing the skill in the natural environment in which the skill is needed. If we do not ensure such practice, we are expecting students who have the least ability to generalize, to generalize across many different environments. The worse case example of this is teaching a student to practice a skill in the isolation of the classroom, and then expecting that student to be able to use that skill in a completely different natural environment. To repeat, the skills being taught must enhance the student's functioning within the school, home, community, work, and recreational environments.

Student and Family Preferences

Students with intellectual disabilities, like all students, are less successful at learning skills they are not interested in than they are in learning skills in which they have a high level of interest. Given the importance of the desire to learn and its relationship to motivation and determination, students with severe disabilities and their families must have an opportunity to be involved in the decisions about what skills the students will learn based on the students' preferences.

Opportunities for Real Work

Educators often opt to place students with significant disabilities into segregated work crews or segregated enclaves with other students with significant disabilities to acquire work experience and vocational skills. Brown (1988) rejects these practices, and instead insists on the importance of placing students with significant disabilities in work situations that reflect the natural proportions concept. Thus, enclaves and crews are unnecessarily restrictive. Thus, when supporting students with disabilities at community vocational sites, it is imperative to attend to natural proportions. As we previously discussed, because approximately 1% of the individuals in society could be labeled with severe intellectual disabilities, student learning environments, including vocational environments, should have a similar proportion of individuals with severe disabilities. In addition, these environments require the presence of students without disability labels—that is, an individual without a disability should be within sight, hearing, and touch of a person with a significant disability for the vocational environment to be defined as an integrated one.

Determining the Most Appropriate Education

To determine the most appropriate education for students with significant disabilities, Brown et al. (1983) suggest using the ecological inventory and discrepancy analysis strategy. This inventory and strategy can assist teachers, students, and parents to develop instructional goals, and to determine the most appropriate skills, activities, and environments for students to reach those goals.

First, educators determine the activities and skills that a same-age, nondisabled peer would be learning, as well as the environments where the same-age, nondisabled peer would be learning these skills. These skill areas focus on five curricular domains: school, vocational, community, recreational, and domestic.

Second, educators then determine if the child with significant disabilities can perform any of these skills independently. That is, the educator determines the discrepancies between the skills and activities that a child without a disability is able to do and those that a child with a disability is capable of completing. Then, the educator makes recommendations as to which skills, activities, and environments will be the primary focus for that particular time period. Appropriate academic and functional objectives can then be determined that are pertinent to the recommendations. It is essential during this process to keep in mind the current and future learning environments that the individual will function within (Brown et al., 1983).

CONCLUSION

In schools and districts where the educational leaders believe in and implement Integrated Comprehensive Services, students with severe disabilities are educated in the same classrooms, schools, and community environments where they would be educated if not disabled. We have heard administrators say, "We actually do Integrated Comprehensive Services in our district." Then we ask, "Do you have students with severe disabilities on the general education teachers' caseloads at the grade level to receive a range of individualized integrated instruction?" Most often, administrators respond by saying, "Oh, well, we don't do it for our students with severe disabilities—they go to a special school or are clustered into special classes in schools around our district." If students with severe disabilities are segregated, then educators are only perpetuating the notion that some students meet our criteria for belonging and other students clearly do not.

Some educators claim that they base their decision to segregate particular students on those students' "individual needs," when in fact the decision is based on the degree of educator creativity and willingness to do what it takes to include students based on the principles described in this chapter. For example, we have witnessed students who have been placed in a segregated, self-contained classroom all day, in a school that is not their home school, and the educators in this district claim the decisions are based on the students' needs. When the family of one of these students moved to a different district that practiced ICS, this student attended the home school and received a balance of integrated school and community instruction. As this example shows, it is not the extent of a student's disability or individual student needs that should determine the degree to which a student will be educated with his or her peers, but rather it is educator creativity and will. If we want to provide integrated school and community instruction for a student with severe disabilities, we will. We cannot claim to be "inclusive" or claim to be practicing ICS when in fact we draw the line to only include particular students at particular times. We must move beyond denying the civil rights of students with severe disabilities. We must walk our talk, and this means putting into practice the principles in this chapter to ensure that literally every single student in the school community, including students with severe disabilities, are full participating members of that school community.

Table 9.1   Chapter 9. Students Who Significantly Challenge Our Teaching

Focus Area	Focus Area Inquiry	Comments: What We Have	Phase of Application
	Home Schools		
1.	Students are attending their home or neighborhood school (e.g., the school they would attend if not disabled).		
	Integrated Classrooms		
2.	Students with significant labels are based in regular education classrooms with peers of a similar age.		
3.	Our school does not have any special rooms set aside just for students with severe disabilities.		
4.	Our school does not have any rooms with home furnishings that are used only by students with disabilities.		
5.	Students with disabilities in our school are transported to and from school and attend field trips with typical peers. They do not have a special bus.		
6.	Students with severe disabilities learn in integrated environments 100% of their school day.		
	Age-Appropriate Placements		
7.	Students with severe disabilities attend their chronological age–appropriate school.		
8.	The chronological age of the student is used to determine how much time should be available for instruction, how much the student has to learn, and where are the most appropriate environments and subenvironments to learn specific activities and skills.		

Focus Area	Focus Area Inquiry	Comments: What We Have	Phase of Application
9.	We use the activities of same-age peers as a benchmark for teaching content for students with significant disabilities.		
10.	Students with severe disabilities are friends with typical students in the school.		
11.	Students with significant needs are involved in age-appropriate extra-curricular activities.		
12.	Teachers teach to the chronological age, not the mental age of students with severe disabilities.		
13.	Students with significant labels use age-appropriate materials to complete their work.		
	Nonschool and Community Environments		
14.	The number of learning environments for students with severe disabilities is the same as for students without disabilities.		
15.	Middle and high school students with severe disabilities spend increasing time in community learning settings.		
16.	Students with severe disabilities receive instruction in four domains: community, vocational, recreational, and domestic.		
	Partial Participation		
17.	Though a student with severe disabilities may not be able to fully participate in a particular activity, the student is given the opportunity to participate partially and thus be included in the activity.		

(Continued)

Table 9.1 (Continued)

Focus Area	Focus Area Inquiry	Comments: What We Have	Phase of Application
	Natural Proportions		
18.	Students with particular labels or needs in the school, classroom, or educational setting reflect the percentage of these students in the overall school setting.		
	Functional Skills		
19.	Students with intellectual disabilities are taught functional skills.		
	Selecting Skills to be Learned		
20.	Skills that are taught to children with significant disabilities are selected because they will assist them in becoming productive members of society and promote independence in the community, home, workplace, and when recreating.		
21.	Students with severe disabilities are provided opportunities to repeatedly practice skills in natural environments with meaningful performance criteria.		
22.	Students with significant needs receive support from collaboration between the grade-level support teacher and IEP team, who jointly examine the individual needs and determine which skills the individual must learn to be independent and what skills and activities are the most important for students in that grade.		
23.	Students are scheduled in integrated community environments to meet their functional needs as part of their schedule, not a unit of study.		
	Student and Family Preferences		
24.	Students with severe disabilities and their families are involved in the decisions regarding what skills the student will learn based on his or her preferences.		

Focus Area	Focus Area Inquiry	Comments: What We Have	Phase of Application
	Opportunities for Real Work		
25.	Students with disabilities are placed in community vocational sites that reflect natural proportions and are integrated environments.		
26.	What is percentage of students with significant labels who receive individualized vocational instruction in integrated, "real" work environments?		
	Determining Most Appropriate Education		
27.	Step 1: Educators determine the activities and skills that a same-age, nondisabled peer would be learning, as well as the environments where the same-age, nondisabled peer would be learning these skills.		
28.	Step 2: The educator determines the discrepancies between the skills and activities that a child without a disability is able to do and those that a child with a disability is capable of completing, and then makes recommendations as to which skills, activities, and environments will be the primary focus for that particular time period.		

Reflective Questions:

1. Given your responses to the focus areas provided, how will your service delivery team address assigning staff and students in support of students with significant disabilities?

2. Given your responses to the focus areas provided, how will grade-level teams assign staff and students in support of students with significant disabilities?

3. Given your responses to the focus areas provided, how will your districtwide team assign staff and students in support of students with significant disabilities?

English Language Learners and ICS

(Cowritten With Martin Scanlan)

We do not have to look far to notice the increasing numbers of students for whom English is not their first language enrolled in our nation's schools. According to the National Center for Education Statistics (NCES) (2004), among youth ages 5–24, "the percentage who were language minorities increased from 9 percent in 1979 to 17 percent in 1999" (p. iii). Looking at the changes over the last two decades of the twentieth century, Crawford (2005) notes that the number of U.S. residents who speak a language other than English at home more than doubled. Nearly every school and district in this country, including rural schools and districts, are experiencing increasing enrollments of students who are English language learners (ELL).

While the linguistic diversity in our schools is increasing, by far the fastest growing group of students who are ELL speak Spanish (National Center for Education Statistics, 2004). According to NCES, two of every three children coming to school from a home where a language other than English is spoken are identified as Latino, and three-quarters of Latino families in the United States speak Spanish at home. This is also the fastest growing group of immigrants (pp. 8–10).

As we have mentioned throughout this book, meeting the needs of students for whom English is not their first language in heterogeneous settings seems to elude even the most social justice–oriented leaders. In many schools, principals are quite proud of the ways they have dismantled pull-out programs that have disproportionately impacted students with disabilities, low-income students, and students of color. In many of these same schools and districts, however, principals cluster their students who are English language learners at all grade levels. That is, elementary school principals often cluster these students into one or two particular classes at a grade level for the entire day, their proportion in these classrooms far exceeding that in the rest of the school. Often these students are clustered with other students who are considered at-risk. In middle schools with the house system, these students are often clustered in a particular house.

At the high school level, these same students often end up spending their entire school day clustered in segregated courses with their language-diverse peers. In some districts, these are called "sheltered English" courses where the content is taught in English or sometimes delivered bilingually. Again, the proportion of these students clustered into these houses and courses far exceeds their proportion in the entire school.

At the district level, students who are English language learners are often bussed across the district and all placed at the same grade-level school. That is, all middle school ELL students are bussed to one particular middle school, or one or two elementary schools receive all the elementary-level ELL students in the district. In many larger districts, all ELL students are sent to particular schools that are called "ESL centers." Thus, in addition to the burden of being bussed outside of their home school, these students end up disproportionately clustered in certain schools.

The negative outcomes of these segregated programs are the same as for any segregated programs. While the practice of segregating ELL students is harmful, families of these students are often left with little choice. If families of students who are ELL wish to enroll their child in their neighborhood school, and this school is not a designated "ESL center," school or district officials inform the family that if their child attends their home school, they will not receive "ESL services." Thus, we are forcing language-diverse families to choose between their neighborhood schools that overtly state they will not meet that student's needs and bussing their child across the district to a segregated school. What kind of "choice" is that? We cannot imagine any school in the country demanding white middle- or upper-class parents to make the same decision for their own child.

A second negative outcome of segregating students who are ELL in particular schools is that even in small rural districts, this segregation is affecting housing patterns in the community. The segregated schools that house the higher numbers of English language learners are the ones that the white, middle- and upper-class families do not want their own children to attend, as these schools are considered "troubled." In turn, these families choose not to move into the attendance areas of these "ESL center" schools, segregating the schools in the districts even further. Thus, the repercussions of segregating English language learners into particular schools in a district will have long-lasting negative outcomes on the students, their families, and the entire community for many generations to come.

A third negative outcome occurs with establishing separate, "sheltered English" classes at the high school level. Though these courses may have been created with good intentions, the outcomes are far from ideal. In our experience, when faced with an entire class of students who are ELL, with varying levels of English fluency and various learning needs, teachers hold lower academic expectations for these students. The slower-paced curriculum leads to a lack of rigor with far less academic engagement during class time. However, across the hall, the all-white, predominantly middle- to upper-class students receive the highly engaging, rigorous, high-expectations curriculum.

The most troublesome thing about all these ways that ELL students are typically educated is that even those who consider themselves social justice leaders and who are implementing ICS principles and practices do not see the problems with clustering ELL students. They do not see that by doing so, they are creating segregated programs for these students that fully contradict the principles and practices of ICS.

School leaders are clustering students who are ELL (with, hopefully, the best of intentions) for three possible reasons. First, some of these students are not proficient in their home language, and research shows (as we will discuss later in this chapter) that these students should learn their home language well, before learning English. Thus, these leaders cannot figure out how to teach these students their home language while they are integrated with their English-speaking peers. Second, these same students must also learn to become proficient English language speakers. Again, leaders cannot figure out how to teach these students English while they are integrated with their English-speaking peers. Third, these students must also learn the content of academic subjects, such as history, mathematics, literature, or science. Leaders cannot figure out how these students can learn the content of, for instance, a history class that is being delivered in English when they do not fully understand the English language.

As we will illustrate in this chapter, the principles of ICS need not be abandoned when it comes to educating ELL students. Literature on best practices for teaching students who are ELL demonstrates that schools have a number of methods at their disposal to effectively integrate these students. Though debates over the best approaches to educate students who are ELL have raged over the past five decades (Crawford, 2000), trends in best practice are clearly emerging. We will discuss how school leaders can apply the principles of ICS to employ these best practices in serving students who are ELL in integrated settings. In Chapter 7, we included specific strategies for working with language-diverse families. In Chapter 14, we discuss federal and state ESL policies that can work against integrated approaches. In that chapter, we explain how to navigate around these requirements in ways that meet the spirit of the requirements but in the end, align with ICS principles and practices. With Grinberg and Saavedra (2000), we critique the pullout programs of traditional approaches to educating students who are ELL as "validating and legitimizing segregation of students as a sound pragmatic practice" (p. 437). We show that educational leaders can navigate the terrain of educating students who are ELL while neither compromising commitments to educational excellence nor abandoning principles of social justice.

Educators should hold three interrelated goals for students who are ELL: (1) bilingual literacy, (2) academic achievement, and (3) socio-cultural integration within the school community (Brisk, 1998). In this chapter, we identify nine best practices to achieve these goals, all of which align with ICS principles and practices. We have grouped these nine practices into three major categories: (1) student placement, (2) curriculum and instruction, and (3) developing teacher capacity. After we describe these practices, we then discuss two key underlying principles for educating ELLs: all students in schools must become bilingual; and bilingual education is an education, not a place. Understanding the practices first is necessary to fully understand these two key principles. We end the chapter with a brief example of exactly what these practices and principles would look like in the life of a school.

STUDENT PLACEMENT

It is impossible to accomplish the three goals for students who are ELL if we segregate these students from their non-ELL peers. The literature shows many reasons for integrating, rather than segregating these students. Students who are ELL are much more apt to succeed when their language and culture are incorporated into the school and their parents and community are viewed as integral to their education (Cummins, 1986). Brisk (1998) points out that schools often introduce ELL students to the English language as well as to U.S. culture and society. Brisk recommends that educators make a priority of "getting to know the students and their families as well as welcoming their languages and cultures" in order to foster a coherent community where these students are understood to be "an integral part of the school" (p. 66). Obviously, it is quite difficult to get to know and welcome families and students if we have booted them out of our attendance area.

Segregating students who are ELL leads to a fragmented education. Torres-Guzman, Abbate, Brisk, and Minaya-Rowe (2001) found that in schools where services were disparate, important data on academic achievement fell through the cracks. They report "a wide range of significant data available," but these data were difficult to summarize and interpret due to their being spread amongst a range of specialists (p. 30). Lopez and Vazquez (2005) make a similar point by showing that when ELL students are pulled out to work with English as a second language (ESL) teachers, the general classroom teachers remain disconnected from the learning process of these children.

Instead of opting for programmatic approaches that favor segregated service delivery, school leaders must apply the same ICS principles and practices to the education of students who are ELL as those that pertain to other traditionally marginalized students in schools. When educating ELL students, leaders need to first remember that these students should always be assigned to their home schools and within these schools, these students should always be assigned to classes and courses in proportions that are similar to that in the school. That is, within schools, educators should not create separate ELL rooms or separate courses for ELL students, but instead, should assign these students to heterogeneous classroom settings.

Home Schools

With no exceptions, all students who are ELL must attend their home school—that is, the school they would typically attend if they were not an ELL. Given that one of the core principles of ICS is that the system needs to accommodate the learner, bussing students across the district is the antithesis of this principle, as bussing proclaims that certain schools will not accommodate students who are ELL. In addition, a core principle of ICS includes meeting individual student needs and not slotting students into predetermined programs, and bussing students across the district defies this basic principle. Thus, districts should not create schools that are "ESL centers" and then bus ELL students across the district to these schools.

School leaders committed to ICS and social justice need to proactively dismantle this practice. Such leaders should request that all students in their neighborhood attendance area attend their school, including all ELL students who are currently bussed to other schools or out of the district. When educating students who are ELL in their home schools, families of students who are ELL do not have to choose between attending their neighborhood school and being told that their child will not be provided language services there or attending a segregated school.

No Separate ESL Rooms or Courses: Heterogeneous Classes

A second best practice for students who are ELL occurs within the school in that no separate rooms or courses are set aside for them. Like students with disability labels, students who are ELL should be heterogeneously assigned to classes across grade levels and across courses in natural proportions. For example, if 10% of the elementary schools are composed of students who are ELL, then when assigning ELL students to the third-grade classes, no class should have more than 10% ELL students. The same would apply to houses or courses at the middle and high school levels.

Some question if it is better to place the maximum proportionate number of students who are ELL in a class. For example, if 10% of the elementary school are ELL students, should one of the third-grade classes receive a full 10%, with the other classes having few or no ELL students? In general, in the spirit of heterogeneous grouping, we think it is best that students are assigned evenly across the different classes; thus, all students and all teachers in that grade experience the benefit of including language diversity in their classroom. We do, however, believe some benefits accrue from more than one or two students who are ELL being enrolled in a class, such as social benefits and support for each other. Further, similar to including students with disabilities, ICS principles would not be congruent with educators designating particular classrooms as the "ELL" rooms, even if the number of ELL students assigned to these rooms were in proportion to the rest of the school. In addition, we think it's best that ELL language levels are mixed within classes, so that, for example, not all students tested at a level 1 are assigned to one class together, but instead there is a heterogeneous mix of levels. This mixed grouping, like any heterogeneous grouping, provides role models as well as natural language teaching and learning between and among students.

CURRICULUM AND INSTRUCTION

After students who are ELL are assigned to their home schools and placed in heterogeneous classes and courses based on their proportion in the school, the teaching and learning in those settings must be addressed. We have identified six critical facets of curriculum and instruction that leaders must incorporate to effectively educate students for whom English is not their primary language: (a) value students' home language, (b) understand language proficiency levels, (c) understand bilingual education versus ESL instruction, (d) use evidence-based ESL teaching techniques, (e) educate students who are ELL as unique individuals with varying needs, and (f) fully integrate highly mobile (migrant) ELL students and their families into the school community.

Value Students' Home Language

In order to be successful with ELL students, the primary curriculum and instruction criterion must be to value students' home language above all other considerations. Research also suggests that students must first become fluent in their home language (Cummins, 1999) before learning English. In their review of the literature on language issues in multicultural contexts, Minami and Ovando (2004) assert that "children's home environments and language communities affect their academic development. How a teacher perceives this background can be crucial to the child's academic success or failure" (p. 582).

Ideally, valuing the home language means ensuring student literacy in that language. As Cummins (1999) puts it, "The trend in much of the data is that programs that aspire to develop bilingualism and biliteracy . . . show much better outcomes than English-only or quick-exit transitional bilingual programs that do not aspire to develop bilingualism and biliteracy" (p. 30). Research shows that if students can become fluent in their home language, this language learning process makes it easier to learn English (Slavin & Cheung, 2004, 2005). Reading proficiency in the language spoken at home has been found to be an important indicator of future performance in English (Garcia, 2000; Reese, Garnier, & Gallimore, 2000). A longitudinal study referred to as the Aguirre report (Ramirez, Yuen, Ramey, & Pasta, 1990) found that among bilingual approaches, students who were provided substantial literacy instruction in their home language and gradually introduced to English achieved highest in mathematics, English language skills, and English reading. The Aguirre report also found that bilingual approaches that make limited use of the home language (e.g., "early-exit" transitional bilingual programs) were no more effective than English immersion programs, which have proven to be ineffective for learning English.

Becoming fluent in their home language has additional benefits for students. First, hearing and learning their home language validates that student's family and culture. These students can then more easily bridge the gap from their homes, families, and cultures to school. Second, becoming fluent in their home language, and then also becoming fluent in English, results in these students becoming fully bilingual in a world that increasingly requires speakers to be bilingual and multilingual if they are to be successful.

Thus, especially in the early elementary grades, ELL students need to be provided plentiful daily opportunities to learn and become fluent in their home language. This learning will require the presence of teachers and ideally peers who can speak the child's language. When students do not first develop literacy and cognitive skills in their native language before trying to learn English, these students often become illiterate or impaired in both languages, which in turn significantly lowers their academic achievement compared to their peers who are not ELL (Calderon & Minaya-Rowe, 2003).

Importantly, some families for whom English is not their home language resist their children learning the home language first, as they fear this will impede them from learning English. As was described more fully in Chapter 7 on school involvement with families, leaders will need to educate these families about the importance and benefits of learning the home language first.

In practice, we can illustrate the critical importance of students becoming fluent in their home language first, before learning English. We worked with one rural school district whose number of Latino students had more than doubled over the last five years. At an elementary school in this district, the principal believed that students who are ELL should only learn English at school. Thus, she allowed these students to only speak English, and forbade them to speak in their home language. To receive services, all the Latino students were required to walk across the street to another elementary school to participate in pullout programs to teach them English. In these programs, though they were staffed by bilingual teachers, some of whom were also Latino and bilingual, the teachers were forbidden to speak in Spanish, and were required to teach and converse with these students only in English. To add insult to injury, the school was then going to retain many of the third- and fourth-grade Latino students based on their low statewide assessment results. This provides one example of how possibly good intentions of the principal for the students who are ELL to learn English resulted in totally inappropriate educational practices, and in the end, the students were punished for the outcomes by being retained.

Understand Language Proficiency Levels

The second curriculum and instruction consideration pertains to language proficiency levels. Students who are ELL are given a language assessment to determine their proficiency in English. Typically, schools learn about children who live in homes where a language other than English is spoken (even if English is also spoken) through a home survey that families complete. Once these students are identified, their English language proficiency is assessed on an annual basis.

Different states use particular scales for English proficiency, but a useful scale is provided by the World-Class Instructional Design and Assessment (WIDA) Consortium (2006). WIDA is an organization "dedicated to the design and implementation of high standards and equitable educational opportunities for English language learners" (n.p.). The WIDA Consortium, established through a federally funded enhanced assessment grant, is a consortium of 10 states with nearly 300,000 students who are ELL. It has developed English language proficiency standards and an English language proficiency test and is also designing a system of alternate academic assessments for students who are ELL.

Language proficiency is determined by attending to the four language domains of listening, speaking, reading, and writing. WIDA (Gottlieb, 2004) defines these domains in the following manner:

- Listening—process, understand, interpret, and evaluate spoken language in a variety of situations
- Speaking—engage in oral communication in a variety of situations for an array of purposes and audiences
- Reading—process, interpret, and evaluate written language, symbols, and text with understanding and fluency
- Writing—engage in written communication in a variety of forms for an array of purposes and audiences (pp. 3–4)

According to WIDA, "[F]ive language proficiency levels outline the progression of language development implied in the acquisition of English as an additional language, from 1, Entering the process, to 5, Bridging to the attainment of state academic content standards" (Gottlieb, 2004, p. 5). These levels indicate how students who are ELL can be expected to perform (see Table 10.1).

Progressing along the English proficiency scales is a long process and can typically take a student five to seven years (Cummins, 1999). A student can also understand what is being said in a second language more easily than the student can express him- or herself in that language. Moreover, a student may be able to read in a second language at a much higher proficiency than write, speak, or verbally understand. A student will also learn social language in another language (levels 2–3) much more quickly than academic content and technical language (level 5). Sometimes teachers assume that because students who are ELL may be able to socially converse in English quite easily, these same students are not trying hard enough in their studies when they struggle with particular subjects or content areas in English. But, given the proficiency levels, this is not the case.

Table 10.1 Performance Definitions for PreK–12 English Language Proficiency Standards*

English Language Proficiency Level	At the given level of English language proficiency, English language learners will process, understand, produce, or use the following:
1 Entering	• Pictorial or graphic representation of the language of the content areas • Words, phrases, or chunks of language when presented with one-step commands, directions, wh-questions, or statements with visual and graphic support
2 Beginning	• General language related to the content areas • Phrases or short sentences • Oral or written language with phonological, syntactic, or semantic errors that *often impede the meaning* of the communication when presented with one- to multiple-step commands, directions, questions, or a series of statements with visual and graphic support
3 Developing	• General and some specific language of the content areas • Expanded sentences in oral interaction or written paragraphs • Oral or written language with phonological, syntactic, or semantic errors *that may impede the communication but retain much of its meaning* when presented with oral or written, narrative or expository descriptions with occasional visual and graphic support
4 Expanding	• Specific and some technical language of the content areas • A variety of sentence lengths of varying linguistic complexity in oral discourse or multiple, related paragraphs • Oral or written language with minimal phonological, syntactic, or semantic errors that *do not impede the overall meaning* of the communication when presented with oral or written connected discourse with occasional visual and graphic support
5 Bridging	• The technical language of the content areas • A variety of sentence lengths of varying linguistic complexity in extended oral or written discourse, including stories, essays, or reports • Oral or written language approaching comparability to that of English-proficient peers when presented with grade-level material

*Modified from WIDA's *English Language Proficiency Standards for English Language Learners in Kindergarten Through Grade 12: Frameworks for Large-Scale State and Classroom Assessment Overview Document* (Gottlieb, 2004)

Understand Bilingual Versus English as a Second Language Instruction

Once students are identified as having a limited proficiency in English, schools are mandated by law to educate them. Some schools offer bilingual education, meaning that the teacher has high competency in the first language of the students being taught. Thus, for example, if students are Spanish speakers, then the teacher is fluent in Spanish and English. Given the importance of students becoming fluent in their first language prior to learning English, it is critical that schools have access to staff who can teach the students in their home language. Student peers who also speak the students' home language can assist with this instruction.

While the bilingual option is advantageous in districts that enroll students with one predominant language other than English, this option is more difficult to provide and sustain when schools and districts have a variety of languages being spoken. Further, all districts, but especially rural districts, are challenged by a shortage of bilingual certified teachers. Because of this, some districts have successfully recruited individuals from the community who are proficient in the language of the students. For example, in schools with a large population of students who are Spanish speakers, they have hired someone from the local Latino community who is not certified to teach, but who has the skills and interests to work with students. These bilingual resource specialists are trained and supported by bilingual and ESL teachers at the school to work successfully with students. These staff also can translate verbal and print communications and serve as a liaison between the school and families. Some districts have then provided ongoing education to the bilingual resource specialists to enable them to become fully certified teachers in the district.

One form of bilingual education occurs in what some refer to as dual or two-way immersion schools (Howard, Sugarman, & Christian, 2003). In these schools, the population is typically composed of one half ELL students and the other half English speakers. Often, the ELL students all have Spanish as their home language. These schools are purposefully constructed, starting in kindergarten when nearly the entire teaching day is taught in Spanish. Translation does not occur for English speakers—they simply are immersed into the Spanish language and learn along with the native Spanish speakers. Importantly, these English speakers come to school fully fluent in English. Thus, they have the background on which to build their Spanish competency. Over the elementary years, the language content shifts in the grades to increasing levels of English spoken, to the point where the day is composed of one half English and the other half Spanish. Over the years, both English and the target language are taught, and students flip between modeling their primary language and learning their second language. This additive approach stresses the value in building language literacy skills first from a core language, then acquiring a second language on top of this. It is important to note that the dual-language approach must be provided at least through fifth grade, and ideally on through middle school. Thus, the main drawback to two-way bilingual programs is that they are effective with students only when the students remain in the same school environment over a series of years. This can be impractical with certain populations of ELL students where mobility rates are high. A student who begins school in a two-way bilingual program but then has to move to a monolingual environment may be disadvantaged.

In a meta-analysis of selected studies on the efficacy of bilingual education, Willig (1985) found that bilingual education programs are consistently more effective for reading, language skills, and mathematics achievement in both English and the home language. A more recent meta-analysis by Rolstad, Mahoney, and Glass (2005) also concludes that "bilingual education is superior to English-only approaches in increasing measures of students' academic achievement in English and in the native language" (p. 590). The research also shows that bilingual education tends to be more effective than English immersion in teaching students who are ELL to read in English (Slavin & Cheung, 2005), and that learning to read in one's native language is a strong predictor of one's ultimate skills in reading in English (Garcia, 2000). Patterns of successful bilingual programs indicate additive bilingual approaches are known to promote academic success as well as promote bilingualism (Cummins, 2000; J. Green, 1998; Krashen, 1999; Ramirez, Yuen, & Ramey, 1991; Thomas & Collier, 2001).

Cognitive benefits to bilingualism include increased creativity and problem-solving skills. Students who are becoming bilingual also tend to know more than their monolingual classmates about the structural properties of the language (sounds, words, grammar). These language strengths are beneficial in reading development because they facilitate decoding academic language. Becoming bilingual enhances one's skills at understanding and communicating with members of other racial, ethnic, and cultural groups and respecting values, social customs, and world views.

It is worth noting that just because someone can fluently speak the language of the ELL learners and is bilingual, he or she does not necessarily have the teaching skills to structure the curriculum and instruction in ways that would help students succeed. The quality of instruction is as important as the language of instruction (August & Hakuta, 1997). Therefore, relying, for example, on a high school or middle school teacher certified to teach Spanish as the sole resource person for Latino speakers in a school will not be sufficient to ensure these students' success.

In addition to bilingual education, many states offer a second area of teacher certification in the area of English as a second language (ESL). Unlike bilingual teachers, ESL teachers may not necessarily be bilingual, but they have been trained to structure the curriculum and instruction in ways that will lead to academic success for students who are ELL. Whether the school offers bilingual or ESL education, both should use evidence-based ESL teaching techniques and both should value and teach students to become fluent in their home language. Often, the phrase "bilingual education" is used to describe any kind of second-language instruction in schools, as compared to English immersion, which does not value or teach the home language and focuses solely on English learning.

In sum, schools that enroll students for whom English is not their first language need to first ensure that these students become literate in their home language. Ideally, they should be taught by a bilingual certified teacher who is fluent in their home language. In the absence of that resource, schools can hire a community person or even family member, provide support from an ESL teacher, and provide resources and materials in the students' language to ensure these students become literate in their home language prior to learning English. While English instruction is a component of bilingual education, all-English programs such as structured English immersion—as recently mandated by English-only laws in California, Arizona, and Massachusetts—do not meet the definition of bilingual education.

Evidence-Based ESL Teaching Techniques

A fourth aspect of curriculum and instruction that leaders need to address for students who are ELL are evidence-based ESL teaching techniques. ESL techniques include introducing key vocabulary associated with the content of the lesson prior to the lesson being taught; providing simple, one-step instead of multi-step directions on assignments; using visuals to illustrate ideas; delivering instruction using a variety of learning modalities, such as always having a visual representation of directions for the lesson; speaking clearly; and offering opportunities for students to engage in hands-on projects or using concrete prompts and objects to illustrate concepts and ideas. In this way, ESL techniques tap into the visual, auditory, and kinesthetic learning modalities of learners—that is, ESL techniques mimic differentiated instruction (see Chapter 8). As such, the teaching techniques that work well with students who are ELL are often quite similar to the ones that teachers of students with disabilities find to be successful. As we have argued previously in this book, the curriculum and instruction that work well with students with identified disabilities can benefit every learner in the classroom. Similarly, ESL techniques can benefit all learners. Thus, there is no mystery and magic in ESL curriculum and instruction. The curriculum and instruction that works well with students who are ELL also works with students with disability labels, and also benefits all students in the classroom, regardless of learning needs. In short, excellent ESL instruction is simply "good teaching" (Ladson-Billings, 1995) for all students.

Educate ELLs as Unique Individuals With Varying Needs

We need to remember that students who are ELL are unique, and all experience U.S. schooling in different ways. Therefore, equity data collection and analysis should be disaggregated across students who are ELL with different home languages. Minami and Ovando (2004) speak to this in detail:

> Some classroom teachers tend to view minority [sic] students as a group, simply ignoring their individual differences. To make matters worse, in such classrooms the "we" (mostly White middle-class teachers) and "they" (minority [sic] students as a bundle) notion of multiculturalism may also exist. Not only is it true that even if they speak the same first language (for example, Spanish) children from one community (Mexico, for instance) and those from another (Puerto Rico) are different; it is also necessary that each minority [sic] student from each community be perceived as a distinct individual. (p. 584)

Research suggests that Spanish-speaking students fare far worse in schools than other students who are ELL. For example, students who come from homes where Spanish is spoken are underserved in schools when compared to other students who are ELL. According to the U.S. Department of Commerce (cited in National Center for Education Statistics [NCES], 2004), 8.8% of students who come from homes where Spanish is spoken have repeated a grade. By contrast, only 4.7% of non-Spanish-speaking students who are ELL have repeated a grade. The difference is even more striking when looking at students who reportedly speak English "very well." Amongst this subset, 9% of students who come from homes where Spanish is spoken have repeated a grade, compared to only 3.4% of non-Spanish-speaking students who are ELL. Considering the strong evidence that grade retention is an ineffective strategy for struggling learners (Hong & Raudenbush, 2005; Jimerson, 2001), this disparate treatment is alarming.

The U.S. Department of Commerce (cited in NCES, 2004) reports similar disparities in high school completion rates. While 9 of 10 non-ELL students graduate, fewer than 7 of 10 ELL students do so. Again, when these data are disaggregated by linguistic differences, students who come from homes where Spanish is spoken are disproportionately hurt. Merely

61% of students who come from homes where Spanish is spoken graduate from high school, versus 90% of non-Spanish-speaking students who are ELL. In other words, while there is no difference in the graduation rates of non-Spanish-speaking ELL students and non-ELL students, there is an immense gap between Spanish-speaking students who are ELL and non-ELL students.

In sum, students who are ELL benefit from ICS in the same manner as all students. Educators need to view students who are ELL as unique members of the classroom community who have distinct learning needs, instead of broadly clustering them as a homogeneous group sharing the same learning needs.

Fully Integrate Highly Mobile Families and Students

One of the most significant factors in the academic success of ELL students is that schools connect with their families (Minami & Ovando, 2004). It is incumbent on the schools to make these connections, for, as Minami and Ovando point out, "contrary to the deficit hypothesis, it is the teacher, not the family, who has the main responsibility for adequate educational support" (p. 584).

One particular population of ELL students who merit attention are highly mobile migrant families. Students from migrant families should receive additional attention from the school to ensure their success (Lopez, 2001; Lopez, Scribner, & Mahitivanichcha, 2001). School leaders often neglect to build connections with these families. Most often, these are Latino families who move to the northern part of the country for the summer and into the fall, and then return to the southern part of the country over the winter to continue their migrant work. These families repeat this cycle annually. Usually, when these families move to a northern state, they return to the same local area of the state, and they also return to the same local area in the south. Thus, though these families are often stereotypically considered "unstable," their lives reflect stability even within the mobility.

An example from practice illustrates these ideas further. An adult learner in one of our courses asked the principal of her school for the number of ELL students in the school, and the principal reported there were zero. Upon further inquiry, the student learned that the district employed a migrant coordinator. This student further learned that approximately 40 migrant students resided in this school attendance area from September through early December each year, and returned to the school attendance area in the late spring. Though these 40 students attended this elementary school during these months, the school district did not count these students in its attendance. In the principal's eyes, these students literally did not exist. Thus, no efforts were made to coordinate with the southern district where these students returned each year. Failure to acknowledge these students resulted in practices such as not including them in any of the holiday program preparations because these students often migrated prior to the program, and the principal did not think it important to slightly shift the program date to include these students. Another migrant student wished to campaign for student council, yet she was prevented from doing so because she would be absent for part of the school year. In another school district, when migrant families made their annual pilgrimage to the south, the district filed truancy petitions against the families and then proceeded to drop them from the school enrollments, even though these families regularly returned each school year.

In these examples, the administrative response to migrant families and students is inexcusable. These negative examples of meeting the needs of migrant families illustrate how critical it is for school leaders for ICS and social justice to possess the basic leadership principles that we describe in Chapter 2, including being advocates for students who are typically marginalized in schools and welcoming and integrating all students fully into the school community.

BUILD TEACHER CAPACITY

Another core principle underlying ICS is that the primary way to prevent student failure and maximize student achievement is to build teacher capacity to teach to a range of diverse needs. As described previously, when ELL students are heterogeneously assigned across classes and courses, the expectation is that all teachers are responsible for all students who are ELL. This expectation is not a small assumption. We have experienced truly exceptional general education teachers who have achieved outstanding success with students with disabilities in their classrooms, but who are quite reluctant to accept ELL students into their schools or classrooms because they truly believe they are incapable of teaching these students. While not all teachers are bilingual, every staff person can learn about ESL curriculum and instruction methods that can benefit all students in the classroom. Thus, leaders must provide extensive professional development to all staff on differentiated, culturally relevant instruction and ESL best practices, and provide plentiful opportunities for staff collaboration and planning, as will be described in Chapter 11, that can significantly build teacher capacity to successfully educate students who are ELL. In addition, some schools that have been successful with ELL students require all new staff hired to also be certified in ESL or in bilingual education.

The length limits of this chapter prevent a thorough explanation of essential teacher skills for students who are ELL that in turn will benefit all students, though we refer the reader to Wong Fillmore and Snow (2000) for such an explanation. These authors believe that all educators need to be literacy experts. Specifically, all educators need to be skilled in oral language development, written language development, and academic English. We now point out a couple of aspects of these authors' detailed explanation that seem most salient for illustrating the critical link between assigning students to heterogeneous learning environments and their academic learning.

The area of English that students who are ELL struggle with the most is the proficiency level 5, or academic English, and problems of academic achievement are often directly rooted in academic English (Wong Fillmore & Snow, 2000). According to Wong Fillmore and Snow, educators need to be sure ELL students are exposed to exemplars of written academic English. Instead, in remedial pullout ELL and reading programs, students are often exposed only to readings composed of choppy sentences and awkward, incoherent, and shallow texts. Paradoxically, this may actually hurt comprehension. Instead, Wong Fillmore and Snow contend, "Well-written texts with grade-level appropriate language can give students access to . . . academic writing. With teachers' help, students can use these texts to learn the vocabulary, grammatical structures, phraseology, and rhetorical devices that are associated with that [academic English] register" (p. 31).

Students who are English language learners must be directly taught to speak, read, and write academic English. ESL techniques on their own, such as visual aids or using simplified English, are not enough. Further, to learn academic English, students who are ELL "must interact directly and frequently with people who know the language well enough to reveal how it works and how it can be used" (Wong Fillmore & Snow, 2000, p. 24). These students rely upon corrective feedback to negotiate and clarify meaning. Thus, clustering students who are ELL together in segregated environments prevents them from hearing the modeling of academic English by their English-speaking peers that would naturally happen in heterogeneous schools and classrooms (Wong Fillmore & Snow, 2000). Further, schools must ensure that students who are in need of the most capable teachers do not end up being instructed by those who are least prepared. Wong Fillmore and Snow explain this critical problem for students:

> [This] problem arises when teachers who do not understand the complexities of English . . . give tutors or teacher aides the responsibility for teaching reading to children who need the most help

(i.e., those in the lowest reading groups). These individuals are far less qualified to teach reading than are teachers. Even more problematic, teachers may assign LEP [Limited English Proficient] children to peer-tutors for help with reading on the grounds that children can communicate more effectively with other children than adults can. It takes a solid understanding of language to teach reading effectively, especially to children who are having the greatest difficulty grasping the abstract and complex relationships between sound and print, and the ideas they represent. (p. 28)

Wong Fillmore and Snow (2000) further caution that by clustering students who are ELL, and providing insufficient direct instruction and support toward developing skills in academic English, schools consign these students to either make little progress toward English proficiency or to develop nonstandard English vernaculars. Students often settle "into a variety of English that is fairly stable and that many of them speak fluently and with confidence. They are no longer language learners, because they are no longer working out the details of English" (p. 24).

We conclude that one of the best ways to develop staff capacity to teach English language learners is to require all staff, including school leaders, to learn a second language themselves—a language spoken by their students. In fact, we urge teacher and administrator preparation programs to require proficiency in a second language as a prerequisite for admission or licensure and as a requirement for faculty hires. In this way, educators and faculty will have firsthand experience of the challenges, frustrations, and nuances of learning a second language and the ways it opens up learning about literacy that will benefit literally all students for generations to come.

PRIMARY PRINCIPLES FOR EDUCATING ELLS

In addition to the three categories of nine practices that can raise the achievement of all learners, including students who are English language learners, we next describe two primary principles that should undergird these practices: all students in schools must become bilingual; and bilingual education is an education, not a place. We then offer one brief example of what these principles and practices could look like in a high school.

All Students in Schools Must Become Bilingual

Nearly all descriptions of various bilingual education models assume that English language learners are the focus and sole beneficiaries of these models, and the goal of these models is often English fluency for students who are ELL (see Ovando, 2003). In this sense, these models reinforce a deficit view of students who are ELL, viewing them as deficient, and suggesting that bilingual education is the way to remedy this deficiency. An ICS perspective of English language learners, on the other hand, views these learners as incredible assets to a school and district. Even learners who are at a level-1 proficiency in English and may be haltingly proficient in their home language are perhaps more developed in their language skills, due to the demands of learning two languages, than their monolingual, English-speaking peers. Even college admissions requirements recognize the value of acquiring more than one language, with nearly all colleges and universities requiring students to have completed two years of a foreign language to be admitted.

Given these university admissions requirements and the fact that nearly all states already require students at the middle and high school levels to complete several years of a foreign language, and given that competency in more than one language advances one's social and cultural capital in ways that will result in greater economic and social gain in today's society, it only makes sense that schools prepare all students to become competent in more than one language. Thus, the focus of bilingual education should not be students who are ELL but all students in the school (including students with disabilities, even students with severe disabilities). In so doing, students who are ELL become resources to the school and their peers in a mutually beneficial way.

In this sense, the ICS application to students who are ELL represents an "additive" rather than "subtractive" model in that the students' home language is valued and forms the basis of learning English. However, ICS extends beyond the additive bilingual models in the literature (Ovando, 2003) to a "multiplicative" model in that ICS principles and practices are additive not just for ELL students but for all students in the school. All students benefit from the language diversity in the classroom and from the instructional strategies that are used to engage these languages. ICS principles and practices would also argue that though the two-way, dual immersion programs may constitute ideal conditions for all students to become bilingual, many aspects of these programs can be naturally incorporated into schools in ways that will increase the likelihood of all students learning more than one language. The disability field already has parallel examples of this. For example, why should two-way immersion schools require equal numbers of English speakers and students who are ELL? We are familiar with schools that have even just one deaf student who uses sign language, and the entire school has learned sign language, effectively becoming bilingual in English and sign. This is just one example of how the promises of two-way immersion can be integrated into all schools.

Bilingual Education Is an Education, Not a Place

Most descriptions of various bilingual education models position them on a continuum from English immersion to two-way immersion (Ovando, 2003; see Table 10.2) as applied to students with Spanish as their home language). These models vary by the amount of time (typically measured in years) spent in segregated environments learning English. As such, these models suffer from the same limitations as the disability placement models. That is, these models conflate place or where students learn with student language learning, assuming that the only place students can receive intensive language instruction is in a segregated pullout program. Thus, these models make the same mistake as the disability models in the past. To remedy this limitation in special education, revisions in the laws clarified that special education is not a place, but a service, and what varies is the intensity of this service within general education classrooms to meet student needs. Similarly, bilingual education is not a place and not even a service, but an education, and the intensity of this bilingual education should vary not by place, but by the level of educational intensity focused on language learning that literally all students receive within heterogeneous classrooms.

In sum, the literature in bilingual education suggests that the goal is English fluency for students who are ELL, and that students must be slotted into one of the models along the continuum. The intensity of services provided is determined by the amount of time in a segregated program. In contrast, with ICS and English language learners, the goal is to create bilingual fluency for all students in the school. The intensity of language instruction is determined not by preset programs, but by the individual needs of students, and is a function of the amount and kind of curriculum, instruction, and support provided in heterogeneous classrooms and courses.

PRACTICES AND PRINCIPLES IN PRACTICE

Given these evidence-based practices related to student placement, curriculum and instruction, and teacher capacity, and principles associated with all students becoming bilingual learners who receive various levels of language-intense instruction in heterogeneous classrooms and courses, how will students who are ELL, who are at a level 2–3 of English language

Table 10.2   Continuum of Approaches to Students Who Are ELL

English Immersion ———————————————————————— Bilingual Education				
English only	Transitional bilingual education "early-exit"	Transitional bilingual education "late-exit"	Maintenance/ developmental bilingual education	Two-way bilingual education
Instruction in English with English as a Second Language (ESL) support	Instruction in English and Spanish	Instruction in English and Spanish	Instruction in English and Spanish	Instruction in English and Spanish
Students who are ELL not segregated	Students who are ELL initially segregated, then mainstreamed in monolingual classes within two years	Students who are ELL initially segregated, then mainstreamed in monolingual classes significantly later	Students who are ELL initially segregated, then mainstreamed in monolingual classes significantly later	Students who are ELL not segregated

proficiency learn in a tenth-grade history class? First, we remind ourselves that the three goals for all students are (a) bilingual fluency, (b) academic achievement, and (c) social and cultural integration.

Based on ICS principles, because the history class is composed of various learners who have been heterogeneously placed (including learners with disability labels, learners who require high academic challenges, learners who struggle with reading, etc.), the class will be taught via a culturally relevant, differentiated curriculum. The teacher is proficient with basic ESL teaching strategies that benefit all learners. Thus, though the students may not be able to fully comprehend all the class content, the curriculum and instruction are such that the student is not totally lost. Concepts and ideas can be reinforced via opportunities for all students in the class to experience individual, small-group, and large-group instructional arrangements. The teacher meets with other grade-level teachers and with the special education and ESL or bilingual teachers assigned to the tenth grade, daily and weekly for collaborative planning. Further, these students will require additional instruction in learning the Spanish language and in learning English, just as their non-ELL peers are learning. With their non-ELL peers, these opportunities can occur before or after school, during study hall, or during the individual and small-group work time in courses throughout the day. In this sense, English and

Spanish language skills are not confined to one pullout course a day, but instead, the students are provided opportunities to learn English and Spanish throughout the entire day within all the courses. Wong Fillmore and Snow (2000) agree that providing language support across the curriculum instead of just in language arts creates a stronger learning environment for students who are ELL:

> [Teachers] need to know something about how language figures in academic learning and to recognize that all students require instructional support and attention to acquire the forms and structures associated with it. . . . Often explicit teaching of language structures and uses is the most effective way to help learners. Teachers must recognize that a focus on language—no matter what subject they are teaching—is crucial. They must engage children in classroom discussions of subject matter that are more and more sophisticated in form and content. And they must know enough about language to discuss it and to support its development in their students. Academic language is learned through frequent exposure and practice over a long period of time from the time children enter school to the time they leave it. (p. 22)

Rather than being confined to a foreign language class, or to an English class for students who are ELL, or to a "sheltered English" content area class, all students learn their home language, whether that is English or another language, as well as a second language, as part of all subject area content. This is reinforced in individual, small-group, and large-group opportunities throughout the day.

In sum, from an ICS perspective, students and families who are language diverse are one of the greatest assets and opportunities that schools have today. Everything we know about learning and student achievement supports the idea of becoming proficient in more than one language. In the next chapter, we address how to develop teacher capacity to meet the needs of all students including students who are ELL.

Table 10.3   Chapter 10. English Language Learners and ICS

Focus Area	Focus Area Inquiry	Comments: What We Have	Phase of Application
1.	Describe the current service delivery model for educating students who are ELL.		
2.	All students who are ELL attend their home school in our district. If not, what is the number and percentage of students who are ELL who do not?		
3.	All the students who are ELL who live in the neighborhood service area of our school attend our school.		
4.	Students who are ELL are not clustered in particular classrooms and courses in our school. These students are heterogeneously assigned to classes and courses.		
5.	Students who are ELL with varying language levels are heterogeneously assigned to classes (e.g., all Level 1s are not assigned to one setting)		
6.	We value students' home language by ensuring that students become fluent in their home language first, prior to learning English.		
7.	We do not assume that because students are socially proficient in English, they are also proficient in academic English.		
8.	Our school has on staff individuals who are fluent in the students' home languages.		
9.	All teaching staff are competent in ESL teaching techniques that are of benefit to all students.		
10.	We collect, analyze, and disaggregate data across students who are ELL, aware of student learning differences among ELL students.		

(Continued)

Table 10.3 (Continued)

Focus Area	Focus Area Inquiry	Comments: What We Have	Phase of Application
11.	We reach out to and fully integrate migrant families and students. We include them in our enrollments the entire school year, and we do not file truancy petitions against them.		
12.	All staff receive extensive professional development opportunities related to students who are ELL, and many regular opportunities for staff collaboration and planning are provided toward this end.		
13.	All newly hired staff are required to hold a license in ESL or bilingual education, are willing to work toward this license, or have extensive proactive experience working with students who are ELL.		
14.	All students who are ELL receive exemplars of academic English rather than remedial-level reading opportunities.		
15.	Students who are ELL are directly taught academic English by the most capable teachers in the school.		
16.	All school staff are learning a second language themselves.		
17.	All students in our school are learning a second language.		
18.	The intensity of instruction for students who are ELL is determined by individual student needs and a function of the amount of curriculum, instruction, and support provided in heterogeneous classrooms/courses.		

11

Developing Teacher Capacity via Hiring, Evaluation, and Teacher Collaboration

To meet the needs of all students in integrated, heterogeneous environments, every decision that school leaders make should be evaluated in terms of the extent to which that decision will increase the teaching capacity of teachers. As we explained in previous chapters, segregating students, by default, de-skills teachers and offers no opportunity for teacher capacity to be strengthened. Even well-intentioned efforts, such as pairing special education and general education teachers in one classroom, do not inherently increase the general education teacher capacity, unless it is the primary goal of that teaching model.

Though the professional development literature addresses staff evaluations, mentoring, and recruitment practices, it does not directly connect these practices to position descriptions or professional development. It also does not take into account the principles and practices associated with meeting student needs in integrated environments. In this chapter, we identify four key practices associated with developing teacher capacity within an ICS model:

1. Educational position descriptions for ICS

2. Professional recruitment, interviewing, and retention

3. Professional continuous learning process (evaluation)

4. Professional development via teacher collaboration

These practices are pivotal for the comprehensive process of moving from programs to services. In schools where the principles of ICS are not integrated into position descriptions, staff evaluations, mentoring, and professional development opportunities, the burden of sustainability is left to informal structures that come and go in schools—mainly people. When schools complete a process of determining how they will provide Integrated Comprehensive Services, they often do not update their staff position descriptions using the principles that support the service delivery model. More candidly, the service delivery model within a school often evolves by default, or based on staff comfort and convenience. In the absence of formal structures, the staff design and school structure then function as an amoeba, taking shape based on the parent, teacher, student, and political pressure within and around the school—sadly enough, not by true design and intent or child need.

As illustrated in Figure 11.1, the four practices for developing teacher capacity are all supported by the Integrated Comprehensive Service delivery principles and are contiguous to each other. The figure illustrates the essential connections between the four practices that can result in developing teacher capacity to teach to a range of student learning needs. We discuss each of these components next.

EDUCATIONAL POSITION DESCRIPTIONS FOR ICS

Often in a school, teachers are hired under a specific district initiative, or to replace a beloved teacher who retired, but with little to no guidance as to the mission of the school and the expectation from other professionals as to their role and responsibilities. State standards and assessment practices have assisted in bringing points of clarity in *what* to teach, but not *how*. Consequently, staff are left to define their role through their educational experiences, interest, and comfort level. For example, a third-grade teacher may be hired to serve a broad range of learners with the expectation that over 70% of his day will be in a collaborative model. Conversely, if the teacher is not comfortable in such a model, there is nothing in the position description that requires him to be more collaborative than he

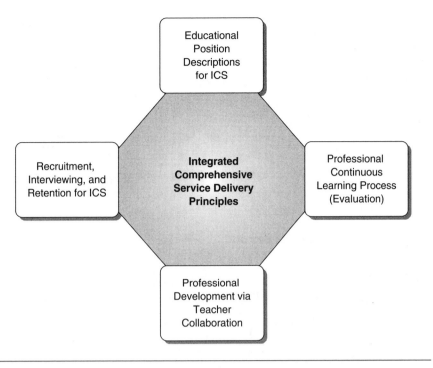

Figure 11.1   Developing Teacher Capacity for ICS

wants to be. Ill-defined positions such as that of a school psychologist may adversely affect the implementation of ICS if the individual hired is interested only in conducting student assessments and in so doing, abandons counseling, teacher support, and other collaborative requirements.

To illustrate the critical nature of redefining position descriptions, imagine another business that would allow its employees to unilaterally define their positions, isolated from the mission and service model. The bottom line is that, if we cannot imagine a company like Pepsi allowing such an ill-defined professional model, how can we as educators, with the welfare of our children in our hands, spend such little time defining the roles and responsibilities of our professionals who are part of a mission to develop ICS?

Thus, a general professional description for each staff position must be based on the service delivery model determined by the School Planning Team and fine-tuned by the Grade-Level Teams. When this rule is followed, all educators are better able to work with each other, as they have all agreed to or defined their own and others' roles. Examples of how professional roles can and should change within ICS can be found in our first book (Capper et al., 2000). In that book, we devoted an entire chapter to how the professional roles and responsibilities of educational staff must change if we are to meet student learning needs in heterogeneous environments. We explained in detail how the specific roles of staff would change within ICS, such as the roles of general educators, special educators, speech/language pathologists, directors of special education, and directors of curriculum and instruction, to name a few.

All position descriptions should include the common ICS principles as the core requirements of the position (see Table 11.1). Following these shared principles and expectations, the position descriptions are individualized to specific roles and responsibilities in these six universal areas:

1. Curriculum for all learners

2. Instruction for all learners

3. Assessment for all learners

4. Professional collaboration

5. Teacher leadership

6. Professional communication

The ICS principles contained within the position description along with these six areas specific to the particular role and responsibilities of the staff member can then be used as an interview protocol for hiring, to help define the responsibilities of the person once hired, and later to evaluate the staff person.

Many schools are aligning their expectations of teachers with their state teacher standards. Likewise, the principles of ICS can be aligned under the core teaching standards to form a cohesive instrument for hiring, supervision, and staff development. Within ICS, all teachers share the responsibilities for all learners, and anyone seeking information about the position or being interviewed for a position will understand that the care for students with specific needs is not just the responsibility of the special education teachers or support personnel but is the responsibility of every staff person in the school.

PROFESSIONAL RECRUITMENT AND RETENTION FOR ICS

We now offer just a few words on recruitment, as others such as Heller (2004) have written exhaustively on attracting and retaining good teachers. We believe that attracting and retaining high-quality teachers is all about providing the necessary supports and respect. Teachers will gravitate

Table 11.1   Position Description in Alignment With ICS

1. The professional educates and supports a full range of differing learners in heterogeneous school and nonschool environments.

2. The professional understands stereotypes and oppression related to race, social class, language, ability, gender, sexual orientation, and religion, as well as other areas of difference, and continues to explore his or her own values and beliefs regarding these issues and their impact on teaching and learning.

3. The professional collaborates and team teaches with a range of teachers and specialists to better meet the needs of the diverse range of learners.

4. The professional cooperatively develops curriculum with universal access in mind for all learners, to assist each learner in making significant progress toward and beyond grade-level standards using a range of individually appropriate assessment options.

5. The professional functions as an active team member of a professional learning community, using data to better support services for all learners in the most integrated comprehensive manner possible.

6. The professional believes that all children are his or her responsibility to teach, and all children can learn in our school given individualized support and the appropriate educational care.

Specific Position Descriptions by Teaching Assignment

- Curriculum for all learners
- Instruction for all learners
- Assessment for all learners
- Professional collaboration
- Teacher leadership
- Professional communication

(See Appendix J for a sample educational professional development plan.)

to schools that are harmonious and supportive. When teachers feel respected, supported, empowered, and entrusted, they will want to work in such an environment. Retention is all about care. When appropriately supported, even teachers who question their ability to provide instruction to a range of students with significant learning needs will be able to provide their insights as well as grow within such an integrated environment.

PROFESSIONAL CONTINUOUS LEARNING PROCESS FOR ICS

To design a continuous professional development process (evaluation), it is imperative that it be aligned with the professional position description.

In this manner, as mentioned previously, the descriptors delineated in the position description become criteria for the formative teacher evaluation. In using the continuous learning process, a teacher may review feedback from her principal as well as her own comments and highlight areas about which she would like more information and professional development.

PROFESSIONAL DEVELOPMENT VIA TEACHER COLLABORATION

Professional development without a doubt is the linchpin of Integrated Comprehensive Services. As we have stated consistently throughout this book, for schools to create this change, educators must leave their comfort zone and design and implement a transformed school where all students are valued and provided equitable curricular options. Commensurately, we know that each professional will require a range of differing support and professional development.

As schools move through the ICS change process, leadership often shifts from administrators holding significant autonomy in leading the school to collaborative models of shared leadership. Though teachers are expected to collaborate more than ever before, they often find it quite difficult to let go of their teaching autonomy. We also contend that the traditional program delivery model for students with special needs inhibits the ability of teachers to collaborate.

Peer collaboration, as defined by Friend and Cook (1991), describes how people work together—not necessarily what they do, but a style of working together to accomplish a shared goal. Importantly, Stainback and Stainback (1996) state that no single educator has all the skills necessary to meet a diverse population of students, which then necessitates collaboration among educators with a broad array of expertise to meet the needs of all learners. Even with the necessity for collaboration, teachers continue to find it quite difficult to collaborate and share their expertise. School leaders can expect teachers to collaborate, yet the teaching milieu is constructed under the assumption of autonomy, where one teacher with a set of information is responsible to bestow that information to prepare students for future employment. Yet, teacher collaboration is essential if educators are to acquire new knowledge and understanding for serving a broad range of diverse learners. In response to the diverse learning needs of students, school leaders often attempt to merge teachers into collaborative configurations without changing the structure of the traditional school, a structure which was developed based on assumptions that teachers would work independently of each other. Therefore, teachers find it difficult to collaborate due to lack of planning time, scheduling, and extended time to work with shared students. Service delivery to students with learning or behavioral challenges that is structured in traditional ways results in three barriers.

Barrier 1: Planning Time

Educators often are concerned about the lack of planning time to collaborate. At the middle and high school levels, we have been able to use houses/teams and block scheduling to build in individual and teacher-team planning time. The situation has not worked as well at the elementary level. Some schools provide an early release once a week to give teachers both individual and team planning time. Early release, however, often means that elementary students with secondary-age siblings who are not offered early release may be left to their own after-school supervision, as child care may be an expensive option for some families. Block scheduling at the elementary level and scheduling related arts classes in such a way to provide planning time for core teachers is one solution to providing additional planning time at the elementary level.

Barrier 2: Scheduling

No one is going to deny that assigning students and teachers is difficult in an Integrated Comprehensive Services delivery model. When Grade-Level Design Teams can meet and work through schedules, everyone wins—even teachers. For example, if a teacher is uncomfortable supporting a small group of students with one member who has autism, that may be a time when one teacher (who is comfortable) leads the instruction, while the other observes and over time participates. In time, often the comfort level, understanding, and teaching skills across a diverse range of learners increase among teachers.

Barrier 3: Frequency of Collaboration Between Teachers

Frequency of collaboration between teachers is inherent within a model supported by the School Planning Team, School Service Delivery Team, and Grade-Level Design Teams because collaboration is not based on the whim of teachers, but on pragmatic restructuring of services within the school. When the school is restructured to support all students in integrated settings with the understanding of collaboration as a must, the consistency and predictability of that collaboration becomes a given.

TYPES OF PROFESSIONAL COLLABORATION FOR ICS

Educators in teacher education have defined a wide range of models of teacher/peer collaboration (see Table 11.2, adapted from Friend & Bursuck, 2002). We identify 13 variables that are necessary for successful teacher collaboration. If one or more of these variables is not present, this does not mean that collaboration cannot occur; it means, just as in any relationship, it will be an area that both teachers will need to improve for the success of all students.

1. Shared vision that all children can and will be successful (just not all at the same time or using the same definition of success)

2. Clear understanding of each other's role that has been determined by the needs of the students and staff availability

3. Mutual respect for each other with the understanding that each person is doing the best that he or she can do at the time

4. Clear understanding of each other's expertise and how it is beneficial in the instructional arena

5. Clear understanding of each other's apprehension in specific areas and a commitment to support one another in these areas both publicly and privately

6. Sufficient time for both long-term planning and short-term planning

7. Clear division of responsibilities based on the configuration model mutually agreed upon

8. Clear communication regarding expectations of each and every learner within the group

9. Clear expectations of assessment and how it will be completed, and what assessments are valued

10. Clear organizational patterns for each teacher and timeliness in completing agreed-upon tasks

11. Specific responsibilities delineated for each teacher in the classroom, which will then be reflected within teacher evaluations

12. Forgiveness—the ability to understand when your partner is not at his or her best

13. Humor—the ability to enjoy the cooperation and bring students into the celebration

Table 11.2   Peer Teaching Configurations

Configuration	Description
One Teacher/One Observer (consultation)	One teacher leads and one teacher observes individual students to better make instructional decisions. This configuration is not implemented for a quarter or a semester, but at intervals to check student learning and understand student needs.
One Teacher/One Drift	One teacher leads the instruction, while the other teacher provides individual support to students. This is often used in large-group settings where one teacher has the content expertise and one teacher has the ability to understand how specific students learn and require specific instructional supports. This type of configuration may also be used when one teacher is split across two classrooms and may not be in the room the entire time to share the actual instructional responsibility equally.
Station Teaching	Teachers develop the curriculum for the specific learners within the classroom and set up stations of instruction where students rotate from one to another. Teachers remain stationary and provide similar instruction with different groups of students. Often a third group may be formed using other support staff, e.g., occupational therapist, physical therapist, speech and language clinician, guidance counselor, Title I teacher, etc. Or, the third group may be formed to provide students with an opportunity for repeated practice or a cooperative assignment.
Parallel Teaching	Teachers divide the group into half and provide the same instruction to a smaller group of learners. They may use different types of instructional techniques with similar content—when the content changes, the configuration is usually defined as "station teaching."
Team Teaching	Teachers develop the curriculum with the understanding of the need for universal access (curriculum developed so that each and every student, even those with significant disabilities, may participate). Teachers then share the instructional responsibility equally, such as one lectures while the other demonstrates an activity.

SOURCE: Adapted from Friend & Bursuck (2002)

Next, we pull together the major ideas in this chapter regarding the importance of hiring, the shift in position descriptions, and teacher collaboration, with an example from practice. This example also illustrates how all these staff changes must occur within a changed service delivery structure. That is, changing how students are served in the school requires changes in hiring, evaluation, and professional development.

In this example, teacher collaboration serves as the cornerstone of professional development in a middle school, and the principal draws from a number of different opportunities to develop teacher capacity. Similar to our description of collaboration in Chapter 8, at this middle school, the sixth grade was composed of eight classes, and the principal divided these classes among four teams. She paired two sets of two rooms together, separated by a door between them. Membership on each team included the two general educators who were paired. The principal also assigned a special educator to each team (the principal reallocated all her resources, including cutting all special education teacher assistants and used the money to hire additional special education staff; see Chapter 12 on reallocating resources for further explanation). Thus, each team of three teachers (two general ed and one special ed) was responsible for 45 students.

At this school, the special education teacher on each team was responsible for (case managed) all the students with disability labels who were placed in these classrooms; however, all three teachers were responsible for all 45 students in the two classes, and all three teachers were responsible for teaching core subjects to the students. So seamlessly did these teachers function across their roles and students that none of the students in these classes knew which teacher was the special education teacher. Importantly, in the student/family handbook, the teaching staff were listed by grade level, with special education teachers included—they were not identified as special education teachers, but simply as members of the teams. The other two sixth-grade teams included both a special education teacher and a bilingual or ESL teacher, depending on the number of ELL students on the team (the way ELL students were assigned to classes is explained in Chapter 10 of this book).

The principal believed that teacher collaboration was the cornerstone of building teacher capacity. Thus, she structured a teaching schedule that afforded as many opportunities as possible to collaborate. These collaborative opportunities, along with additional strategies, resulted in 10 different ways she developed teacher capacity at her school, starting with the hiring of staff.

In addition to seeking staff who were appropriately certified, the principal looked for individuals who were pleasant, hardworking, willing to collaborate and co-plan instruction, open to discussions and self-reflection on race and white privilege, and comfortable with students with high needs (including students with severe, challenging behaviors). Importantly, in the interview process, the principal made clear to the prospective teacher the types of students with whom he or she would be expected to work, providing specific examples of students and their behaviors, and she asked questions to learn about the teacher's history and capacity to be successful with these students.

Beyond hiring, five strategies the principal drew from to develop teacher capacity were directly related to teacher collaboration. First, all the teachers received daily individual planning time. Individual planning time is important because teachers should not feel like they must choose between individual and collaborative planning time. Second, while students attended allied arts courses such as art, band, or foreign language, each team of teachers received daily common planning time. Thus, each day, the two general educators and the special educator received time in which they could plan together. Third, the principal provided weekly or every-other-week planning with a facilitator who guided the team through a planning session focused on such items as curriculum, student needs, and resources the teachers needed.

The facilitator's job was to help these teachers meet the needs of the wide range of students in their classrooms. The facilitator role was filled by various individuals (the same individual met with the same team over the entire year, however), including the school psychologist, the learning coordinator, or a curriculum specialist who was hired through a comprehensive school reform grant.

A fourth way the principal provided collaborative teaching opportunities that then served to develop teacher capacity was by setting aside funds for teachers to apply for extended planning time during the school year. With the funds, the team was able to take a day away from school, and with the help of a facilitator, spend the entire day collaborating and planning a universal curriculum and instruction for all the students on their team. A fifth opportunity for teacher collaboration was provided by giving teachers the opportunity to apply for funding from the school to meet and plan with a facilitator during the summer months.

In addition to these teacher collaboration opportunities that developed the teaching capacity of all the teachers on the team—general, special ed, and ESL teachers across the entire range of students and subject areas—the principal expected student services support staff, such as the speech/language pathologist, to work with their students within the general education classroom (except for students who needed intensive instruction on saying particular sounds). For example, the speech pathologist modeled to the classroom teachers ideas for them to integrate into their own teaching that would increase the language skills of not only the students identified for speech/language services, but for all the students in the classroom.

The principal also encouraged teachers to take advantage of professional development opportunities in the district and elsewhere, but would only approve opportunities that were directly aligned with the school's mission and goals and objectives for the year. Another way that the principal developed the capacity of her staff was by sending small groups of teachers to make presentations on their outstanding teaching at the National Middle School Conference. A final and indirect way that the principal promoted and supported teacher collaboration resulted from the fun activities that were structured for the students in the school. These included faculty-student basketball games, theme dances where all staff and students wore dance theme clothing to school, "chillin' out" parties that the staff held to celebrate the end of each quarter, and Friday afterschool socials for faculty. These activities encouraged social connection among the staff, which in turn supported staff collaboration within and across classrooms and grade levels at the school.

As can be seen by this one example, teacher collaboration across special education, general education, bilingual education, literacy, and other areas extends far beyond assigning a special education and general education teacher to coteach with each other. In fact, if a hierarchy existed that depicted levels of teacher collaboration, simply pairing a general and special education teacher—while obviously a step beyond isolationist, segregated teaching—would be at the bottom. Schools that believe they have "arrived" at their inclusion goal by providing opportunities for special education and general education teachers simply to teach together still have a long way to go.

This middle school provides more support for the fact that ICS is not about one change in the school, such as differentiated curriculum, or creating team-teaching opportunities between general and special educators. ICS requires an entire rethinking of the school structure, and this change in structure then requires a total rethinking of professional roles and responsibilities. This chapter has also argued that these professional role changes require hiring educators intentionally and purposively into these transformed roles, creating position descriptions that match these new identities, and aligning teacher evaluation to these transformed position descriptions. In addition, leaders for ICS and social justice must provide as many intentional and structured opportunities as possible for teachers to collaborate and to share roles and responsibilities with each other as a means to develop teacher capacity. Additional professional development opportunities must be directly linked to the school mission and goals, and successful teachers in the school should have opportunities to share their expertise with others. Finally, providing opportunities for staff to meaningfully engage with each other and students in informal ways serves as one way to develop a proactive school climate (see Chapter 6), which in turn can nurture and support collaborative teacher relationships. In so doing, teacher capacity is strengthened to be able to meet the wide range of student needs in the classroom—the bottom-line goal of ICS.

Table 11.3   Chapter 11. Developing Teacher Capacity

Focus Area	Focus Area Inquiry	Comments: What We Have	Phase of Application
1.	Position descriptions are written in support of the role that each individual will play within the school, based on the school/district mission and staff design in support of ICS, i.e., all must work together to meet the individual needs of each student.		
2.	Position descriptions are provided for individuals who are interviewing for the position and presented as part of each posting and recruitment fair.		
3.	The unions and school board approve position descriptions, which align the school/district mission and staff design in support of ICS.		
4.	The first five to six descriptors on the position description are supported by the national and state administrator and teacher standards, as well as those specific expectations that fulfill the mission of the school in support of ICS. In doing such, a unification of expectations around ICS is formed.		
5.	Components of the position description are used for individualized staff evaluation forms in addition to the school/district supervision and goal-setting portfolios.		
6.	Recruitment postings are written specifically based on the position descriptions that incorporate ICS principles.		
7.	Recruitment postings are worded in a manner to support the ICS staff assignment, such as working with other educators, etc.		

(Continued)

Table 11.3 (Continued)

Focus Area	Focus Area Inquiry	Comments: What We Have	Phase of Application
8.	Recruitment efforts use the position description to determine appropriate interviewing questions, using a common set of questions formulated from the first five to six descriptors.		
9.	What percentage of position descriptions have been rewritten and school board approved in support of the school mission and staff design for ICS?		
10.	What percentage of evaluations are completed using the evaluation tool that parallels the position description in support of ICS?		
11.	What percentage of administrators are comfortable completing interviews and evaluations in this manner?		
12.	Assess the history of staff turnover in your school. To what extent is your school a place where teachers who support ICS would want to work?		
13.	Assess the time available for planning and collaboration in your school. Based on the example in the chapter, how can planning time be increased?		
14.	Based on the list of peer teaching options, which options are utilized in your school and to what extent? To what extent should this be changed in support of ICS?		
15.	To what extent are the 13 variables necessary for teacher collaboration present in your school? What needs to change and how could this change happen?		
16.	List all the opportunities available for professional development, including all the opportunities available for teacher collaboration. Assess this list based on ICS.		

Focus Area	Focus Area Inquiry	Comments: What We Have	Phase of Application
17.	To what extent are professional development opportunities directly linked to school goals/mission?		
18.	Assess the opportunities for staff to meaningfully engage with each other in informal ways.		

Reflective Questions:

1. When you review your data, is there a disconnect between position descriptions, teacher evaluations, and building teacher capacity?

2. Can you find where the disconnect is in the system?

3. What steps can you take to begin to build a connection?

CORNERSTONE 4

Implementing Change: Funding and Policy

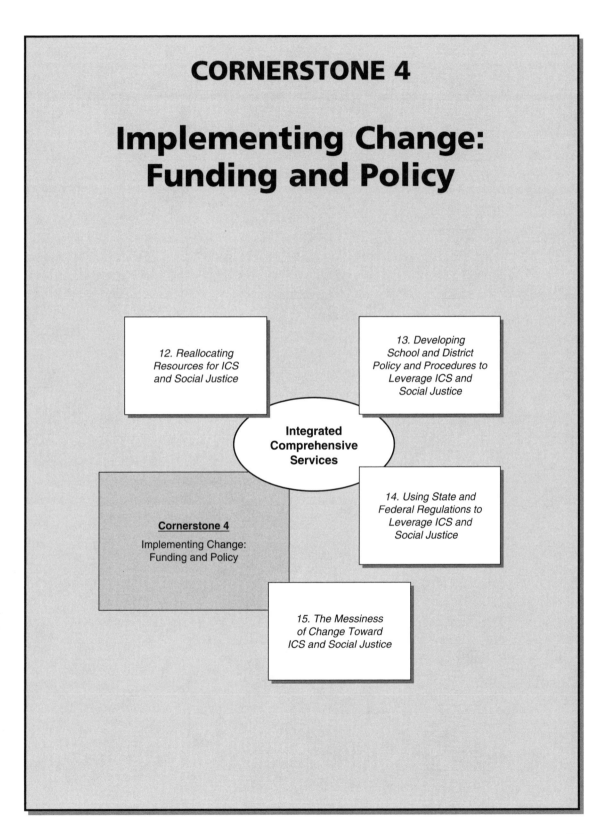

12. Reallocating Resources for ICS and Social Justice

13. Developing School and District Policy and Procedures to Leverage ICS and Social Justice

Integrated Comprehensive Services

Cornerstone 4

Implementing Change: Funding and Policy

14. Using State and Federal Regulations to Leverage ICS and Social Justice

15. The Messiness of Change Toward ICS and Social Justice

Reallocating Resources for ICS and Social Justice

It seems we are constantly blaming the crisis in public education on the lack of or misallocation of funds. Principals have said to us, "Yes, I would be happy to lead a movement toward Integrated Comprehensive Services if my district had the money to back it—but we don't." An underlying assumption prevails among administrators and teachers that to better serve a range of different learners will cost money—money schools do not have. On top of this, educators argue that because of federal mandates, such as those associated with the No Child Left Behind Act, they cannot possibly take on another unfunded initiative such as ICS.

Educators assume that to implement ICS will be quite costly, requiring additional funding in a time of severe economic crisis in education. Educators also assume that providing services to students in integrated environments will cost more than segregated options. We always find it interesting that educators, and at times the public, believe that we do not have enough money for education. They point to these unfunded and underfunded federal mandates for which districts are not provided enough funding to comply.

For example, educators point to the federal special education laws that require districts to meet the needs of students with disabilities, but the federal government has decreased financial support for these programs over time. In response, educators and policy makers, conservative and progressive, have demanded increased special education funding.

This perceived lack of funding for special education has resulted in ironies in practice in local districts. Many educators believe that special education is underfunded, but at the same time, they and some community members point out that special education receives more funding than general education. This perception results in general educators and families of general education students blaming district budget shortfalls on students with disabilities and the services they require. Similarly, educators and some community members also blame budget shortfalls on the costs of educating other students who sometimes struggle in schools, such as students of color, low-income students, and students for whom English is not their first language. Again, educators and community members argue that these students require more support and funding than general education students, and that this takes away from funding that could go toward higher achieving, white, middle- to upper-class students. Such blaming is more prevalent in suburban; small town; and rural, predominantly white districts whose demographics are changing as families of color, low-income families, and families for whom English is not their first language are moving into these districts.

This budget crisis and the blaming of typically marginalized students and families for contributing to it, and the appeal to policy makers to increase funding for these populations in particular and for education in general, take place in an interesting context. While the budget debate wages on, districts seem to be able to find the money to create segregated, separate programs, which, as we argued in Chapter 1, are the most expensive, least effective way to provide services to students.

For example, when dealing with increases in student enrollment, we have witnessed school communities debate for months on end whether to add onto an existing high school to create one really large high school, or to build a separate high school resulting in two smaller high schools. The argument is often put forth that the large high school will be more cost effective. However, we know from research (Lee & Smith, 1997) that the most effective and efficient high school size is 600 to 900 students. Beyond this size, students become lost in the crowd and achievement suffers (Osterman, 2000). Thus, when large schools are built at the elementary, middle, or high school levels, in part to save costs, over the long term, these large complexes cost the taxpayers much more money than smaller schools. As students inevitably struggle in these large education complexes, educators will set up segregated special programs to meet student needs. For example, one district argued they did not have enough money to build a separate high school rather than add onto the existing high school. But when the one large high school could not meet the needs of all its students, they built a brand new alternative high school. In addition to establishing segregated programs in or out of schools to respond to the problems that result from large schools, we spend thousands of federal and local dollars trying to transform these large complexes into smaller learning communities (Osterman, 2000).

Thus, though educators cry out for more funding for education in general, and special education in particular, we are always amazed how there seem to be plenty of funds to create and sustain expensive segregated programs, to bus students and cluster them within particular schools in a district, to transport students to an entirely different district, to hire additional teaching assistants, and to evaluate and label students. Thus, in this chapter, we argue that lack of funding is not the problem when it comes to implementing ICS. Instead, we need to stop spending money on inefficient, ineffective programs and reallocate the resources we currently have.

As we explained in Chapter 1, in segregated programs, separate funding sources are accessed and policies are written to support each program for each eligibility area, causing replication of services and soaring costs. These policies and programs are focused on fixing what are perceived as student deficits. Often, policies are compliance driven and not quality driven, resulting in meeting the letter of many nondiscrimination regulations but never reaching the spirit in which the regulations were written. These separate programs are expensive due to the costs involved in identifying students as well as duplication of staff and materials between schools and programs and across programs. Separate programs are quick fixes and not focused on long-term solutions, which inevitably results in higher costs in the long run. For example, as we previously stated, separate programs, by default, do not build teacher capacity to teach to a range of student needs. To illustrate, if the second-grade teacher sends students out of the room for reading help, the next year, when students need reading help, she will send students out again. Sending students out of the room this year will not increase her capacity to teach students reading next year. Thus, the way that separate programs de-skill teachers and limit their growth is yet another hidden cost of segregated programs.

In addition, the multidimensional nature of resources keeps all of us trying to figure out how to better meet the disparate needs within and across our public schools. The inequities of school funding are at an all-time high. Educators end up either perpetuating the status quo through identified expenditures or feeling trapped by earmarked dollars for specific programs. Our response to this dilemma is to reallocate current funding and expenditures. As we discussed in Chapter 2 regarding leadership, we must first believe that we can do it—more than that, we must believe that we have an ethical, moral, legal, and social responsibility to create Integrated Comprehensive Services for all learners before we can even begin our discussion about funding.

Before we lay out some of the current realities and facts associated with school funding, we will first argue that every teacher leader, school leader, and district administrator must become an expert in school finance. In successful ICS schools, leaders do not shy away from learning about how federal, state, district, and local funding works and do not abdicate their responsibility for knowing this to school or district administrators who are in charge of the school finances. This information is critical for them to know how to draw from the variety of funding available and how to merge existing resources in ways that derive maximum benefit for all students. In addition, these leaders are quite shrewd about tapping into private grants and local resources to support their ICS and social justice efforts. From working with their local PTO, to tapping private foundations, to collaborating with the neighborhood senior center for volunteers, these leaders know a critical part of their work includes raising funds and acquiring resources for their vision. Aligned with Odden and Archibald's (2001) work, these leaders view resources broadly to include not only external funding, but also all the school staff who could be repositioned or reallocated in ways to support ICS.

Not being afraid to dig into the details of the finances (external as well as human resources), and knowing how to shrewdly and wisely use and manage revenues and expenditures, are critical skills of a servant leader for social justice. In fact, as leaders who are supported by public taxpayer money, we have a moral and ethical responsibility to the students to manage the funds in the best way possible that will ensure student success. We also have a moral and ethical responsibility to the taxpayers to be stewards of the highest standards with this money and use it to bring about the greatest impact on democracy and toward social justice ends.

To know how to reallocate existing resources, leaders need a sense of understanding about some financial realities, including the disparity of funding across districts and the responsibility to play a role in moving state and local funding formulas in the direction of equity. We also are aware of the number of unfunded and underfunded mandates causing pressure on school personnel. In addition, we will attend to the allocation of funds within a district and school and discuss how money is often allocated in districts and how much money is spent on a model of services to keep students "out" versus "in."

DISPARITY IN SCHOOL FUNDING

Schools are funded through federal, state, and local resources, yet according to Biddle and Berliner (2002), because nearly half of those funds comes from local property taxes, the system generates large funding differences between wealthy and impoverished communities. Such differences exist among states, among school districts within each state, and even among schools within specific districts. For example, in 2003 in the state of Wisconsin, the total cost per pupil ranged from $6,632 to $14,438 across districts. That is, some districts fund their schools at more than double the amount per pupil than other districts. The relationship between funding disparities and student achievement is well documented. The National Center for Education Statistics (1998, cited in Biddle & Berliner, 2002) says their data show that communities where student poverty is rare tend to have well-funded schools, whereas schools in communities where student poverty is rampant tend to receive much less funding. In addition to school district funding inequities, educators are also faced with underfunded legislative mandates. We discuss this next.

UNDERFUNDED MANDATES

Between the lack of funding of No Child Left Behind and the underfunding of the Individuals with Disabilities Act (IDEA), school personnel believe that it is virtually impossible to meet the needs of every child. As to the latter legislation, we identify two major variables to attend to when looking at the need for increased funding under IDEA. First, the amount of dollars granted to districts over the past 25 years has decreased, while the population of students with disabilities has increased (Individuals with Disabilities Education Improvement Act [IDEIA], 2004). Second, the type of funding formula used by states to distribute categorical aid to districts may foster the over-labeling of students with disabilities. For example, in Wisconsin over the past 25 years, special education aid to districts has dropped by 37%. In those same 25 years, the number of students eligible for services has doubled at the same time the number of students without disabilities in our public schools has steadily increased in some districts and declined in others (U.S. Department of Education, 2000). Thus, in Wisconsin, the way the state distributes special education funding to districts may increase the propensity of educators to label students with disabilities.

Since IDEA 1997 and IDEIA 2004, there has been a call for states to support a neutral-placement funding formula—that is, a funding formula that does not perpetuate the placement of students in segregated settings or encourage the eligibility of students for special education. Currently, states use either a teacher-weighted, student-weighted, or block funding formula, with poverty and high-need students factored into the equation. A teacher-weighted formula means that districts receive financial reimbursement from the state for teacher salaries. The more students who are labeled with disabilities, the larger the number of special education teachers who are partially funded by the state. However, in Wisconsin, the state pays 28% of the cost of teacher salaries, while the district must absorb the other 72%. Thus, in this case of teacher-weighted formulas, it is not fiscally smart to over-label students with disabilities. A student-weighted funding formula means that districts receive financial reimbursement from the state, based on the number of students labeled for special education. The problem with student-weighted funding is that it can encourage districts to over-label students with disabilities to receive additional funding.

The most equitable manner to distribute funds has been a block formula with a poverty factor and high-needs cost factored in. Through block-funding formulas, the district receives a percentage of funding based on the typical percentage of students in this country who are labeled with a particular disability. Thus, for example, if students with severe disabilities typically comprise 1% to 3% of the school population nationally, then every district would receive funding reimbursement based on this same percentage of the entire student population in the district (not just students with disabilities). If the district has more than 1% to 3% percent of its entire student population with severe disabilities, they would receive the same amount as if they had less than this. As another way of explanation, if 12% of the students in the United States typically have disabilities (which is the case), and 2% of the 12% have severe disabilities, then 10% of the total population of students in the district are funded, for example, at $3,000 per student and the other 2% are funded at $12,000. The district receives funding for 12% of its entire student population whether they have 8% students labeled with disabilities or 16%. In this way, districts are not tempted to over-label students with disabilities because there is no financial incentive to do so.

If a district has labeled only 8% of its students with disabilities, but receives funding based on 12% of its student population, then the district could use the additional funds for early intervention, emphasis on literacy, professional development, and other practices discussed in this book that prevent student struggle. Districts receive funds and a financial incentive for prevention practices, rather than only receiving funds after students fail and are labeled. In this way, the cycle of blaming students for their own failure and over-labeling these students with disabilities could be stopped, teacher capacity to teach to a range of students could be increased via the practices discussed in this book, and the national and local incidence of students with disabilities could be significantly reduced.

The advantage of this funding formula is that districts would not be encouraged to over-label students with disabilities. Moreover, districts that meet a particular poverty level would receive additional funding. Thus, each district would receive a set amount of dollars based on the national percentage of students with particular disabilities and the poverty factor, completely disconnected from the number of students the district labels, the type of disability, and the type of services provided. Unfortunately, this formula also spurs the most controversy, since most states that use such a formula—Pennsylvania, for example—believe that their funding mechanism should take into consideration the actual number of students meeting eligibility instead of a projection based on the percentage of individuals who typically have disabilities in our country. The underlying assumption, however, is that block formulas assume that the students who meet eligibility requirements are truly disabled, and this eligibility determination had nothing to do with teacher ability, early childhood experiences, or the lack of other more flexible supports in integrated environments, to name a few of the relevant factors.

In contrast, the teacher- or student-weighted formula for funding in some states could be aligned to an increase in student eligibility as it is tied to an increase in funding. Such funding often provides an incentive for teachers to label because they do not know what else to do, and at least they will get additional dollars to provide additional services, albeit special education.

Consequently, before we blindly go forth and increase funding to underfunded mandates and fund those mandates that come without such provisions, we need to consider the following. First, we believe that fully funding special education will perpetuate a movement to label even more students than are currently labeled. Second, the increase in the number of students with disabilities and the associated increase in costs are due, in large part, to the inflexible manner in which services are provided based on student failure and slotting that we discussed in the second chapter. Third, shifting to ICS will, in the long haul, prove that our current funding amounts are enough to meet the needs of all students in heterogeneous, integrated environments.

In short, we must address how students become eligible for services or student labeling, the placement of these students, and how services are provided, before we can unequivocally come to an economically efficient and effective means to offset special education costs. We provide four examples next to illustrate our point.

First, educators need to determine why the increase in the numbers of students labeled for special education in many districts is often greater than the increase in students to the district. Research shows that often the number of students labeled for special education or who are labeled eligible for other services is a result of poor instructional practices rather than within-child deficits. For example, Chynoweth (2004) studied two rural school districts in the same state with similar demographics, but one district labeled more than twice the number of students with disabilities as compared to the other district. Her study showed that it was not student need, but educator and family assumptions about disabilities, their perceptions of special education, and district policies and practices that determined the extent to which students were labeled.

Second, we need to determine what services will be provided to better meet the needs of all learners. Choosing cross-categorical support by grade level will cost less than grouping children with similar labels together into separate classrooms only for students labeled with emotional disturbance or classrooms only for students labeled with cognitive disabilities or autism, to offer a few examples. Unfortunately, many states require districts to label a minimum number of students with a particular label before the state will fund a teacher to teach these students. Relatedly, providing teacher assistant support for several low-incidence students and also developing natural supports for students in the classroom (i.e., peer support, classroom structure support) cost less than providing individual assistants for these students. In addition, providing seamless support for all learners across special education, general education, at-risk, ESL, and federal Title I services costs less than providing separate units/teachers and administrative support for these differing student service areas.

Third, educators need to determine where students with a range of needs will best be served. Serving each and every child within the schools they would attend if not disabled costs less than transporting students to other schools or districts and paying increased administrative costs. At the school level, educating students in different types of learning groups (e.g., small-group, individual, and large-group instruction) throughout the day costs less than placing students with similar labels in homogeneous, self-contained classrooms and resource rooms.

Fourth, educators need to determine how they will teach all learners. That is, school districts will continue to spend too much on special education when the only way students can access a differentiated curriculum that meets their needs is outside of general education settings. Thus, we argue that the underfunding of special education is not the problem. Rather, we need to focus on how we use the funding we currently receive in more cost-effective ways that reflect evidence-based practices.

The lack of funding for NCLB cannot be discussed in isolation of the law requirements. Often, many educators and the general public complain about the underfunding of NCLB without taking time to really think about what we are asking our legislatures to fund. Certainly, funding qualified teachers and research-based methodologies is admirable—but what we really want funding to cover is the high-stakes testing that may not be so admirable. Instead of requesting additional funding for testing, we can advocate for funding practices that would pay off over time in both the generation of income and the support of bridging the equity gap in this country.

In sum, blindly increasing the funding for underfunded federal mandates is not the solution for meeting the needs of all students in our schools. We do argue that funding disparities between schools, districts, and states should be addressed. However, we cannot wait for these disparities to be erased before taking responsibility for the funding and expenditures in our own schools and districts. In fact, we argue that enormous financial gain can be made to the benefit of all students in the district, even under current financial constraints, by reallocating district resources. We discuss this next.

ALLOCATION OF DISTRICT MONIES

The monies at the district level are currently allocated in most districts to perpetuate a fragmented, segregated model of program delivery supported by federal mandates that are meant to alleviate nondiscrimination (i.e., special education, Title 1, and ESL, to name three such mandates). In most districts, educators spend an inordinate amount of money to segregate students and then claim it is impossible to reallocate the funds for integrated services. Once we integrate students who need full-time support, we then define the model as costly. However, it only seems costly because we are now being intentional about spending and can consciously see the use of our money within the district.

To take one example, educators often send a student with severe needs to another district to be served, costing the district $35,000 for the out-of-district placement, $15,000 for bussing, and another $8,000 for overhead and administrative cost, for a total of $58,000. When district educators spend money in this way, they are not reminded daily of how much money that individual costs the district. Given that there are 180 school days, in this case, the district is spending $322 per day to send this student to another district, supposedly to meet his needs. In so doing, this practice often demoralizes the student and family or, at the least, promotes the idea that some district students are more dispensable than others.

In contrast, by serving this student in the district, even with a full-time teaching assistant, and with no special transportation required, the total cost to the district is closer to $30,000 plus a percentage of teacher time, which adds another $8,000 for a total of $38,000. Thus, the out-of-district placement costs $58,000 compared to a $38,000 in-district placement. The in-district placement amounts to $211 per day compared to the $322 per day for the out-of-district placement. For the $38,000, district educators have daily contact with the student, can be supportive and inclusive, and the student and family can experience a sense of belonging.

This case example illustrates that educators need to come clean with taxpayers. Some educators are not being honest when they insist that they cannot "deal with" certain types of students in their own district, and they tell the public to do so would be "way too expensive." Then, administrators ship the student to another district, a placement that is typically more costly. Beyond the allocation of existing district resources, we must also consider the merger and reallocation of disparate funding sources. We discuss this next.

THE MERGER AND REALLOCATION OF RESOURCES AT THE DISTRICT LEVEL

To merge resources, it is important to know the different funding sources, what we have control of at the local level, what we need to advocate for at the state and federal level, and how we need to analyze our expenditures. Funding from the district/state should be prorated across schools as discussed previously in this chapter, based on the percentage of students with disabilities nationally. This practice would allow educators to make decisions about use of and allocation of funds as close to local need as possible.

In Table 12.1, we provide an example of an analysis of local school district expenditures related to selected student services areas in at-risk and special education. We examined three specific expenditures and determined ways these expenditures could be reduced. In the table, "tuitioned-out" means sending a student to another district. When a student is sent to a different district for services, the student's local district must pay tuition for that student to the other district. When we refer to the "cooperative" in the analysis, this is the name of the regional service agency that provides services to students with disabilities in a particular region. Many states employ this model of services, including New York State, Wisconsin, and Iowa among many others. Typically, local school districts pay money to the cooperative for these services, or the cooperative receives a particular percentage of the district's state special education funding. In addition, based on this scenario, students should attend the schools they would attend if not disabled and should be on regular transportation busses as often as possible (based on their IEP). In this example, examining just three areas of student services—one related to at-risk students and the other two associated with special education—could result in a net savings of $200,000 to the district. Odden and Archibald (2001) offer additional examples of how school and district resources can be reallocated. To summarize, if schools were funded based on a formula that supported a typical national percentage of students' disabilities with district/school poverty taken into consideration, then personnel could more easily merge resources and support at the district level.

THE MERGER AND REALLOCATION OF RESOURCES AT THE SCHOOL LEVEL

School administrators should work closely with the School Planning Team and School Service Delivery Teams when developing the budget. Funding at the school level should be merged as much as possible to better meet the needs of all learners in support of ICS. For example, principals of successful ICS schools have drawn across funding sources, such as from Title I, special education, district minority achievement money, comprehensive school reform grant funds, and ESL funds, to support their ICS efforts. Administrators should begin developing their budget first by allocating funds for staff. Next, they should allocate funds to support the individual needs of students. The Grade-Level Design Teams should determine student needs based on individual service plans (ISPs) or individualized education plans (IEPs) and request appropriate materials/funding for these students. Third, administrators should allocate funds specifically for building teacher capacity. To that end, it is critical for all special education staff to be certified or working toward certification in special education to obtain the optimal categorical aid from the state.

We offer a case example to illustrate these three steps. In one high school, all staff and their areas of certification were listed to help us determine which staff could more easily be assigned to heterogeneous classes. For example, at this high school, all ESL staff were also certified in an academic subject area. Thus, an ESL staff person also certified in history could be assigned a heterogeneously grouped history class that included students who were ELLs and students with disabilities, the numbers assigned to the class being in proportion with their overall percentage in the school. Assigning staff in this way represented a more efficient way of using teacher resources. Prior to this decision, these dually certified ESL teachers cotaught with a history teacher with no other certifications, creating teaching and funding redundancy in the classroom. At the same time, other ESL teachers staffed a Writing Center each period of the day in which no ESL students volunteered to attend to receive help. Thus, some

Table 12.1 Analysis of Funding Reallocation for ICS

Area of Analysis	Current Status	Inquiry	Recommendations for ICS Based on Principles	Recommended Timeline/Resources
Supporting students considered at-risk	$171,000—Amount of funds in general budget to buy 2 full-time teachers for at-risk students $59,299—Amount of funds for 2 students "at-risk" tuitioned out to a regional cooperative agency $30,000 spent on bussing the 2 students $1,100 in supplies	Why are there 2 full-time positions in at-risk in addition to the $59,299 used for the 2 students tuitioned out through the cooperative in addition to bussing costs? Over $163,811 is spent on at-risk students.	Carefully determine how to better service children with at-risk learning needs within the district—possibly part of a District Service Delivery Team discussion. Over time, you may want to discontinue tuition-out services through county cooperative agency (savings of nearly $100,000, including transportation).	Spring of current school year Discussion during the current school year by the District Service Delivery Team
Contracting out for budget support	District special education entitlement is set at $122,769 by the state. However, only $92,845.88 is actually allocated to the district. The remainder of the money is used by the cooperative to oversee the grant ($29,924).	Is it worth $29,924 to have the county cooperative agency oversee the grant?	Writing and monitoring of the entitlement accounts are not difficult; worth a savings of $30,000 to the district to be better spent.	Spring of the current school year for the following year's budget

Area of Analysis	Current Status	Inquiry	Recommendations for ICS Based on Principles	Recommended Timeline/Resources
Tuitioned-out students to other districts	8 students currently tuitioned out to other districts comes to $182,571. This sum does not include transportation, at $50,000 or more.	Is it possible to return any of the students back to the district?	At this point, an average of $22,821 is spent on each of the 8 students currently tuitioned out. Each student certainly does not need an assistant—however, there is plenty of money to bring the students back and staff appropriately with 2 teachers and 2 assistants, resulting in at least a savings of $20,000 plus transportation cost for a total savings of $70,000.	Current school year

ESL staff had three to four periods a day out of seven periods when they literally had nothing to do. In this resource-inefficient context, students who were ELL scored quite low on achievement tests, and their dropout rate was double that of the white student population. Thus, allocating funds for staff needs to take place after staff have been assigned in ways that reflect ICS principles. After funding for staff has been completed and students have been assigned to heterogeneous classes, grade-level design teams can then determine funding for student needs and for developing teacher capacity.

Educators should set funds aside to be able to realign staff for temporary periods of time to support students with significant behavioral needs. Funds should also be set aside for new students who may move into the school or district and may have significant needs.

Funding and the reallocation of resources are critical areas of knowledge for school leaders to implement ICS. Even with the financial inequities between schools and districts, and even with the pressures of underfunded or unfunded federal and state mandates, school leaders have no excuse for not fully implementing ICS. ICS requires rethinking service delivery for all students in ways that will maximize student achievement and growth. As leaders for social justice, we can no longer ethically continue to develop and sustain segregated programs for students when there are more effective and efficient alternatives.

Table 12.2   Chapter 12. Reallocating Resources for ICS and Social Justice

Focus Area	Focus Area Inquiry	Comments: What We Have	Phase of Application
1.	We do not blame budget shortfalls on students with disabilities or other students with different learning needs in our school.		
2.	When faced with the question of whether to build one large school or two smaller ones, educators support two smaller schools because in the long run, these are more effective for students and more cost efficient.		
3.	We are analyzing district and school expenditures and targeting those that segregate students (such as separate bussing, segregated programs, sending students out of district, etc.) for reexamination of their educational effectiveness and cost efficiency.		
4.	All school and teacher leaders are or are becoming experts in school finance and reallocating resources. They do not abdicate this responsibility to someone else.		
5.	Our school leaders are skilled at obtaining additional funds and resources (human and financial) from private grants and local resources.		
6.	We do not use the fact of underfunded or unfunded mandates as excuses for not providing evidence-based practices for all students.		
7.	We agree that fully funding special education is not a solution and can exacerbate the problems of labeling and segregation.		
8.	We agree that the increase in the number of students with disabilities is due, in part, to the failure of schools to meet the range of students' learning needs, and not due to inherent disabilities in students.		

(Continued)

Table 12.2 (Continued)

Focus Area	Focus Area Inquiry	Comments: What We Have	Phase of Application
9.	The percentage of students labeled with disabilities in our school/district is not greater than 10%–12% (federal averages), regardless of the demographics of our district. If it is greater than that, we are working to reduce this number.		
10.	We are quite prudent about the hiring and use of teaching assistants for individual students, and are limiting their hiring or are cutting or reassigning these staff.		
11.	We are implementing cross-categorical support for students rather than segregating students into separate special education categories (e.g., ED class) because the former is more educationally effective and cost efficient.		
12.	We are providing seamless support across special ed, general ed, at-risk, ESL, Title 1, etc. (sharing staff and resources across these areas) because this is more educationally effective and cost efficient.		
13.	All students in our district attend their neighborhood school or the school they would attend if they did not have a label (instead of bussing students with particular labels to particular schools) because this practice is more educationally effective and cost efficient than not doing so.		
14.	All students in our school receive a differentiated curriculum in heterogeneous learning environments because this practice is more educationally effective and cost efficient than sending students to resource rooms or other pullout options.		
15.	We do not use funding disparities between schools, districts, and states as an excuse to not take full responsibility for the funding and expenditures in our own school, and we are reallocating resources to this end.		

Focus Area	Focus Area Inquiry	Comments: What We Have	Phase of Application
16.	We are conscious of and make public the full cost of educating students in out-of-district or out-of-school placements (such as sending students with a particular disability to another district, or to an alternative school within district, etc.).		
17.	Leaders initiate their budget by allocating funds for staff, then for particular student needs, then for professional development.		
18.	All special education staff are certified or working toward certification to obtain optimal state aid.		
19.	We set aside funds to realign staff for temporary periods of time to support students with significant behavioral needs.		
20.	We set aside funds for new students who may move into the school or district with significant needs.		
21.	Funding from the district/state has been prorated across schools to allow for funding decisions to be made as close to the school needs as possible.		
22.	Funding at the school level is merged to better meet the needs of all learners in support of ICS.		
23.	All teachers/teacher teams take responsibility to determine student needs based on individual service plans (ISPs) or individualized education plans (IEPs) and request appropriate materials/funding.		
24.	Individual schools receive their prorated amount of special education funding based on the students enrolled in their schools who generate the revenue, versus all funding received going into a district general account.		

Reflective Questions:

1. Is the district paying for any students to receive services outside of the district using a tuition agreement?

2. Is the district using any contract agency to assist in the provision of services and charging an overhead or administrative cost as well as a cost for services?

3. Is the district using any type of specially designed transportation?

Developing School District Policy and Procedures to Leverage ICS and Social Justice

13

District policies and procedures are the glue that keeps the implementation of the school mission and Integrated Comprehensive Services aligned to support practice. In many litigious districts with active school boards, policies and procedures become some of the most attended to activities. In other districts, the policies and procedures become outdated or out of alignment with the school mission and implementation of services over time. It is essential that all policies and procedures are aligned to the mission of the school. For example, if the mission states, "we believe all children can learn and be successful," the policy on discipline and suspensions and expulsions must consider the fact that when students are suspended or expelled, they are not able to learn from content teachers. When we begin to align our policies and procedures with the move toward Integrated Comprehensive Services, we provide the glue that is needed to allow the services to be sustained over time.

In many districts, specific district policies are aligned to an appropriate central office administrator who ensures the policies are followed. In addition, many schools then use district policy to define specific school-based policy. These school-based policies are communicated via published procedures, student/staff handbooks, and newsletters, to name a few venues. The superintendent often becomes the keeper of the school board policy books. However, we suggest a school principal review the district policy manual annually to determine whether there are board policies that could inhibit the implementation and sustainability of ICS principles and practices.

If, upon review, the principal identifies district policies that work in opposition to ICS, then he or she should conduct a deeper analysis of the policies that do so. This analysis should include identifying who is in support of the current policy, when it was last revised and approved, when would be the appropriate time to inquire about the lack of alignment, and who else would be supportive of revisions.

Here we provide examples of four policies and procedures that could work against ICS and offer strategies to remedy them. (In Table 13.1, we review these examples and offer additional examples related to individual student plans, district and state assessment practices, and student discipline.) First, policies that require students to be retained are not supported by ICS principles, practices, or retention research. Thus, district policy regarding retention must recognize the severe impact that retention has on students and that the practice always blames students and neglects school responsibility. In this sense, retention should be rarely if ever used. The decision should require a range of assessments, and students should receive individualized service plans that support progress toward grade-level standards and beyond. Retention policies should be clearly worded regarding the teacher's responsibility to meet the individual needs of students rather than retaining students when they have not been successful.

Second, policies and procedures regarding student discipline, especially those having to do with student suspension and expulsion, should be carefully examined to ensure they align with ICS principles and practices. From an ICS perspective, the goal of student discipline should not be to "get rid of" troubled students but to problem solve different strategies in support of their success. Therefore, student suspension policies should be for in-school suspensions only. Relatedly, expulsion policies should be worded in ways that collaborate with juvenile county and city recommendations and supports—not in isolation from legal undertakings.

Third, student harassment policies should be clearly stated and continually assessed to determine their effectiveness. Students model what they see—therefore, anti-harassment policies need to extend to all adults in the school and be continually assessed to determine their effectiveness.

As a fourth and final example, the entire procedure to assess children to determine their eligibility for specific programs is extremely flawed and often works against the development of Integrated Comprehensive Services. Educators employ many different individualized assessment procedures for a student to meet eligibility for a specific program. That is, special programs such as special education, at-risk, English as a second language, Reading Recovery or Read 180, and gifted and talented all require unique procedures to determine student eligibility. When the process for referrals to the various programs uses different forms, different expectations for obtaining parent permission, different assessment practices, and differently licensed staff, the process symbolizes and perpetuates separate programs. Though our intentions are positive, these procedures create confusion for staff and families. These disparate procedures perpetuate segregation of students and thus work against ICS principles. Therefore, District and School Service Delivery Teams should find ways to align all the procedures for services, which in turn will align the services themselves. We explain one way to do so next.

In one of the schools we worked with, we began by merging the referral-to-service process across all the different programs. First, the School Service Delivery Team located all the forms for each program area, then went over the differences in each form, and then discussed what had to be done legally. IDEA legislation requires the most details for referral procedures when compared to other programs. Therefore, the staff began merging the process for referral following the legal requirements of IDEA. As a result, a parent could request additional assistance for his or her child, which would automatically trigger a meeting of a proactive intervention team. (In some schools, this team is referred to as a prereferral team and in the context of ICS, can function at the school level as a subteam of the School Service Delivery Team or can function at specific grades as a subteam of the Grade-Level Design Team, discussed in Chapter 5.) At this meeting, the team could request additional information and complete a referral for generic services; that is, the referral would not be automatically for special education. Thus, this process resulted in one funnel or one point of access to determine eligibility for special education services, at-risk services, ESL services, gifted services, and reading supports, to name a few examples. In addition, in this way, students were not predetermined to be eligible for any type of service before the initial assessment.

Based on the concerns listed in the referral, the school psychologist could assist in the development of a team of experts that would always include the student's primary teacher and one or more specialized teacher(s) in the area(s) of concern. For example, for a student with needs in the areas of reading and behavior, the team could include the reading teacher and the cross-categorical teacher at the child's grade level. The team would meet with the student's family and review current performance reports to determine what type of additional assessment they would complete, if any; discuss any other concerns; and set a date to share the results of the assessments or to share additional information with the family.

At this next meeting, if the child met eligibility for special education, an individualized education plan (IEP) would be developed. If the student did not meet eligibility for special education, but met eligibility for reading supports, the team would develop an individualized service plan (ISP), which would include defining the appropriate curriculum and materials, setting appropriate goals, and establishing a follow-up date to review the student's progress in reading. Changing the policy and procedures for acquiring support for a student into a streamlined process that reflects ICS principles and practices reduced the process from eight different referral-to-service options with varying assessments and procedures to one access point to numerous services, limited only by the creativity of the teaching team.

Table 13.1 District Policy and Procedure Analysis to Align With ICS

Current Procedures/Policies	Example of Conflict With ICS Principles	ICS Recommendations
Different eligibility practices for • Special education • Title 1 • At-risk • English as a second language • Gifted and talented	• Policies perpetuate segregated programs. • Policies assume students must qualify and be labeled before they receive services. • Staff do not have the opportunities to build each other's capacity.	• Follow the most legally sound referral-to-services process (often IDEA) and begin to build an integrated referral process via paperwork and procedures. • Apply legal requirements across different policies (e.g., parent permission for all types of student assessment, not just special education referrals).
Different student service plans for different programs—or no service plans for different programs. For example, special education has an IEP; however, at-risk, ESL, G&T do not have student plans, but students who are eligible for section 504 have an individualized service plan. District and state student assessment practices are completed differently for different subgroups of students according to their eligibility in a program.	• Policies perpetuate segregated programs. • Legal requirements are not used to leverage ICS. • Teaming around all learners is lacking. • Student support is not seamlessly tied to and grounded in core teaching and learning. • Homogeneous grouping patterns by eligibility symbolically set the tone in opposition to flexible grouping patterns.	• Complete service plans for any student who is eligible for any service as well as those students who require the continuity in instruction across teaching staff. • Use similar forms to IEPs (refer to electronic forms in Capper et al., 2000). • Support all students in proactive ways in creating assessment procedures that are legally sound—but allow students to be seen as individuals, not labels.

Current Procedures/Policies	Example of Conflict With ICS Principles	ICS Recommendations
	• Students are assumed to be different when in fact student needs typically overlap across different labels.	• The approved modifications for most standardized assessments may go across many subgroups, and these modified assessments can be completed in small-group, integrated environments.
Discipline procedures are applied differently across students eligible for special education and those who are not eligible (e.g., suspension, behavioral protocols, and expulsion procedures).	• Policies are in opposition to the ICS principle that the source of student failure is the system, not the child. When a student is not able to function within the school, the school has failed that particular child, for whatever reasons.	• Uniformly apply discipline procedures across all students. Policies and procedures must set the expectation that all children can be successful and that all school personnel will continue to individualize instruction until they can meet each learner's needs.
Retention policy advocates student retention.	• Policies assume student is the source of failure. • Policies do not acknowledge culturally relevant curriculum. • Student has to meet eligibility to receive assistance or be retained.	• Retention is rarely the answer, since it is not an instructional intervention. • Teachers must better understand how a child learns, and then teach to their learning style using culturally relevant curriculum and flexible grouping practices.

In sum, for deep, second-order change to occur via ICS, the core of the education system has to be completely assessed and realigned to the principles of ICS. If we continue to maintain our current structure, policies, funding mechanisms, and instructional practices, and occasionally apply particular practices, such as differentiated curriculum, and define that as Integrated Comprehensive Services, we will fail miserably, continue to blame the student, and revert back to our traditional practices that continue to perpetuate the status quo. Given that the status quo is not scoring well on assessment data, post-secondary success, graduation rate, and even equity, we have no choice but to create deep change through the analysis of policies and procedures and to leverage these policies and procedures toward ICS and social justice.

Table 13.2   Chapter 13. Developing School District Policy and Procedures to Leverage ICS and Social Justice

Focus Area	Focus Area Inquiry	Comments: What We Have	Phase of Application
1.	We have reviewed our school policies and procedures, and they each align with ICS principles and practices.		
2.	A school leader reviews the district policy manual annually to determine whether there are board policies that could inhibit the implementation and sustainability of ICS principles and practices.		
3.	Our retention policies are aligned with ICS principles and practices.		
4.	Our suspension policies are aligned with ICS principles and practices.		
5.	Our student and adult harassment policies are aligned with ICS principles and practices.		
6.	We have eliminated separate eligibility policies and procedures for students to receive support and developed one simplified policy and procedure.		
7.	Separate federal legislative policies are integrated throughout all district/school policies with a goal to reflect ICS principles.		
8.	The use of IEPs and plans for students who are eligible for Section 504 support (Rehabilitation Act, 1973) have been united with individualized service plans for each learner.		
9.	Our student discipline policies are unified and applied across all students.		
10.	District and state assessment policies that allow for accommodations for particular students are extended to all students who need them.		

Reflective Question:

Based on your analysis, what school and district policies do not align to the principles of ICS, and what process or course will your team take to update those policies and procedures?

14

Using State and Federal Regulations to Leverage ICS and Social Justice

Educational leaders for ICS and social justice are savvy about leveraging all state and federal regulations in ways that will support ICS principles and practices. As we previously stated, these leaders are clear about their focus and their agenda and do not get caught up in blaming the latest waves of policy changes for the lack of student success in their schools. Thus, with the reauthorization of IDEIA (the Individuals with Disabilities Education Improvement Act of 2004) and No Child Left Behind (NCLB), we have a responsibility to leverage these federal and state regulations to meet the needs of each learner in an integrated comprehensive manner.

The federal IDEA and NCLB regulations share many common features. First and most predominantly, both laws require qualified teachers to teach students. Second, both laws require rigorous standards for the inclusion of all students in assessments. Third, both laws require the inclusion of students in content-based instruction. Both regulations, however, also contain pitfalls that can work against ICS (see Table 14.1). For educational leaders to live out an ICS mission, the pitfalls of the regulations must be known and negotiated, not unknowingly used to perpetuate segregation.

Table 14.1   Regulatory Pitfalls

No Child Left Behind (NCLB)	Individuals with Disabilities Education Act (IDEA)
1. Often results in students being placed into segregated groups to remediate for the purposes of increased test score performance	1. A regulation that looks for disability instead of understanding the pedagogy of differences
2. Blames students in need for low test scores, thus building a culture of those who are "wanted" and those who are "unwanted"	2. A regulation that assesses students after the student fails instead of gaining knowledge of how all children learn as a way to offer appropriate services for the prevention of failure
3. Can perpetuate a pedagogy of testing proficiency instead of a pedagogy of passion, awareness, learning, new knowledge, application, and evaluation	3. Categorizes students by abilities and disabilities, as if they require different instructional, curricular, and assessment techniques for each category
4. Applies educational Band-Aids (even those that are research-based) for all learners such as, Read 180, direct instruction, and mastery learning, instead of requiring the hard work of changing school structures and requiring high levels of teaching across diverse learners	4. A regulation that asks teachers to individualize goals based on teacher limitations and a narrow knowledge set
5. Cultivates a culture of licensed teachers that are content-based experts, with little knowledge about how a range of learners learn or the ability to assist children in showing what they know in the way they can the most often	5. A regulation that is geared more toward paperwork cutbacks than allowing teachers to create IEPs that actually show, in stages, the steps to meet the annual goal
6. Suggests we have failed students with a significant disability if we have not brought them to grade level	6. A regulation that still promotes a continuum of placement options that includes segregated placements—which often extend throughout the child's day, month, year, and life—even though IDEA 1997 clarified that special education was a service, not a place

TOWARD AN INTEGRATED FEDERAL EDUCATION ACT

We advocate for uniting IDEA and the Elementary and Secondary Education Act as a way to best serve the broad range of students in schools. That is, we believe that all students should be provided with the practices associated with IDEA, not just students labeled with disabilities. As the federal regulations regarding IDEA and NCLB are reauthorized, we believe the requirements of these two regulations will continue to be merged. We are hopeful that court cases involving students for whom English is not their first language and legislation regarding homeless students will also be incorporated into IDEA and NCLB. A merger of these acts would clarify ambiguities and provide an integrated platform from the top down. Based on the recent reauthorization of IDEA and NCLB, our recommendations for an integrated federal education act would include but not be limited to the following regulations:

- Provide all students with access to a Free and Appropriate Public Education (FAPE).
- Provide services in the least restrictive environment to all students.
- Hold high educational standards and require accountability for each and every learner.
- Require highly qualified teachers, and require all teachers to become certified in more than one area. That is, all content teachers would also be required to be certified to work with a range of student needs (i.e., special education, ESL, etc.).
- Require that all children be assessed in a culturally relevant manner to obtain meaningful information about each child's specific learning and behavioral needs.
- Ensure that all children in need of individualized services receive those services in an integrated comprehensive manner.
- Support the rights of families to be equal participants in directing their child's education and ensure due process rights when that does not occur.
- Require districts to be block funded to proactively support the learning of all children through Integrated Comprehensive Services.
- Provide all students with individualized educational service plans.
- Require the condition of suspension to be limited to 10 days for all learners and for students who have been expelled, educational services would continue in a different fashion versus the absence of all services.
- Provide transitional services to post-secondary environments for all learners.

These are just a few of our suggestions for a merged federal education act. An integrated federal educational regulation would allow for a unified educational platform that would end the confusion between acts and the separation of programs and enable schools to clearly function in support of students in a proactive, meaningful manner. If we apply the requirements of IDEIA to all students, then students would not be separated and treated differently based on having a label or not, or based on what kind of label a student has been given. In this way, all students benefit from universal access to federal nondiscrimination regulations.

Though NCLB and IDEA regulations are moving closer together in principle and in requirements and practice, to truly see a merger of both regulations may take decades. School leaders cannot wait for this to happen. They must forge ahead with creating new paths at the school and district level and provide examples to state and federal policy makers of how merging federal policies in a comprehensive and seamless manner could occur for the success of all learners. We cannot allow fragmented and inconsistent regulations to create turmoil and failure in our schools. We must use the regulations to leverage the support for Integrated Comprehensive Services on behalf of our children and society. Next, we offer a list of the possible ways that school leaders can merge the federal and state regulations at the district and school levels, and continue to be in compliance with the individual acts themselves. We grouped our suggestions under teacher qualifications, academic achievement, student assessment, and school involvement with families.

Teacher Qualifications

1. All students receive instruction from content-certified teachers.

2. All teachers are certified or working toward certification.

3. Incentives are provided to teachers to obtain certification in an area that addresses the needs of typically marginalized students (e.g., certification in special education, bilingual education, English as a second language, remedial reading, etc.).

4. Teachers who wish to be hired into the school/district must have dual certification or be willing to seek a dual certification (per number 3 in this list).

Academic Achievement and Discipline

1. Starting in fifth grade, all students receive career guidance and course planning for middle and high school via a three-way meeting between the student, a family member, and a teacher or counselor. The career and course planning is updated annually via a similar meeting.

2. All students 16 and older have met with a counselor or IEP teacher to begin their transition to post-school opportunities and integrated adult service options.

3. IEPs/ISPs clearly articulate the academic, social, and emotional goals for each child.

4. All IEPs/ISPs are updated (progress to date) at least four times a year.

5. Each child's IEP/ISP clarifies percentage of services necessary to meet the student's individual needs.

6. Each child's IEP/ISP is reviewed annually to determine appropriateness of services, as well as small-group, one-to-one, and large-group instructional placements.

7. Discipline policies are the same for all students, regardless of label.

Student Assessment

1. All students are assessed (within 90 days) as to how they learn, and instruction is determined based on appropriate learning modalities.

2. Teachers complete individualized service plans based on assessment results and as a means to demonstrate progress toward grade-level standards and beyond through both standard- and performance-based assessments.

3. All students are given annual proficiency tests in the areas of reading, math, social studies, and science.

4. School performance data are disaggregated based on disability, poverty, race, and language diversity.

5. School meets Adequate Yearly Progress (AYP) requirements.

School Involvement With Families

1. Parent permission is obtained before an assessment is conducted with any student.

2. All parents have due process rights regarding the education of their children.

3. Ample time is provided when reviewing assessment results with students and parents.

4. All parent meetings are scheduled at mutually agreed-upon times and places, and child care, transportation, and interpreters are provided by the school as needed.

CONCLUSION

Throughout this book, we have presented the principles of ICS and how to develop such services. Schools must first develop the core principles from which they will function and use the federal and state regulations to support those principles. We can no longer afford the practice of creating and leading schools based on changing political forces at the state and federal level. We know that leaders for ICS and social justice have the resolve and the commitment to children and the ability to set a vision of comprehensive equitable services. These leaders do not let the whims of political leaders become the educational leader's excuse to continue to fail students of color, of poverty, of disability, or any other students who are typically devalued. All forces—both political and legal—should be used to strengthen and leverage the core principles of ICS for social justice.

Table 14.2   Chapter 14. Merging Federal Regulations to Leverage ICS and Social Justice

Focus Area	Focus Area Inquiry	Comments: What We Have	Phase of Application
1.	We do not blame federal regulations for the lack of student achievement in our school/district.		
2.	We do not get stuck in criticizing federal regulations, but instead, use these regulations to leverage ICS principles and practices.		
	Teacher Qualifications		
3.	All students receive instruction from content-certified teachers.		
4.	All teachers are certified or working toward certification.		
5.	Incentives are provided to teachers to obtain certification in an area that addresses the needs of typically marginalized students (e.g., certification in special education, bilingual education, English as a second language, remedial reading, etc.).		
6.	Teachers who wish to be hired into the school/district must have dual certification or be willing to seek a dual certification (per number 3 in this list).		
	Academic Achievement		
7.	Starting in fifth grade, all students receive career guidance and course planning for middle and high school via a three-way meeting between the student, a family member, and a teacher or counselor. The career and course planning is updated annually via a similar meeting.		

(Continued)

Table 14.2 (Continued)

Focus Area	Focus Area Inquiry	Comments: What We Have	Phase of Application
8.	All students 16 and older have met with a counselor or IEP teacher to begin their transition process.		
9.	IEPs/ISPs clearly articulate the academic, social, and emotional goals for each child.		
10.	All IEPs/ISPs are updated (progress to date) at least four times a year.		
11.	Each child's IEP/ISP clarifies percentage of services necessary to meet the student's individual needs.		
12.	Each child's IEP/ISP is reviewed annually to determine appropriateness of services, as well as small-group, 1:1, and large-group instructional placements.		
	Student Assessment and Discipline		
13.	All students are assessed (within 90 days) as to how they learn, and instruction is determined based on appropriate learning modalities.		
14.	Teachers complete individualized service plans based on assessment results and as a means to demonstrate progress toward grade-level standards and beyond through both standard- and performance-based assessments.		
15.	All students are provided annual proficiency tests in the areas of reading, math, social studies, and science.		
16.	School performance data are disaggregated based on disability, poverty, race, and language diversity.		
17.	School meets Adequate Yearly Progress (AYP) requirements.		

Focus Area	Focus Area Inquiry	Comments: What We Have	Phase of Application
18.	School discipline policies are the same for all students, regardless of label.		
	School Involvement With Families		
19.	Parent permission is obtained before an assessment occurs with any student.		
20.	All parents have due process rights regarding the education of their children.		
21.	Ample time is provided when reviewing assessment results with students and parents.		
22.	All parent meetings are scheduled at mutually agreed-upon times and places, and child care, transportation, and interpreters are provided by the school as needed.		
Reflective Questions:			
Based on the response to the above assessment, how will your school bring about a merger in the regulations at the school level? What first steps will you take?			

The Messiness of Change Toward ICS and Social Justice

After learning about ICS and believing in the merits of changing the structure and culture of schools toward this end, most leaders want to know where to begin. In this chapter, we first discuss the different ways we have seen school leaders move toward ICS. Next, we discuss the difference between leading for compliance (first-order change) and leading beyond compliance (second-order change). In so doing, we make suggestions for how this book can be used to bring about second-order change.

The schools and districts that are moving toward ICS have initiated this process in varying ways. How one begins making change in a school/district depends on the context. In one middle school with whom we have worked, the principal was hired mid-year into a school that was in extreme and utter chaos (i.e., behavior of many students out of control, low staff morale, a revolving door of principals in and out, and angry and dissatisfied parents). In this case, the principal needed to take swift and decisive action from the first day on the job. In her contract negotiations, she requested and received an extra assistant principal whom she hand picked, and she hand picked a learning coordinator to assist her with curriculum changes and professional development. She convened a school climate action team that included parents, community members, staff, and students to create behavior expectations for students and staff and to develop a schoolwide behavior management plan. She paired these actions with developing positive behavior supports such as schoolwide dances and faculty-student basketball games. She communicated her behavior expectations via a weekly school newsletter and family listening sessions. She also worked with the school parent organization to upgrade and clean up the school facilities that were literally falling apart. She, like our other examples to follow, also collected extensive data on the current status of the school's students. She explained that she did not include staff in the collection and analysis, but staff collaborated on goals, curriculum, instruction, and professional development, based on these data.

As a second example, a new principal was placed at a school with increasing numbers of students of color, students for whom English was not their first language, and students in poverty. The educators at this school served students with special needs via a plethora of pullout programs. Importantly, this principal did not stand up at his first faculty meeting and announce he was going to transform the school with an "inclusion initiative." Instead, the implementation of ICS principles and practices ultimately led to students being educated in heterogeneous learning environments, but as this book discusses, ICS moves beyond merely placing students in general education classrooms. To begin, this principal clearly communicated his vision about the importance of all students belonging and the importance of equity and social justice with the educators in the school via faculty meetings, school newsletters, and conversations with staff and families.

At this same school, the principal knew it was important that staff have a deep understanding of their current practices and the outcomes of those practices. Early in his tenure at the school, at a faculty meeting, he drew on the board the current status of service delivery at the school. He drew a series of small squares forming a rectangle that depicted the actual layout of the school classrooms. He then drew arrows to show where students in each of these classrooms traveled throughout the day to get their needs met. The myriad of arrows and lines crisscrossing the board that illustrated the current service delivery structure made obvious the inefficiencies and inequities of this structure. This illustration then began a series of questions and conversations with the staff, conveying that if they wanted students to feel part of a community and to belong, and if they wanted students to gain in student achievement, they could not continue the mess that was depicted on the board. Importantly, the principal listened to the teacher concerns about the current service delivery and the aspects that were not working, and used these concerns to make changes in the system. In addition, the principal began working with the staff to collect data on the current status of the students in the school, using similar data collection instruments and a similar process to those described in Chapter 4. The staff then had conversations about the collected data.

In just a matter of three years, this principal transformed the school practices into ones that reflected ICS and significantly raised student achievement for all typically marginalized students at his school.

At another elementary school, the principal was hired to help a staff learn to meet the needs of changing student demographics, with increasing numbers of students of color and students for whom English is not their first language. She took advantage of the superintendent requiring the staff to engage in a strategic planning process to ask questions and begin conversations about the discrepancies between how staff wanted to work with students and what was currently happening in the school. That is, the staff were concerned that many students were being sent out of their classrooms to receive help elsewhere, and they were also concerned about the large size of their classes. Over a period of two years, with the support of a Comprehensive School Reform grant, this school came to reflect the principles and practices of ICS, including serving students with disabilities and students for whom English was not their first language in integrated classroom settings.

These three examples illustrate eight considerations when implementing ICS. First, these three examples show that there is not one primary starting point for implementing ICS. One common factor among the three examples is that the school leaders used current data (see examples of these data in Chapter 4) and also used concrete illustrations of the school's current service delivery models to help staff have a clear understanding of the current status of their school regarding the education of students who typically struggle. The leaders were then able to help their staff see the discrepancies between the current status of their school, and their mission, vision, or expectations of how they wished to be as educators or as a school. To help this to occur, all the end-of-chapter evaluations in this book can also be used as a way to assess the current status of service delivery and to uncover the discrepancies in educator beliefs and practices. In schools that are in chaos, as in the first example, this discrepancy will not be difficult to see, and in fact, little time and effort will be needed to point out the glaring inadequacies in the current system and that something different needs to be done.

In other settings, however, educators, families, and community members may take great pride in their school and student achievements and believe nothing at all needs to change—nothing, that is, except how to "deal with" the increasing number of students of color and students who are ELL. The fact that students are segregated does not upset anyone as long as most of the students are achieving at satisfactory levels. In all school settings, but especially in settings such as these, it will be important for leaders to point out and to build on the existing strengths of the school to leverage ICS. At the same time, staff and families will need to see the areas that could make their "good" school even better for all students.

Second, each of these examples illustrates, as we have repeated in this book, that implementing ICS principles and practices is not just one particular change, but instead, requires multiple changes at the macro and micro level of the school, all of which emanate from central core ICS values and principles. ICS is not about standing up at a faculty meeting and announcing that "We are now going to be an inclusive school." As this book shows, ICS is so much more than that. At the same time, while multiple aspects of the school will evolve and change toward ICS, educators still need to prioritize and focus their efforts and need to be quite strategic in doing so.

A third leadership consideration that these examples show is that, contrary to the leadership literature, transformative change does not have to take a decade. In fact, in six schools we have studied, moving toward ICS occurred in one, two, or three years at most. In schools that were most in crisis, the transformation happened more quickly. Though there can never be a rigid timetable for change, leaders cannot assume that deep change takes a long time. In fact, the reality of student needs and student struggles behooves leaders to acknowledge the urgency of the situation for many students and families. We cannot let these students continue to struggle and fail, and leaders need to move forward in as timely a way as possible.

A fourth lesson about change that we have learned regarding implementing ICS in schools is that engaging in such leadership does not require a leader to have extensive school leadership experience. We learned this lesson by happenstance. In our research, we set out to study schools that had significantly raised student achievement for low-income students, students of color, students with disabilities, and students for whom English was not their first language—and they had raised this achievement by also eliminating segregated programs. First we located the schools, and then we interviewed and collected data from the leaders in these schools. In all six schools, the leaders were new to their school leadership positions; only one had served as principal for a few years prior to transforming the school. One principal did not yet hold her license and was obtaining it while serving in the position. Thus, new school leaders need not be timid about moving toward ICS. In addition, faculty in preparation programs need to hold much higher expectations for the accomplishments of new leaders in the field.

A fifth lesson we have learned from these leaders is the importance of having a team structure in place that can share decisions and, frankly, share the responsibility for changes in the school. All these leaders convened a leadership team to help them make the necessary changes in the school. We refer back to Chapter 5 for ideas about these teams, including the School Planning Team and the School Service Delivery Team as two key possibilities for initiating change.

A sixth consideration about implementing ICS concerns the inevitable resistance that leaders will face when doing so (Theoharis, 2004). It is critical that leaders come to expect resistance to their efforts, perhaps excruciatingly major resistance. In every school we studied, not every staff member agreed with the change efforts. In each school, a few staff did not believe in or agree with the changes wrought by ICS principles and practices. The fact that not all staff supported the change did not prevent the change from happening. When (not if, but when) resistance from staff, families, community members, district administration, union leadership, or state leadership happens, leaders should not take it that they have done or are doing something wrong. Upturning an educational standard such as segregated programs is no small thing. Resistance does mean it is critically important that leaders continue to educate staff, families, and communities about ICS; continue to engage in conversations with individuals who resist these efforts; and continue to collect and use data in ways that can support their efforts.

A seventh and related consideration is that any change, but especially implementing ICS principles and practices, will require leaders to take good care of themselves in the process. Social justice work is long-haul work, not for the faint of heart. It requires your clearest mind, strongest body, purest heart, and a calm emotional center. In all the schools we have studied, the leaders labored many long hours and days at their work. Leading for compliance can more than fill up the hours in a week; leading *beyond* compliance requires even more (though we advocate for leveraging compliance regulations for social justice as described in Chapter 14). Advocating for students who struggle in their own schools was these leaders' life passion, to the point that when the changes were not happening fast enough and teachers were resisting changes and students continued to struggle, these leaders took this on personally. They agonized over it. Thus, it is critical that leaders have personal plans of action for self-care when they embark on this leadership. As part of this plan, leaders need to identify at least one other leader for ICS and social justice with whom they can share ideas, provide support, and hold each other accountable for their work.

A final consideration we have learned from these leaders is that the change process is never finished. New students and families with new needs enroll in our schools every year. Every year is a new year, and every day is a new day. In that case, we can say that we may never fully "arrive" because there will always be new challenges. At the same time, we cannot use the never-finished change process to rest on our laurels and not persistently keep moving forward.

We all know that change brings with it some measure of chaos. Most teachers and administrators that we have worked with want to know exactly what will happen as they move through the transformation of a segregated program model to a proactive service delivery model. We typically respond with, "Let's take these first few steps and then we can see where we are and where we need to go." Richard DuFour, a school principal at Adlai Stevenson High School District in Lincolnshire, Illinois, agrees and explains further his experience with educational change:

> Most educators have not been trained in initiating, implementing, and sustaining change. They have moved too quickly, or they have lost momentum by not moving quickly enough. They have thought too big—or too small. They have neglected the process of creating a critical mass of support or have failed to proceed because of the mistaken notion that they needed unanimous support before launching an initiative. They have regarded conflict as a problem to avoid rather than an inevitable and valuable byproduct of substantive change. They have failed to anchor the change within the culture of the school. They have considered a change initiative as a task to complete rather than an ongoing process. In short, school practitioners have not learned how the complexities of the change process transform organizations. (DuFour & Eaker, 1998, pp. 14–15)

We also encourage leaders not to take all the components of the ICS formative process (as depicted in Figure 0.3) in the introduction to this book, place them in a linear format, and then attempt to follow each one step by step. If they do, they will surely become frustrated and disillusioned. With this book, we have offered a pragmatic, interconnected process; we have not offered a step-by-step magical tool to create schools of social justice.

Instead, this book offers a means to initiate conversations about how service delivery is structured in schools. These conversations about ICS and social justice are not only invaluable, but necessary to bring ICS to fruition. When we begin asking questions, we start having conversations with others about values and beliefs and student learning, and only then can we begin our transformation from programs to services.

Ironically, we, as educators in schools, often operate at the other end of the spectrum from a linear process. We let ourselves be subjected to federal and state regulations that often send our schools into one tailspin after another. Sadly enough, this is what most school districts believe is pragmatic change. That is, many educators in schools function as a repository for federal regulations, voiceless to the inadequacies, and feeling powerless about the requirements, allowing for complete chaos, absent of vision truly on behalf of all learners, and in so doing, define the mess as making adequate yearly progress.

At the same time, we have witnessed schools implementing a few of the domains that we have addressed in this book with little to no critical reflection on the core values that should undermine these domains (as described in Chapter 2, on leadership). Throughout this book, we are asking school leaders to assess the current status of their schools across the domains in each chapter within the context of a school educational plan, and then to determine their interconnectedness. The 15 components of ICS each comprised a chapter in this book and were summarized in the book's introduction; all these components are important to create change toward social justice for all learners. In Figure 0.3 in the introduction, we visually depicted these 15 aspects of ICS as a circle where one aspect may feed into the next one, or an educator may go back and connect one aspect with a previous domain, or make a major connection with one across the circle. Our intent was to establish a process that is clearly nonlinear.

While engaged in this nonlinear process, we must move beyond compliance with state and federal mandates where only first-order change is initiated and the status quo is either knowingly or unknowingly maintained (Meyer, Brooks, & Goes, 1990). When leading for compliance, first-order change is used to improve on the efficiency and effectiveness of the system without any disruption to the system or without altering the way teachers and students routinely behave—the bottom line being that disruption and conflict are sidestepped (R. L. Green, 2004). What we are asking school leaders to do is to pragmatically move into discontinuous and second-order change, challenging the core of the system that has perpetuated the segregation of students and staff without question.

We believe this change can only and must only happen through a passion for social justice first and foremost, inquiry about the status quo, and an overwhelming commitment from our inner core about the value of all students. This is where the work is not about who we are, but what the world needs. We must be able to move beyond ourselves to model the change we wish to see in this world. Politics, ego, self-interest, competition, and life nuances must be moved to the side. We have the ability, the passion, and the inquiry to take the higher road—we ask you to take this walk with us.

Table 15.1   Chapter 15. The Messiness of Change Toward ICS and Social Justice

Focus Area	Focus Area Inquiry	Comments: What We Have	Phase of Application
1.	We have specified the context of our change process (i.e., school in chaos, stable school with little incentive to change, etc.).		
2.	We communicate about the various changes using a variety of formats and media, including personal conversations, newsletters, faculty meetings, parent meetings, etc.		
3.	We are using data (such as the end-of-chapter evaluations and the equity audit questions in this book) to assess the current status of our school and to communicate this status to others.		
4.	We are using data to illustrate the discrepancies and gaps between what educators believe and think is best for students, and what is actually occurring in practice.		
5.	We are using data to initiate conversations with staff, families, students, and community members about the gaps between what we believe and what we do.		
6.	We understand that ICS is more than just differentiating the curriculum, or integrating students in classrooms.		
7.	Though ICS requires substantial change, we realize it is possible for change to evolve fairly quickly over several years. For students who are struggling, we know there is an urgency to our efforts.		
8.	The leadership required to change toward ICS is not about years of experience, but about vision and communication, and working proactively with staff, families, and the community.		
9.	We have clear team structures in place to share the change decisions and responsibilities.		

Focus Area	Focus Area Inquiry	Comments: What We Have	Phase of Application
10.	When we encounter resistance to the change efforts, we know we do not need 100% agreement to move forward; we consider individual concerns, and consider resistance part of the change process and an indication to continue to listen and to communicate.		
11.	We each have individual plans of healthy self-care, and we each have a colleague who will help support us and hold us accountable for our work.		
12.	We know that this work is never done, but do not use that as an excuse for the inequities that persist in our system.		
13.	A formative analysis is completed to assist in the multidimensional levels of change for each section of the school educational plan.		
14.	We know that change must be organic—there must be a structure, but within the structure there must be time for individuals to think, process, discuss, and evaluate.		
15.	The change is owned by the majority of individuals within the school.		

Reflective Questions:

1. How can your team begin the change process within your school?

2. What will be the barriers and supports for the change? How can you mitigate the barriers and maximize the supports?

Appendix A

ICS Evaluation Interview

Determine to What Extent a School/District Is Oriented Toward ICS Principles and Practices

CORE PRINCIPLES: FOCUSING ON EQUITY

1. In this district/school/classroom (depending on the interviewee), when a student fails or struggles, why is that so?

2. What is your philosophy for addressing and/or preventing student struggle?

EQUITABLE STRUCTURES: LOCATION

District Level

1. Do all students in this district attend their neighborhood school (this includes disabilities, ESL, at-risk, gifted, etc.)? If not, which ones do not?
   a. What have been the barriers to doing this?
   b. What have been the supports for doing this?

2. Do you tuition out any of your students to other districts?

3. Do you accept students from other districts?

School Level

1. Are there any rooms set aside for labeled students? If so, which ones? Why?

2. Are there any lower track classes or higher track classes (i.e., AP, basic math, basic science, etc.)? If so, why?

3. How are students placed at each grade level or assigned to classes?

4. What are the barriers to placing students in heterogeneous classrooms?

5. What are the supports for doing so?

ACCESS TO HIGH-QUALITY TEACHING AND LEARNING: EDUCATOR ROLES

1. How is it decided which staff work with which students? Do all staff work with all students or are there specialty areas? Why?

2. What are the barriers to staff working with all students?

3. What has been provided to staff to support them in their efforts?

4. How are staff prepared to work with a range of students?

ACCESS TO HIGH-QUALITY TEACHING AND LEARNING: CURRICULUM AND INSTRUCTION

1. How are the students' various learning needs met in each classroom?

2. What are the barriers and supports to this?

IMPLEMENTING CHANGE: FUNDING

1. To what extent are funding and resources merged to serve a range of students?

2. What are the barriers and supports to this?

Appendix B

Equity Audit Data Collection and Analysis

General and Social Class Data and Analysis (Report fraction and percentage for each as applicable)	
1. Number of students in your district:	
2. Number of staff in your school (certified and noncertified):	
3. Number of students in your school:	
4. Number of students who transferred or moved into the school the last academic year (disaggregate by race, disability, gender, ESL, and free/reduced lunch):	
5. Students who transferred out of the school in the last academic year (disaggregate by race, disability, gender, ESL, and free/reduced lunch):	
6. Fraction and percentage of staff in your school who are associated with student services (e.g., special education, special education assistants, counselors, psychologists, nurses, bilingual specialists, reading specialists, gifted and talented specialist):	
Status of Labeling at Your School **(Report total number [fraction] and percentage)**	
1. Students labeled "gifted" in your school:	
2. Students labeled "at-risk" in your school:	
3. Students labeled with a disability in your school:	
4. Students labeled ESL or bilingual in your school:	
5. Students who attend an alternative school/setting:	
6. Students with any other kind of label in your school (include the label):	
7. Total students who are labeled in your school (adding together questions 1–6):	

(Continued)

Appendix B (Continued)

Discipline Data	
1. Students who were suspended in the past year (disaggregate these data by gender, race, disability, free/reduced-price lunch, and English language learners; divide into in-school and out-of-school suspensions):	
2. Students who were expelled in the past year (disaggregate by gender, race, disability, free/reduced-price lunch, and English language learners; divide into in-school and out-of-school suspensions):	
3. Students who were placed in an Alternative Interim Placement in the past year (disaggregate by gender, race, disability, free/reduced-price lunch, and English language learners):	
4. Low attendance and/or truancy (disaggregate by race, free/reduced-price lunch, ESL, disability, and gender):	
5. Other relevant discipline data:	
General Achievement Data	
1. Fourth-grade achievement (disaggregate by race, free/reduced-price lunch, ESL, disability, and gender):	
2. Eighth-grade achievement (disaggregate by race, free/reduced-price lunch, ESL, disability, and gender):	
3. Tenth-grade achievement (disaggregate by race, free/reduced-price lunch, ESL, disability, and gender):	
4. Graduation rate (disaggregate by race, free/reduced-price lunch, ESL, disability, and gender):	
5. Graduated with an academic diploma (disaggregate by race, free/reduced-price lunch, ESL, disability, and gender):	
6. Drop-out rate (disaggregate by race, free/reduced-price lunch, ESL, disability, and gender):	
7. Participation in ACT, SAT, Advanced Placement exams (disaggregate by race, free/reduced-price lunch, ESL, disability, and gender):	
8. Test results of ACT, SAT, Advanced Placement exams (disaggregate by race, free/reduced-price lunch, ESL, disability, and gender):	
Social Class (Report fraction and percentage)	
1. Students receiving free and reduced-price lunches in your educational setting:	
2. Students receiving free/reduced-price lunches in other schools in your district at the same level (elementary, middle, secondary):	

3. Students identified for special education (all categorical areas) in your educational setting:	
4. Of the number of students identified for special education, what fraction and what percentage receive free/reduced-price lunches? *Note: We have found that most districts do not gather or report this information. It may be possible, however, to find such data or to calculate this information by hand.	
5. How does the response to Item 4 compare to Item 1? The answers should be similar. If, for example, 60% of students identified for special education also qualify for free and reduced-price lunches (#4), and your educational setting has 20% of its students receiving free/reduced-price lunches (#1), students who receive free/reduced-price lunches are overrepresented in special education. Further, this means that, in this setting, if a student is from a lower socioeconomic class family, he or she is three times more likely to be labeled for special education than other students. What social class myths support these data?	
6. Students identified as "gifted" (e.g., TAG) in your setting who receive free/reduced-price lunches. Compare the response to Item 1. (If students are not labeled gifted, investigate related student groups in the school, such as Academic Decathlon, advanced placement classes, Algebra classes, etc.)	
7. Students identified as "at-risk" in your setting who receive free/reduced-price lunches. Compare your response to Item 1. (If students are not labeled "at-risk," investigate related student groupings in the school, such as remedial reading, summer school, general math, etc.)	
8. Report two pieces of academic achievement data in your setting (preferably reading and math) as they relate to social class.	
9. Collect social class comparison data on at least two other areas in your school/setting (e.g., parent-teacher organization, student council, safety patrol, band).	
10. Social Class Data Analysis Do not exceed one page. (University students, support the analysis thoroughly with the literature.) What do these social class data mean? In your analysis, include the strengths and areas for improvement in serving students of lower social classes within your school's curriculum, instruction, and culture, and other learning opportunities. Identify concrete, specific ideas for remedying the weaknesses.	

Appendix B (Continued)

Race and Ethnicity Data and Analysis

Race and Ethnicity (Report fraction and percentage for each)	
1. Students of color in your school: How does this compare to other schools in the district?	
2. Students of color in the total district:	
3. Students labeled for special education:	
4. Of the number of students labeled for special education, what fraction and percentage are students of color?	
5. How does this number and percentage compare with those in Item 1?	
6. Of the number and percentage of students labeled "at-risk," what fraction and percentage are students of color? Compare the response with that for Item 1.	
7. Of the number and percentage of students labeled "gifted," what fraction and percentage are students of color? Compare the response with that for Item 1.	
8. Total staff who are people of color in your school: Compare the response with that for Item 1.	
9. Certified staff who are people of color in your school:	
10. Uncertified staff who are people of color in your school:	
11. People of color serving on the school board:	
12. (a) Report two pieces of academic achievement data (preferably reading and math) as they relate to race/ethnicity. (b) Collect race/ethnicity comparison data on at least two other areas in your school/setting.	
13. Race and Ethnicity Data Analysis Refer to the social class section for directions. Include the following: Discuss the problems with the phrase, "I don't even see the person's color," and "But we do not have, or have very few, students of color in our school/district, so race isn't an issue here."	

English Language Learners (ELL) and Bilingual Data and Analysis

ELL (Report fraction and percentage for each)	
1. How many English language learners are in your school and what languages do they speak? How does this compare to other schools in your district?	
2. How many English language learners are in the total district?	

3. How many students are labeled for special education?	
4. Of the number of students labeled for special education, what fraction and percentage are English language learners?	
5. How does this fraction and percentage compare with those in Item 1?	
6. Of the number of students labeled "at-risk," what fraction and percentage are English language learners? Compare the response with that for Item 1.	
7. Of the number and percentage of students labeled "gifted," what fraction and percentage are English language learners? Compare the response with that for Item 1.	
8. What is the English language learner service delivery model used in your school?	
9. What is the total number of certified and uncertified staff who are bilingual in your setting? Compare the response with that for Item 1.	
10. What is the total number of staff who serve as bilingual or ESL teachers or teaching assistants in the school?	
11. Bilingual people serving on the school board:	
12. Report two pieces of academic achievement data (preferably reading and math) as they relate to this area of diversity.	
13. Collect student English language learner comparison data on at least two other areas in your school/setting.	
14. English Language Learner and Bilingual Data Analysis (see directions for Social Class Data Analysis)	

(Dis)ability Data and Analysis

Students With (Dis)abilities (Report fraction and percentage)	
1. Number of students labeled with (dis)abilities in each grade level in your school:	
2. Number of students labeled with disabilities in your school: How does your school compare with other schools in your district?	
3. Fraction and percentage of students by disability label, i.e., behavioral challenges, cognitively disabled, learning disabled, severely disabled, and so on:	
4. Number of students labeled with disabilities in your district:	

Appendix B (Continued)

5. Number of special education referrals each year: How has this changed over time?	
6. Of those students referred, what fraction/percentage were then identified for special education?	
7. Do all students with disabilities in your school community attend the school they would attend if they were not labeled? Explain.	
8. Do some students with (dis)abilities who do not live in your attendance area attend your school or district? Explain.	
9. Report two pieces of academic achievement data (preferably reading and math) as they relate to (dis)ability.	
10. Collect (dis)ability information in at least two other areas in your school/setting.	
11. (Dis)ability Data Analysis (see Social Class Data Analysis for directions)	

Gender Data and Analysis

Gender (Report fraction and percentage for each)	
1. Females on the teaching staff at the elementary level: middle school level: high school level:	
2. Females teaching science and math classes at the middle/high school level:	
3. Females teaching English (and related courses) at the middle/high school level:	
4. Females teaching history (and related courses) at the middle/high school level:	
5. Females teaching the highest level of math students at your school:	
6. Females teaching advanced placement courses at the high school:	
7. Out-of-school suspensions or expulsions by gender:	
8. Females/males with an emotional disability:	
9. Females/males on the administrative team:	
10. Females/males at the elementary, middle, and high school administrative level:	

11. Females/males on school board:	
12. (a) Report two pieces of academic achievement data (preferably reading and math) as they relate to this area of diversity. (b) Collect gender comparison data on at least two other areas in your school/setting.	
13. Gender Data Analysis (see Social Class Data Analysis for directions)	

Sexual Orientation and Gender Identity Data and Analysis

1. Does your district have any active policies that address sexual orientation and gender identity?	
2. Assess your school or district's anti-harassment policy. To what extent does it address sexual orientation and gender identity?	
3. How many staff are open about their LBGT identity to other staff? to students? to families and community?	
4. What percentage of teachers in your school would be proactive in supporting LGBT staff, students, and families? What percentage would be neutral? What percentage would oppose being supportive of LGBT staff, students, and families?	
5. Does your school/district provide domestic partner benefits to its employees?	
6. To what extent are invitations to school functions, staff gatherings, and so forth, inclusive of LGBT relationships?	
7. How and to what extent does your district's curriculum provide instruction related to sexual orientation and gender identity?	
8. If a group of students approached your building principal and requested to begin a Gay/Straight Alliance, how would your principal and/or district respond?	
9. Does your middle/high school have a Gay/Straight Alliance? If not, why not? If so, assess the efforts of this group.	
10. Assess your school's library/media holdings related to sexual orientation and gender identity. To what extent do students in your school have access to information about sexual orientation and gender identity, and what is the nature of this information?	
11. To what extent are school enrollment forms inclusive of nontraditional families?	

Appendix B (Continued)

12. To what extent has professional development addressed sexual orientation and gender identity?	
13. To what extent do students at the elementary level receive information about and have access to information about nontraditional families (i.e., when the early elementary grades complete family units, how many books and materials are available to these classrooms about nontraditional families)?	
14. To what extent are students teased or called names because of their gender identity or sexual orientation in your school? How do you know? To what extent are data collected on this?	
15. To what extent are students at your school required to adhere to a gender-specific dress code (e.g., at holiday concerts, are girls required to wear dresses and boys required to wear suits)?	
16. Sexual Orientation Data Analysis (see Social Class Data Analysis for directions)	

Appendix C

All Learners Learn Best When . . .

As an individual or with a group of people, brainstorm a response to the following open-ended sentence: We know that all learners learn best when . . .

Expect the brainstorm to take up to one hour; it is best not to go longer than that. Record everyone's responses on newsprint or in a format that allows all to view the results. At the next meeting, build consensus on the list by either having the entire group work on it or having small groups work on sections. To do so, use the "fist to five" method of consensus building. Ask whether everyone agrees with each descriptor. Point to the first descriptor and ask to what extent each person agrees with it. It is important not to have discussion of each item. Holding up a fist means "I cannot agree," all five fingers up means "I am in full agreement," and fewer fingers mean lesser degrees of agreement. Mark the descriptors for which all participants hold up three, four, or five fingers. Set aside the descriptors on which there is disagreement. Descriptors on which there is agreement or mixed agreement can serve as discussion items at later meetings. Descriptors on which there is widespread disagreement may be set aside for now.

Next, it can be helpful to categorize the agreed-on descriptors under major headings such as curriculum, instruction, social/emotional, and services, among others. Finally, the list can be compared with similar lists supported by research. Of course, this activity may be adapted for your specific needs, such as those related to group size and time.

The list that you or your group generates and agrees on should be typed up and copied for all participants. Gaining clarity about how each student learns best is a crucial first step. The rest of this book will help translate into action this internal wisdom about what works for students.

Appendix D

**Urban High School Service
Delivery Model Prior to ICS**

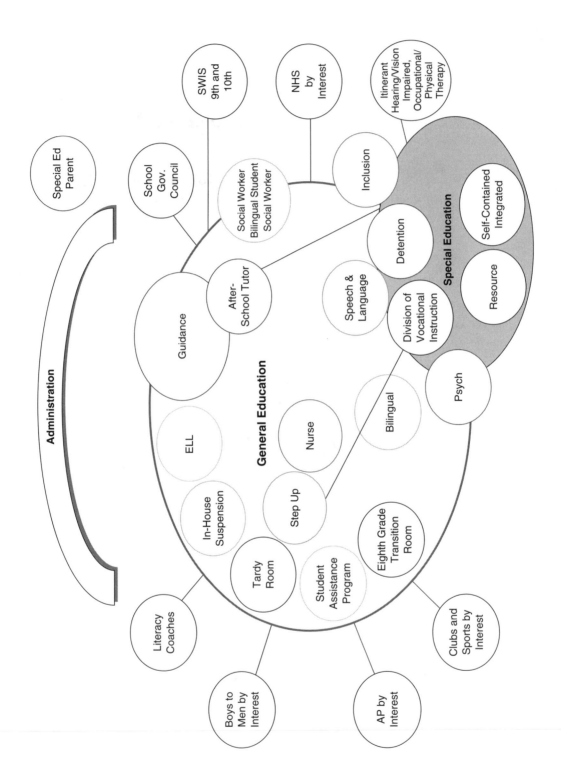

Appendix E

Individualized Service Plan

Age/Grade Cluster	Curriculum Standard (long-term objective)	Related Benchmarks for Stated Standard	Primary Methodology for Instruction	Assessment Options	Performance Level
Grade 2–4	Reading Read to acquire information.	• Summarize key details of informational texts, connecting new information to prior knowledge. • Identify a topic of interest and seek information about it by investigating available text resources.	Experiential ☐ Functional ☐ Small group ☐ Cooperative ☐ Tutorial ☐ Other ☐	Performance-based ☐ Functional ☐ District assessment with modification ☐ Portfolio ☐ Observation ☐ Other ☐	Advanced ☐ Proficient ☐ Basic skills ☐ Developing skills ☐ Supplanting skills ☐ Other ☐
Grade 2–4	Math Construct or select and use a variety of appropriate strategies to solve problems.	• Solve problems using different strategies such as draw a picture, build a model, act out, or look for a pattern. • Write number sentences to solve problems. • Solve problems using computer software, calculators, and/or math manipulatives.	Experiential ☐ Functional ☐ Small group ☐ Cooperative ☐ Tutorial ☐ Other ☐	Performance-based ☐ Functional ☐ District assessment with modification ☐ Portfolio ☐ Observation ☐ Other ☐	Advanced ☐ Proficient ☐ Basic skills ☐ Developing skills ☐ Supplanting skills ☐ Other ☐

Appendix F

Schedule for Integrated Comprehensive Services

Middle School, Seventh Grade, 110 Students, One House

Block Schedule

Students:

10 students with LD, 2 at-risk, 1 with autism, 2 with cognitive disabilities, and 2 with behavioral needs

(17 total—15 eligible for special ed, 2 not eligible)

Staffing:

4 general educators

1 special educator

1 assistant

Other support: bilingual resource teacher, school psychologist, reading resource teachers, etc.

Staffing Configuration	Block 1: 8:15–9:45 Math/Sci	Block 2: 9:45–11:15 FamilyEd/Spanish	Block 3: 11:15–12:30 Lunch/Tech	Block 4: 12:30–2:00 Lang/History	Block 5: 2:00–3:30 PhysEd/Health
General Educators (2)	Supporting 1 student with high behavioral needs and 1 student with autism (who is very academically capable)	Planning time for General Ed and Special Educator First part of meeting is on universal access: second part, Special Ed teacher leaves to provide support in Spanish	Lunch/Lunch Duty	Same as Block 1	Health—Team taught
General Educators (2)	Supporting 3 students with LD—team lesson codeveloped for universal access with Special Educator and school psych	Planning time	Lunch/Hall Duty	Same as Block 1	Phys. Ed—Support with assistant
Special Educator	Support across 2 rooms supporting 9 students (7 with LD, 1 at-risk, and 1 with behavioral needs) Some large- and some small-group instruction in integrated spaces	Meeting, followed by support in Spanish	Lunch/Community Prep with student with autism and 1 student with LD—significant	Team teaching—both classrooms are moved together	Teaming in Health

Staffing Configuration	Block 1: 8:15–9:45 Math/Sci	Block 2: 9:45–11:15 FamilyEd/Spanish	Block 3: 11:15–12:30 Lunch/Tech	Block 4: 12:30–2:00 Lang/History	Block 5: 2:00–3:30 PhysEd/Health
Assistant	Community with 1 student with CD and 1 with behavioral needs. Prep in the school library followed by instruction in the community	Assistant supporting in Family and Consumer Ed	Lunch/Supporting lunch room—to assist in friendships/prevent bullying, etc.	Community Instruction for Vocational with 1 other teacher from the HS and 1 other HS student	Assisting in Phys. Ed
Other Support (Bilingual Resource Assistants\Psych, Reading Resource, etc.)	Student with CD working in the office—supported/supervised by the school psych	Other student with CD is working at the elementary school, guidance counselor at the elementary provides supervision			Resource Reading Teacher working in small group with student with autism and 3 students who are academically gifted and 1 student at-risk of failure, to develop a school project

Appendix G

Sample Lesson Plan for All Learners

Big Picture: Weather

Key Concept: Cloud Type

Standard: Science Fourth Grade

E.12.a. Describe the weather commonly found in Wisconsin in terms of clouds, temperature, humidity, and forms of precipitation, and the changes that occur over time, including seasonal changes.

E.12.b. Observe, measure, compare, and contrast weather changes over time

Learner Materials	Assessment	Benchmark	Content	Instructional Intelligence	Instructional Format	Resources
Descriptors/ Attributes	**Performance Functional Portfolio**	**Coached/ Independent Advanced Proficient Basic Skill Developing Skill**	**Specific Curriculum**	**Auditory Visual Kinesthetic**	**Cooperative Tutorial Small Group Large Group Experiential**	
Learner 1 & 1a: Nonreaders, low average readers, students needing hands-on experience in comprehending new concepts, students w/minimal science experience, students	Portfolio: Weather folder w/cloud booklet and learning journal Functional: Record cloud types in weather brochure (picture or word).	Developing Skill: Associate cloud type by description to type of weather, utilizing guide booklet for resource. Basic Skill: Associate cloud type by description to type of weather, i.e., Fluffy clouds indicate	Four most common cloud types 1. Cumulus 2. Cumulonimbus 3. Stratus 4. Cirrus Explain what clouds are made of and how clouds are formed.	Visual: Overheads w/discussion Create booklets w/match of description and picture. Identify and record cloud types of daily weather in weather brochure (picture or word).	Large group (35) and small groups (varies) Divide class into two random sections (17 each).	Overheads of 4 cloud types Premade blank booklets for students to create cloud picture and write description of each cloud type Weather brochure Cotton balls/paper Metal spoons Shaving cream

Learner Materials	Assessment	Benchmark	Content	Instructional Intelligence	Instructional Format	Resources
Descriptors/ Attributes	**Performance Functional Portfolio**	**Coached/ Independent Advanced Proficient Basic Skill Developing Skill**	**Specific Curriculum**	**Auditory Visual Kinesthetic**	**Cooperative Tutorial Small Group Large Group Experiential**	*Resources*
needing high structure and teacher direction	<u>Performance:</u> Match cloud type to descriptive words.	*nice weather;* dramatize, draw, or orally describe how clouds are formed. <u>Proficient:</u> Name cloud type and general weather pattern w/o cue. Orally w/drawing or in writing identify what clouds are made of. <u>Advanced:</u> All proficient criteria and self-generated projects negotiated w/teacher—"what I know, what I want to know/learn, and what I have learned" (KWL).		Match game: picture to description <u>Kinesthetic:</u> Make cloud types w/cotton balls Lesson: What Are Clouds Made of? Drops Get Together <u>Auditory:</u> Repetition of matching picture to verbal description Tape of weather songs		Toothpicks Eyedroppers Blue-tinted water Pictures w/descriptions Pictures w/o descriptions Match game (cards) of picture and description Magnetic match game (large pictures) See bibliography.

(Continued)

Appendix G (Continued)

Big Picture: Weather

Key Concept: Cloud Type

Standard: Science Fourth Grade

E.12.a. Describe the weather commonly found in Wisconsin in terms of clouds, temperature, humidity, and forms of precipitation, and the changes that occur over time, including seasonal changes.

E.12.b. Observe, measure, compare, and contrast weather changes over time.

Learner/Materials	Assessment	Benchmark	Content	Instructional Intelligence	Instructional Format	Resources
Descriptors/Attributes	**Performance Functional Portfolio**	**Coached/ Independent Advanced Proficient Basic Skill Developing Skill**	**Specific Curriculum**	**Auditory Visual Kinesthetic**	**Cooperative Tutorial Small Group Large Group Experiential**	
Learner 2: Average readers with independent work skills, emerging study skills	Portfolio: Weather folder w/cloud booklet. Performance: Identify cloud type and weather pattern; identify what clouds are made of and explain how clouds are formed.	Proficient: Name cloud type and general weather pattern. In writing, identify what clouds are made of. Advanced: All proficient criteria and self-generated project negotiated w/teacher—"what I know, what I want to know/learn, and what I have learned" (KWL).	Four most common cloud types 1. Cumulus 2. Cumulonimbus 3. Stratus 4. Cirrus Associated weather patterns Process of cloud formation	Visual: Overheads w/ discussion Create booklets w/match of description and picture. Identify and record cloud types and predictable weather patterns daily in weather brochure.	Large group (35) and small groups (varies) Study skills: Practice using booklet as study guide. Writing in group Explanation of cloud formation	Overheads of 4 cloud types Premade blank booklets for students to create cloud picture and write description of each cloud type Weather brochure Metal spoons Shaving cream Toothpicks Eyedroppers

Learner Materials	Assessment	Benchmark	Content	Instructional Intelligence	Instructional Format	Resources
Descriptors/ Attributes	**Performance Functional Portfolio**	**Coached/ Independent Advanced Proficient Basic Skill Developing Skill**	**Specific Curriculum**	**Auditory Visual Kinesthetic**	**Cooperative Tutorial Small Group Large Group Experiential**	
				<u>Kinesthetic:</u> Lesson: What Are Clouds Made of? Drops Get Together <u>Auditory:</u> Tape		
<u>Learner 2a:</u> Science oriented, motivated by curiosity, independent learner	<u>Portfolio:</u> Weather folder w/cloud booklet and independent project, weather brochure <u>Performance:</u> Identify cloud type and weather pattern. Independent weather project	<u>Proficient:</u> Identify cloud type and general weather pattern. In writing, identify how clouds are formed and what they are made of. <u>Advanced:</u> All proficient criteria and self-generated project negotiated w/teacher—"what I know, what I want to know/learn, and what I have learned" (KWL).	Same as above	Same as above Through KWL activity, student determined modality of interest in independent study.	Same as above Cooperative groups and/or independent work time	Blue-tinted water See bibliography. Same as above Library books Internet access

(Continued)

Appendix G (Continued)

Lesson Plan

Weather—Cloud Type

Note:

Day 1	Day 2	Day 3	Day 4	Day 5
Large group (1&2): "Weather Watch": Brainstorming session Chart student ideas. Introduce calendar of events. Create weather folder (pictures for non-drawers to paste on cover).	*Large group (1&2):* Flip books 1s—picture & words on single page 2s—picture w/words on reverse side Note: cotton balls for some 1s for hand-on experience of differences 2a's Activity—"what I know, what I want to know/learn, and what I have learned" (KWL)	*Large group* (divided into 2 random sections for experiments) What Are Clouds Made of? Drops Get Together Extra time—review flip book and types of clouds w/partners	*Large group (1&2):* Introduce weather brochure. Model resources for weather identification: Internet, paper, phone, observation, and instruments. 1s match game (card and magnetic) 2s study skills—how to use flip booklet as study guide 2a's—20 minutes to discuss KWL results and think about self-initiated project	*Study Skills/Assessment* Teach each group of learners how to use flip chart for resources for self-study. Demonstrate match game for 1s for repetition and practice in studying. 2a's—Review timeline and/or structure of independent project.
Comments:	Comments:	Comments:	Comments:	Comments:

Appendix H

Process for Functional Behavioral Assessment

Establish a collaborative team that includes the student, at least one student peer (if appropriate), a sibling, and other family members important in the student's life.

1. List all positive or appropriate behaviors the student has and all his or her individual strengths. These behaviors can be classified under the multiple intelligence frames of interpersonal skills, intrapersonal skills, music, mathematics, linguistic, nature, humor, and spirit.

_____

2. List all challenging behaviors in observable terms—communicative intent, frequency, and duration of the behavior. Finally, describe the school's typical responses to the behavior and rate the behavior according to seriousness:

Behavior	Observable Terms	Communicative Intent (perceived purpose of behavior/history)	Frequency of Behavior	Duration of Behavior	What Preceded Behavior (time, places, with whom, etc.)	Typical Response and Outcome at School/at Home	Rate by Seriousness (distracting, disruptive, destructive, etc.)

3. Determine the top three behaviors that the team will address:

_____

_____

4. Develop a Behavioral Plan (sample is provided in Appendix I). Determine on-task behavior, first-teacher response, second-teacher response, etc.

Appendix I

Sample Behavioral Plan

BEHAVIOR PROTOCOL: Sawyer

Ground Rules for Success:

- Allow time for Sawyer to process information (min. 15 seconds).
- Present information both orally and visually.
- Provide intermittent positive reinforcement.

Student Behavior	Initial Adult Response	Follow-Up Adult Response (+/–)
Engaged in Work • Quiet • Mindful • May stand up, but on task	• Verbal reinforcement • Primary reinforcements • Don't overdo it—does not want to be recognized.	• Continued reinforcement • Or reinforcement plan
Behavior 1: Signs of Being Off Task • Out of seat/walks around with no direction • Constantly verbal • Looks confused	• Redirect to the task both orally and visually (e.g., "Look on the board, Sawyer. That is what you're supposed to do.") • Touch lightly on the arm. • Process time, 15 seconds	• Modify the task so that Sawyer can meet with success. • Modify the environment—check for sensory difficulties. • Allow Sawyer to take a break; encourage him to verbalize need.
Behavior 2: Signs of Agitation • Becomes argumentative when redirected • Initiates arguments with other students	• Ask Sawyer what he needs: "You look like you need _____." • Use the problem/solution chart. • Use social story.	• Redirect to another physical setting for a large motor activity—give him 2 win-win choices, i.e., small gym or outside. • Follow Sawyer (but do not chase) if he leaves the classroom.

Student Behavior	Initial Adult Response	Follow-Up Adult Response (+/−)
• Not logical • Dark circles under eyes become apparent	• Offer options for exit to a less stimulating environment. • Do not touch Sawyer. • Remove all stimuli (including teacher voice and eye contact). • With two trained staff, remove all stimuli. • Provide an environment for Sawyer to walk it off (gym, outdoors, hallways, track, etc.). • Provide tangible options for sensory integration support (do not verbalize options).	• Use walkie-talkies to notify office that Sawyer's in level 3/2 (third level of behavior/2nd teacher intervention). • Line up predetermined backup supports. • If behaviors persist (over 1 hour and 30 minutes), arrange for Sawyer to exit the school grounds. • Page mom; if not available, page county support person.
Behavior 3: Signs of Noncompliance • Hits things, kicks, throws • Runs/bolts • Engages in verbal challenges		
Signs of Resolution • Sawyer allows staff to walk with him • Becomes logical	• Discuss what could have happened differently. • Return to sensory diet.	• Sawyer returns to his typical schedule. • Staff debriefs after school to provide recommendations or changes in plan.

Appendix J

Educational Professional Development Plan Template

PROFESSIONAL   _____

GRADE/SUBJECT   _____

OBSERVATIONS   _____

MEETINGS AND
DISCUSSIONS   _____

NOTE: Professional goals/action plans or items that have been
mutually agreed upon to evaluate should be attached to this form.

SIGNATURES (indicating review of this report):

_____
Date   Professional Signature

_____
Date   Supervisor Signature

Appendix J (Continued)

Responsibilities for All Professionals	Ability	Professional Comments Date	Evaluative Comments Date	Areas Requiring Additional Support and Type of Information/Format
1. The professional supports and services a full range of differing learners in the most heterogeneous school and nonschool environments.	5 4 3 2 1 ☐ ☐ ☐ ☐ ☐			
2. The professional collaborates and team teaches with a range of teachers and specialists to better meet the needs of the diverse range of learners.	5 4 3 2 1 ☐ ☐ ☐ ☐ ☐			
3. The professional cooperatively develops curriculum with universal access in mind for all learners, to assist each learner in making significant progress toward and beyond grade-level standards using a range of individually appropriate assessment options.	5 4 3 2 1 ☐ ☐ ☐ ☐ ☐			
4. The professional functions as an active team member of a professional learning community using data for inquiry to better support services for all learners in the most integrated comprehensive manner possible.	5 4 3 2 1 ☐ ☐ ☐ ☐ ☐			
5. The professional believes that all children are his or her responsibility to teach, and all children can learn in our school given individualized support and the appropriate educational care.	5 4 3 2 1 ☐ ☐ ☐ ☐ ☐			

Rating Scale

5—Area of Strength, Exceeds Expectations
4—Meets Appropriate Expectations
3—Needs Attention Through Goal Setting
2—Has Not Met Expectations
1—Deficit Area

Responsibilities for All Professionals	Ability	Professional Comments Date	Evaluative Comments Date	Areas Requiring Additional Support and Type of Information/Format
TEACHER–STUDENT RELATIONSHIPS				
Positive teacher-student relationships are demonstrated when the teacher				
1. Recognizes/identifies individual students and their needs.	5 4 3 2 1 ☐ ☐ ☐ ☐ ☐			
2. Facilitates students' decision making.	5 4 3 2 1 ☐ ☐ ☐ ☐ ☐			
3. Provides opportunities for all students to achieve.	5 4 3 2 1 ☐ ☐ ☐ ☐ ☐			
4. Uses positive, encouraging, and supportive communication.	5 4 3 2 1 ☐ ☐ ☐ ☐ ☐			
5. Is responsive to students' feelings and behaviors.	5 4 3 2 1 ☐ ☐ ☐ ☐ ☐			
6. Displays an appropriate sense of humor.	5 4 3 2 1 ☐ ☐ ☐ ☐ ☐			
7. Demonstrates mutual respect and trust.	5 4 3 2 1 ☐ ☐ ☐ ☐ ☐			
8. Is accessible and approachable for students.	5 4 3 2 1 ☐ ☐ ☐ ☐ ☐			
9. Other:	5 4 3 2 1 ☐ ☐ ☐ ☐ ☐			

Rating Scale
5—Area of Strength, Exceeds Expectations
4—Meets Appropriate Expectations
3—Needs Attention Through Goal Setting
2—Has Not Met Expectations
1—Deficit Area

(Continued)

Appendix J (Continued)

Encouraging Learning	Ability	Professional Comments Date	Evaluative Comments Date	Areas Requiring Additional Support and Type of Information/Format
Effective motivation/stimulation techniques are demonstrated when the teacher				
1. Demonstrates a positive, enthusiastic approach to teaching/learning.	5 4 3 2 1 ☐ ☐ ☐ ☐ ☐			
2. Established/sustains attention with activities appropriate to students' levels.	5 4 3 2 1 ☐ ☐ ☐ ☐ ☐			
3. Accommodates students' learning styles/differences.	5 4 3 2 1 ☐ ☐ ☐ ☐ ☐			
4. Recognizes/encourages intrinsic motivation in students.	5 4 3 2 1 ☐ ☐ ☐ ☐ ☐			
5. Monitors and positively reinforces students' behaviors/progress.	5 4 3 2 1 ☐ ☐ ☐ ☐ ☐			
6. Other:	5 4 3 2 1 ☐ ☐ ☐ ☐ ☐			

Rating Scale

5—Area of Strength, Exceeds Expectations
4—Meets Appropriate Expectations
3—Needs Attention Through Goal Setting
2—Has Not Met Expectations
1—Deficit Area

Planning for Learning	Ability	Professional Comments Date	Evaluative Comments Date	Areas Requiring Additional Support and Type of Information/Format
To demonstrate an understanding of the importance of content and thinking, the teacher should				
1. Establish immediate and long-range objectives designed to fit the developmental needs of students.	5 4 3 2 1 ☐ ☐ ☐ ☐ ☐			
2. Demonstrate current knowledge of subject matter.	5 4 3 2 1 ☐ ☐ ☐ ☐ ☐			
3. Incorporate learning outcomes in planning curricular experiences.	5 4 3 2 1 ☐ ☐ ☐ ☐ ☐			
4. Establish daily lesson plans and comprehensive unit plans.	5 4 3 2 1 ☐ ☐ ☐ ☐ ☐			
5. Express appropriate rationale for teaching procedures educating a range of students with differences in general educational and community environments.	5 4 3 2 1 ☐ ☐ ☐ ☐ ☐			
6. Exhibit an operative knowledge of the developmental processes of the IEP.	5 4 3 2 1 ☐ ☐ ☐ ☐ ☐			
7. Exhibit an operative knowledge of a multidisciplinary team approach.	5 4 3 2 1 ☐ ☐ ☐ ☐ ☐			
8. Convey knowledge of special educational referral system including least restrictive environment.	5 4 3 2 1 ☐ ☐ ☐ ☐ ☐			
9. Demonstrate knowledge concerning the annual review and due process procedures.	5 4 3 2 1 ☐ ☐ ☐ ☐ ☐			

Rating Scale
5—Area of Strength, Exceeds Expectations
4—Meets Appropriate Expectations
3—Needs Attention Through Goal Setting
2—Has Not Met Expectations
1—Deficit Area

(Continued)

Professional Responsibilities	Ability	Professional Comments Date	Evaluative Comments Date	Areas Requiring Additional Support and Type of Information/Format
Professional responsibilities encompass long-term activities, including				
1. Consistent communication with parents regarding students' progress.	5 4 3 2 1 ☐ ☐ ☐ ☐ ☐			
2. Demonstrating promptness and accuracy with reports and records.	5 4 3 2 1 ☐ ☐ ☐ ☐ ☐			
3. Using available educational resources within the building, district, and community.	5 4 3 2 1 ☐ ☐ ☐ ☐ ☐			
4. Participating in the formulation and implementation of classroom, building, and district policies/strategic plan.	5 4 3 2 1 ☐ ☐ ☐ ☐ ☐			
5. Demonstrating dependability regarding school hours, meetings, and conferences.	5 4 3 2 1 ☐ ☐ ☐ ☐ ☐			
6. Contributing to the development and improvement of curricular programs.	5 4 3 2 1 ☐ ☐ ☐ ☐ ☐			
7. Engaging in professional development activities.	5 4 3 2 1 ☐ ☐ ☐ ☐ ☐			
8. Demonstrating cooperative work skills.	5 4 3 2 1 ☐ ☐ ☐ ☐ ☐			
9. Displaying adaptability to changing institutional circumstances.	5 4 3 2 1 ☐ ☐ ☐ ☐ ☐			
10. Supporting related service programs (e.g., Student Assistance Programs, developmental guidance, resource programs).	5 4 3 2 1 ☐ ☐ ☐ ☐ ☐			
11. Appropriateness of assessment tool selection (from norm-referenced to functional assessments).	5 4 3 2 1 ☐ ☐ ☐ ☐ ☐			
12. Quality of administration.	5 4 3 2 1 ☐ ☐ ☐ ☐ ☐			

Professional Responsibilities	Ability	Professional Comments Date	Evaluative Comments Date	Areas Requiring Additional Support and Type of Information/Format
13. Quality of results analysis and interpretation.	5 4 3 2 1 ☐ ☐ ☐ ☐ ☐			
14. Analyzing data obtained from evaluative instruments for the purpose of planning objective, and needed supports.	5 4 3 2 1 ☐ ☐ ☐ ☐ ☐			
15. Writing instructional goals based on assessment information.	5 4 3 2 1 ☐ ☐ ☐ ☐ ☐			
16. Translating instructional goals into sequential objectives that are a. Chronological-age appropriate b. Environmentally appropriate c. Functionally or otherwise appropriate d. Behaviorally written e. Academically appropriate.	5 4 3 2 1 ☐ ☐ ☐ ☐ ☐			
17. Identifying techniques of instruction appropriate for a variety of learning styles.	5 4 3 2 1 ☐ ☐ ☐ ☐ ☐			
18. Selecting appropriate methods of data collection.	5 4 3 2 1 ☐ ☐ ☐ ☐ ☐			
19. Demonstrating the ability to collect and utilize data within the classroom and community environments.	5 4 3 2 1 ☐ ☐ ☐ ☐ ☐			
20. Utilizing data to analyze effectiveness of instruction and make appropriate changes.	5 4 3 2 1 ☐ ☐ ☐ ☐ ☐			
21. Other:	5 4 3 2 1 ☐ ☐ ☐ ☐ ☐			

Rating Scale
5—Area of Strength, Exceeds Expectations
4—Meets Appropriate Expectations
3—Needs Attention Through Goal Setting
2—Has Not Met Expectations
1—Deficit Area

(Continued)

Environmental Effectiveness	Ability	Professional Comments Date	Evaluative Comments Date	Areas Requiring Additional Support and Type of Information/Format
An effective classroom environment includes				
1. A classroom characterized by on-task behavior.	5 4 3 2 1 □ □ □ □ □			
2. Establishing clear parameters for student conduct.	5 4 3 2 1 □ □ □ □ □			
3. Maintaining clear parameters for student conduct.	5 4 3 2 1 □ □ □ □ □			
4. Facilitating the development of self-discipline and instilling responsibility for an orderly classroom.	5 4 3 2 1 □ □ □ □ □			
5. Encouraging students to incorporate decision-making skills and to assume responsibility for their choices.	5 4 3 2 1 □ □ □ □ □			
6. Responding effectively to situations requiring intervention.	5 4 3 2 1 □ □ □ □ □			
7. Other:	5 4 3 2 1 □ □ □ □ □			

Rating Scale

5—Area of Strength, Exceeds Expectations
4—Meets Appropriate Expectations
3—Needs Attention Through Goal Setting
2—Has Not Met Expectations
1—Deficit Area

Teaching Techniques	Ability	Professional Comments Date	Evaluative Comments Date	Areas Requiring Additional Support and Type of Information/Format
A teacher who is using effective techniques				
1. Exhibits clarity in communication.	5 4 3 2 1 ☐ ☐ ☐ ☐ ☐			
2. Makes objectives of lessons clear to students.	5 4 3 2 1 ☐ ☐ ☐ ☐ ☐			
3. Uses variety in materials, activities, approaches (i.e., cooperative learning, individualized projects, mentorships, etc.), and presentations.	5 4 3 2 1 ☐ ☐ ☐ ☐ ☐			
4. Provides preview/review to focus learning.	5 4 3 2 1 ☐ ☐ ☐ ☐ ☐			
5. Uses transitional/transfer techniques to facilitate learning.	5 4 3 2 1 ☐ ☐ ☐ ☐ ☐			
6. Provides guided practice opportunities.	5 4 3 2 1 ☐ ☐ ☐ ☐ ☐			
7. Encourages student participation.	5 4 3 2 1 ☐ ☐ ☐ ☐ ☐			
8. Encourages interdisciplinary applications of learning.	5 4 3 2 1 ☐ ☐ ☐ ☐ ☐			
9. Uses appropriate levels of question (e.g., critical thinking).	5 4 3 2 1 ☐ ☐ ☐ ☐ ☐			
10. Focuses students' thinking at appropriate levels.	5 4 3 2 1 ☐ ☐ ☐ ☐ ☐			
11. Assesses students' achievement according to curricular outcomes.	5 4 3 2 1 ☐ ☐ ☐ ☐ ☐			

Rating Scale

5—Area of Strength, Exceeds Expectations
4—Meets Appropriate Expectations
3—Needs Attention Through Goal Setting
2—Has Not Met Expectations
1—Deficit Area

References

Adams, M., Bell, L. A., & Griffin, P. (Eds.). (1997). *Teaching for diversity and social justice: A sourcebook.* New York: Routledge.

Allen, A. (1997). Creating space for discussion about social justice and equity in an elementary classroom. *Language Arts, 74*(7), 518–524.

August, D., & Hakuta, K. (Eds.). (1997). *Improving schooling for language minority children: A research agenda.* Washington, DC: National Research Council, Institute of Medicine.

Ayers, W., Hunt, J. A., & Quinn, T. (1998). (Eds.). *Teaching for social justice.* New York: The New Press and Teachers College Press.

Baumgart, D., Brown, L., Pumpian, I., Nisbet, J., Ford, A., Sweet, M., et al. (1980). The principle of partial participation and individualized adaptations in educational programs for severely handicapped students. *Journal of the Association for the Severely Handicapped, 7*(2), 17–27.

Biddle, B., & Berliner, D. (2002). Unequal school funding in the United States. *Educational Leadership, 59*(8), 48–59.

Blackorby, J., & Wagner, M. (1996). Longitudinal postschool outcomes of youth with disabilities: Findings from the National Longitudinal Transition Study. *Exceptional Children, 62*(5), 399–413.

Borman, G. D., Hewes, G. M., Overman, L. T., & Brown, S. (2003). Comprehensive school reform and achievement: A meta-analysis. *Review of Educational Research, 73,* 125–230.

Brantlinger, E., (1993). *The politics of social class in secondary school: Views of affluent and impoverished youth.* New York: Teachers College Press.

Brantlinger, E. (1997). Using ideology: Cases of nonrecognition of the politics of research and practice in special education. *Review of Educational Research, 67*(4), 425–459.

Brantlinger, E., Majd-Jabbari, M., & Guskin, S. L. (1996). Self-interest and liberal educational discourse: How ideology works for middle-class mothers. *American Educational Research Journal, 33*(3).

Bremer, C. D., Clapper, A. T., Hitchcock, C., Hall, T., & Kachgal, M. (2002). *Universal design: A strategy to support students' access to the general education curriculum* (Volume 1, Issue 3). Minneapolis, MN: National Center on Secondary Education and Transition.

Brisk, M. E. (1998). *Bilingual education: From compensatory to quality schooling.* Mahwah, NJ: Erlbaum.

Brown v. Board of Education, 347 U.S. 483 (1954).

Brown, L. (1988). Who are they and what do they want? In L. Brown, E. Frattura Kampschroer, A. Udvari-Solner, P. Schwarz, P. VanDeventer, G. Courchane, et al. (Eds.), *Educational programs for students with severe intellectual disabilities, Vol. XVIII*. Madison, WI: Madison Metropolitan School District.

Brown, L., Branston, M., Hamre Nietupski, S., Pumpian, I., Certo, N., & Gruenewald, L. (1979). A strategy for developing chronological age appropriate and functional curricular content for severely handicapped adolescents and young adults. *Journal of Special Education, 13*(1), 81–90.

Brown, L., Long, E., Udvari-Solner, A., Davis, L., VanDeventer, P., Ahlgren, C., et al. (1989). The home school: Why students with severe intellectual disabilities must attend the schools of their brothers, sisters, friends and neighbors. *The Journal of the Association for Persons With Severe Handicaps, 14*(1), 1–7.

Brown, L., Nisbet, J., Ford, A., Sweet, M., Shiraga, B., York, J., et al. (1983). The critical need for nonschool instruction in educational programs for severely handicapped students. *The Journal of the Association for Persons With Severe Handicaps, 8*(3), 71–77.

Brown, L., Schwarz, P., Udvari-Solner, A., Frattura Kampschroer, E., Johnson, F., & Jorgensen, J. (1991). How much time should a student who is severely intellectually disabled spend in regular education classrooms and elsewhere? *The Journal of the Association for Persons With Severe Handicaps, 16*(1), 39–47.

Brown, L., Shiraga, B., Rogan, P., York, J., Zanella Albright, K., McCarthy, E., et al. (1988). The "why question" in educational programs for students who are severely intellectually disabled. In S. Calculator & J. Bedrosian (Eds.), *Communication assessment and intervention for adults with mental retardation* (pp. 139–153). San Diego, CA: College Hill Press.

Brown, L., Udvari-Solner, A., Long, E., Davis, L., & Jorgensen, J. (1990). Integrated work: A rejection of the segregated enclave and mobile work crew. In L. H. Meyer, C. A. Peck, & L. Brown (Eds.), *Critical issues in the lives of people with severe disabilities* (pp. 219–229). Baltimore: Brookes.

Burrello, L. C., Lashley, C., & Beatty, E. E. (2000). *Educating all students together: How school leaders create unified systems*. Thousand Oaks, CA: Corwin Press.

Calderon, M. E., & Minaya-Rowe, L. (2003). *Designing and implementing two-way bilingual programs*. Thousand Oaks, CA: Corwin Press.

Capper, C. A. (1993). *Educational administration in a pluralistic society*. Albany: State University of New York Press.

Capper, C. A., Frattura, E., & Keyes, M. W. (2000). *Meeting the needs of students of all abilities: How leaders go beyond inclusion*. Thousand Oaks, CA: Corwin Press.

Capper, C., & Young, M. D. (in press). *Educational leaders for social justice*. Thousand Oaks, CA: Corwin Press.

Causton-Theoharis, J. N. (2003). Increasing interactions between students with severe disabilities and their peers via paraprofessional training. *Dissertation Abstracts International 64*(08), 2839A. (UMI No. 3101362)

Chambers, J. G., Parrish, T. B., & Harr, J. (2002). *What are states spending on special education services in the United States, 1999–2000? Advance Report #1, Special Education Expenditure Project (SEEP)*. Washington, DC: U.S. Department of Education.

Chambers, J. G., Parrish, T. B., Lieberman, J. C., & Wolman, J. M. (1998). What are we spending on special education in the U.S.? *CSEF Brief No. 8*. Palo Alto, CA: Center for Special Education Finance.

Chasnoff, D., Ben-Dov, A. J., & Yacker, F. (Producers). (2000). *That's a family!* [Videocassette]. United States: Women's Educational Media.

Chin Y., & Capper, C. A. (1999, October). *Contradictions in inclusion.* Paper presented at the Leadership Conference, Department of Educational Administration, University of Wisconsin–Madison.

Chynoweth, J. (2004). *The policies, practices, and beliefs of educators that influence the identification of students with disabilities.* Unpublished doctoral dissertation, University of Wisconsin–Madison.

Cochran-Smith, M. (1995). Color blindness and basket making are not the answers: Confronting the dilemmas of race, culture, and language diversity in teacher education. *American Educational Research Journal, 32*(3), 493–522.

Cochran-Smith, M. (2004). Defining the outcomes of teacher education: What's social justice got to do with it? *Asia-Pacific Journal of Teacher Education, 32*(3), 193–212.

Conchas, G. (2006). *The color of success: Race and high-achieving urban youth.* New York: Teachers College Press.

Conzemius, A., & O'Neil, J. (2001). *Building shared responsibility for student learning.* Alexandria, VA: Association for Supervision and Curriculum Development.

Crawford, J. (2000). Language politics in the United States. In C. Ovando & P. McLaren (Eds.), *The politics of multiculturalism and bilingual education: Students and teachers caught in the crossfire* (pp. 106–125). Boston: McGraw-Hill.

Crawford, J. (2005). *Making sense of census 2000.* Retrieved February 3, 2006, from http://www.nabe.org/research/demography.html

Cummins, J. (1986). Empowering minority students: A framework for intervention. *Harvard Educational Review, 56*(1), 18–36.

Cummins, J. (1999). Alternative paradigms in bilingual education research: Does theory have a place? *Educational Researcher, 28*(7), 26–32.

Cummins, J. (2000). Beyond adversarial discourse: Searching for common ground in the education of bilingual students. In C. Ovando & P. McLaren (Eds.), *The politics of biculturalism and bilingual education: Students and teachers caught in the crossfire* (pp. 126–147). Boston: McGraw-Hill.

Darling-Hammond, L., French, J., & Garcia-Lopez, S. P. (Eds.). (2002). *Learning to teach for social justice.* New York: Teachers College Press.

Darling-Hammond, L., & Youngs, P. (2002). Defining "highly qualified teachers": What does "scientifically-based research" actually tell us? *Educational Researcher, 31*(9), 13–25.

Dentith, A., & Frattura, E. (2004). *Barriers and supports to integrated services for all students: Examining roles, structures, and processes in one urban district* [online]. Available at http://coe.ksu.edu/ucea/bytitle.htm

Deschenes, S., Cuban, L., & Tyack, O. (2001). Mismatch: Historical perspectives on schools and students who don't fit them. *Teachers College Record, 103*(4), 525–537.

Dewey, J. (1902). *The child and the curriculum: The school and society.* Chicago: University of Chicago Press.

Donnellan, A. (1984). The criterion of the least dangerous assumption. *Behavior Disorders, 9,* 141–150.

Donovan, M. S., & Cross, C. T. (2002). *Minority students in special and gifted education.* Washington, DC: National Academy Press.

Doyle, M. B. (2002). *The paraprofessional's guide to the inclusive classroom: Working as a team.* (2nd ed.). Baltimore: Brookes.

DuFour, R. & Eaker, R. (1998). *Professional learning communities at work: Best practices for enhancing student achievement.* Bloomington, IN: National Educational Service.

DuFour, R., Eaker, R., & Karhanek, G. (2004). *Whatever it takes: How professional learning communities respond when kids don't learn.* Bloomington, IN: National Educational Service.

Durtschi, E. (2005). *Elementary school principals' involvement in special education: Roles, attitudes, and training.* Unpublished doctoral dissertation, University of Wisconsin–Madison.

Dwyer, D., & Hecht, J. (1992). Minimal parental involvement. *School Community Journal, 2*(2), 53–66.

Families and Schools Together (FAST). (2004). *FAST impact and research.* Retrieved February 16, 2006, from http://www.wcer.wisc.edu/fast/research/index.html

Freire, P. (1970). *Pedagogy of the oppressed.* New York: Continuum.

French, J. (2002). Idealism meets reality. In L. Darling-Hammond, J. French, & S. P. Garcia-Lopez (Eds.), *Learning to teach for social justice* (pp. 59–65). New York: Teachers College Press.

Friend, M., & Bursuck, W. (2002). *Including students with special needs: A practical guide for classroom teachers.* Boston: Allyn & Bacon.

Friend, M., & Bursuck, W. (2006). *Including students with special needs: A practical guide for classroom teachers* (4th ed.). Boston: Allyn & Bacon.

Friend, M., & Cook, L. C. (1991). *Interactions: Collaboration skills for school professionals.* Boston: Allyn & Bacon.

Fullan, M. (1999). *Change forces: The sequel.* Philadelphia: Falmer.

Garcia, G. (2000). Bilingual children's reading. In M. L. Kamil, P. B. Mosenthal, P. D. Pearson, & R. Barr (Eds.), *Handbook of reading research* (Vol. 3, pp. 813–834). Mahwah, NJ: Erlbaum.

Gaudelli, W. (2001). Reflection on multicultural education: A teacher's experience. *Multicultural Education, 8*(4), 35–37.

Gottlieb, M. (2004). *English language proficiency standards for English language learners in kindergarten through grade 12.* Madison, WI: WIDA Consortium.

Green, J. (1998). *A meta-analysis of the effectiveness of bilingual education.* Claremont, CA: Tomas Rivera Policy Center.

Green, R. L. (2004). *Practicing the art of leadership: A problem-based approach to implementing the ISLLC standards.* Upper Saddle River, NJ: Merrill/Prentice Hall.

Greenleaf, R. K. (1977). *Servant leadership: A journey into the nature of legitimate power and greatness.* New York: Paulist Press.

Grinberg, J., & Saavedra, E. R. (2000). The constitution of bilingual/ESL education as a disciplinary practice: Genealogical explorations. *Review of Educational Research, 70*(4), 419–441.

Heller, D. (2004). *Teachers wanted: Attracting and retaining good teachers.* Alexandria, VA: Association for Supervision and Curriculum Development.

Holloway, J. (2002). Extracurricular activities and student motivation. *Educational Leadership, 60*(1), 80–81.

Hong, G., & Raudenbush, S. (2005). Effects of kindergarten retention policy on children's cognitive growth in reading and mathematics. *Educational Evaluation and Policy Analysis, 27*(3), 205–224.

Hosp, J. L., & Reschly, D. J. (2002). Predictors of restrictiveness of placement for African-American and Caucasian students. *Exceptional Children, 6*(2), 225–238.

Howard, E., Sugarman, J., & Christian, D. (2003). *Trends in two-way immersion education: A review of the research* (Report No. 63). Baltimore: Center for Research on the Education of Students Placed at Risk.

Hoy, W. K., & Miskel, C. G. (2001). *Educational administration: Theory, research, and practice.* Boston: McGraw-Hill.

Huefner, D. (2000). *Getting comfortable with special education law: A framework for working with children with disabilities.* Norwood: MA: Christopher-Gordon.

Hunt, J. A. (1998). Of stories, seeds and the promises of social justice. In W. Ayers, J. A. Hunt, & T. Quinn (Eds.), *Teaching for social justice* (pp. xiii–xv). New York: The New Press and Teachers College Press.

Individuals with Disabilities Education Act of 1997, Pub. L. No. 105–17.

Individuals with Disabilities Education Improvement Act of 2004, Pub. L. No. 108–446.

Jimerson, S. (2001). Meta-analysis of grade retention research: Implications for practice in the 21st century. *The School Psychology Review, 30*(3), 420–437.

Johnson, R. S. (2002). *Using data to close the achievement gap: How to measure equity in our schools.* Thousand Oaks, CA: Corwin Press.

Jorgensen, C. M. (Ed.). (1998). *Restructuring high schools for all students: Taking inclusion to the next level.* Baltimore: Brookes.

Krashen, S. D. (1999). *Condemned without a trial: Bogus arguments against bilingual education.* Portsmouth, NH: Heinemann.

Ladson-Billings, G. (1994). *The dream keepers: Successful teachers of African American children.* San Francisco: Jossey-Bass.

Ladson-Billings, G. (1995). "But that's just good teaching!" Toward a theory of culturally relevant pedagogy. *American Educational Research Journal, 32*(3), 465–491.

Ladson-Billings, G. (2001). *Crossing over to Canaan : The journey of new teachers in diverse classrooms.* San Francisco: Jossey-Bass.

Lee, V., & Smith, J. (1997). High school size: Which works best and for whom? *Educational Evaluation and Policy Analysis, 19*(3), 205–227.

Lewison, M., Flint, A. S., & Van Sluys, K. (2002). Taking on critical literacy: The journey of newcomers and novices. *Language Arts, 7*(5), 382–392.

Littky, D., & Grabelle, S. (2004). *The big picture: Education is everyone's business.* Alexandria, VA: Association for Supervision and Curriculum Development.

Lopez, G. R. (2001). The value of hard work: Lessons on parent involvement from an (im)migrant household. *Harvard Educational Review, 71*(3), 416–437.

Lopez, G. R., Gonzalez, M. L., & Fierro, E. (2005). Educational leadership along the U.S.–Mexico border: Crossing borders/embracing hybridity/building bridges. In C. Marshall & M. Oliva (Eds.), *Leadership for social justice: Making revolutions in education* (pp. 64–84). Boston: Pearson.

Lopez, G. R., Scribner, J. D., & Mahitivanichcha, K. (2001). Redefining parental involvement: Lessons from high-performing migrant-impacted schools. *American Educational Research Journal, 38*(2), 253–288.

Lopez, G. R., & Vazquez, V. (2005). *"They don't speak English": Interrogating racist ideologies and perceptions of school personnel in a Midwestern state.* Paper presented at the National Conference of University Council of Educational Administration, Nashville, Tennessee.

Losen, D. J., & Orfield, G. (Eds.). (2002). *Racial inequity in special education.* Cambridge, MA: Harvard Education Press.

Makler, A. (1994). Through teachers' eyes: Teaching about justice and injustice. *Update on law-related education, 18*(1), 15–20.

McKenzie, K. B., & Scheurich, J. J. (2004). Equity traps: A useful construct for preparing principals to lead schools that are successful with racially diverse students. *Educational Administration Quarterly, 40*(5), 601.

McLeskey, J., & Waldron, N. L. (2000). *Inclusive schools in action: Making differences ordinary.* Alexandria, VA: Association for Supervision and Curriculum Development.

Meyer, A., Brooks, G., & Goes, J. (1990). Environmental jobs and industry revolution: Organizational responses to discontinuous change. *Strategic Management Journal, 11,* 93–110.

Meyer, L., Peck, C., & Brown, L. (1991). *Critical issues in the lives of people with severe disabilities.* Baltimore: Brookes.

Minami, M., & Ovando, C. J. (2004). Language issues in multicultural contexts. In J. Banks & C. McGee Banks (Eds.), *Handbook of research on multicultural education* (2nd ed., pp. 567–588). San Francisco: Jossey-Bass.

Moroder, M. (2000, March 21). Unpublished lesson plan. Stoner Prairie Elementary School, Verona, Wisconsin.

National Center for Education Statistics. (2004). Language minorities and their educational and labor market indicators: Recent trends. Washington, DC: U.S. Department of Education. Available online at http://nces.ed.gov/pubs2004/2004009.pdf

National Organization on Disability. (2000). *2000 N.O.D./Harris Survey of Americans with Disabilities.* Washington, DC: Author. Retrieved September 1, 2004, from http://www.nod.org/content.cfm?id=1076#educ

No Child Left Behind Act of 2001, Pub. L. No. 107–110.

Oakes, J. (1985). *Keeping track.* New Haven, CT: Yale University Press.

Oakes, J., & Lipton, M. (1999). *Teaching to change the world.* Boston: McGraw-Hill.

Oakes, J., Quartz, K. H., Ryan, S., & Lipton, M. (2000). Becoming good American schools. *Phi Delta Kappan, 81*(8), 568–576.

Odden, A., & Archibald, S. (2001). *Reallocating resources: How to boost student achievement without asking for more.* Thousand Oaks, CA: Corwin Press.

Odden, A., & Picus, L. (2000). *School finance: A policy perspective* (2nd ed.). New York: McGraw-Hill.

Office of Special Education and Rehabilitative Services (OSERS). (2002). *OSERS 23rd annual report to Congress on the implementation of the IDEA.* Washington, DC: U.S. Department of Education.

Osterman, K. (2000). Students' need for belonging in the school community. *Review of Educational Research, 70*(3), 323–367.

Ovando, C. (2003). Bilingual education in the United States: Historical development and current issues. *Bilingual Research Journal, 27*(1), 1–25.

Perry, E. (1997). Is equity always best? Educational stakeholders lash out. *Journal of Educational Administration, 35*(5), 451–465.

Peterson, M., & Hittie, M. M. (2003). *Inclusive teaching: Creating effective schools for all learners.* San Francisco: Allyn & Bacon.

Philpott, J. (2003). *Transition and adaptation to the maternal role: Women's perceptions of themselves as mothers to children with significant disabilities.* Unpublished doctoral dissertation, University of Wisconsin–Madison.

Plessy v. Ferguson, 163 U.S. 537 (1896).

Portes, A., & Hao, L. (2004). The schooling of children of immigrants: Contextual effects on the educational attainment of the second generation. *Proceedings of the National Academy of Sciences of the United States of America (PNAS), 101*(33), 11920–11927.

Quality Counts (2004). Count me in: Special education in an era of standards [Special issue]. *Education Week, 23*(17). Available online at http://counts.edweek.org/sreports/qc04/

Quinn, R. (2000). *Change the world.* San Francisco: Jossey-Bass

Quinn, R. (2004). *Building the bridge as you walk.* San Francisco: Jossey-Bass.

Rainforth, B., & Kugelmass, J. W. (2003). *Curriculum and instruction for all learners: Blending systematic and constructivist approaches in inclusive elementary schools.* Baltimore: Brookes.

Ramirez, J. D., Yuen, S., & Ramey, D. R. (1991). Final report: Longitudinal study of structured immersion strategy, early-exit, and late-exit transitional bilingual education programs for language-minority children. *NABE Journal, 8,* 15–34.

Ramirez, J. D., Yuen, S., Ramey, D. R., & Pasta, D. (1990). *Final report: Longitudinal study of immersion strategy, early-exit, and late-exit transitional bilingual education programs for language-minority children* (Contract No. 300–87–0156, U.S. Department of Education). San Mateo, CA: Aguirre International.

Rea, P. J., McLaughlin, V. L., & Walther-Thomas, C. (2002). Outcomes for students with learning disabilities in inclusive and pullout programs. *Exceptional Children, 68*(2), 203–223.

Reese, L., Garnier, H., & Gallimore, R. (2000). Longitudinal analysis of the antecedents of emergent Spanish literacy and middle-school English reading achievement of Spanish-speaking students. *American Educational Research Journal, 37*(3), 633–662.

Reeves, D. B. (2004). *Accountability for learning: How teachers and school leaders can take charge.* Alexandria, VA: Association for Supervision and Curriculum Development.

Rehabilitation Act, 29 U.S.C. § 794(a), Section 504 (1973).

Riehl, C. J. (2000). The principal's role in creating inclusive schools for diverse students: A review of normative, empirical, critical literature on the practice of educational administration. *Review of Educational Research, 70*(1), 55–81.

Riester, A. F., Pursch, V., & Skrla L. (2002). Principals for social justice: Leaders of school success for children from low-income homes. *Journal of School Leadership, 12*(3), 281–304.

Rolstad, K., Mahoney, K., & Glass, G. V. (2005). The big picture: A meta-analysis of program effectiveness research on English language learners. *Educational Policy, 19*(4), 572–594.

Sailor, W. (Ed.). (2002). *Whole school success and inclusive education: Building partnerships for learning, achievement, and accountability.* New York: National Professional Resources.

Scheurich, J. J. (1998). Highly successful and loving, public elementary schools populated mainly by low-SES children of color: Core beliefs and cultural characteristics. *Urban Education, 33*(4), 451–491.

Scheurich, J. J., & Skrla, L. (2003). Leadership for equity and excellence: Creating high achievement classrooms, schools, and districts. Thousand Oaks, CA: Corwin Press.

Skrla, L., Scheurich, J. J., Garcia, J., & Nolly, G. (2004). Equity audits: A practical leadership tool for developing equitable and excellent schools. *Educational Administration Quarterly, 40*(1), 133–161.

Skrtic, T. M. (Ed.). (1995). *Disability and democracy: Reconstructing (special) education for postmodernity.* New York: Teachers College Press.

Slavin, R. E. (2002). The intentional school: Effective elementary education for all children. In S. Stringfield & D. Land (Eds.), *Educating at-risk students* (Vol. 101, pp. 111–127). Chicago: University of Chicago Press.

Slavin, R. E., & Cheung, A. (2004). How do English language learners learn to read? *Educational Leadership, 52*–57.

Slavin, R. E., & Cheung, A. (2005). A synthesis of research on language of reading instruction for English language learners. *Review of Educational Research, 75*(2), 247–284.

Stainback, S., & Stainback, W. (1996). *Inclusion: A guide for educators.* Baltimore: Brookes.

Suárez-Orozco, M., Suárez-Orozco, C., & Doucet, F. (2004). The academic engagement and achievement of Latino youth. In C. A. M. Banks & J. A. Banks (Eds.), *Handbook of research on multicultural education* (2nd ed., pp. 420–437). San Francisco: Jossey-Bass.

Theoharis, G. (2004). *At no small cost: Social justice leaders and their response to resistance.* Unpublished doctoral dissertation, University of Wisconsin–Madison.

Thomas, W., & Collier, V. (2001). *A national study of school effectiveness for language minority students' long-term academic achievement.* Washington, DC: Center for Research on Education, Diversity, and Excellence.

Thousand, J. S., Villa, R. A., & Nevin, A. (2002). *Creativity and collaborative learning: The practical guide to empowering students, teachers, and families* (2nd ed.). Baltimore: Brookes.

Thurlow, M. L., Elliott, J. L., & Ysseldyke, J. E. (1998). *Testing students with disabilities: Practical strategies for complying with district and state requirements.* Thousand Oaks, CA: Corwin Press.

Tomlinson, C. A. (2001). *How to differentiate instruction in mixed-ability classrooms* (2nd ed.). Alexandria, VA: Association for Supervision and Curriculum Development.

Tomlinson, C. A., & Allan, S. D. (2000). *Leadership for differentiating schools and classrooms.* Alexandria, VA: Association for Supervision and Curriculum Development.

Tomlinson, C. A., & Reis, S. (Eds.). (2004). *Differentiation for gifted and talented students.* Thousand Oaks, CA: Corwin Press.

Torres-Guzman, M., Abbate, J., Brisk, M. E., & Minaya-Rowe, L. (2001). Defining and documenting success for bilingual learners: A collective case study. *Bilingual Research Journal, 26*(1), 23.

Traudt, K. (2002). Survey says . . .: Can white teacher effectively teach students of color? In L. Darling-Hammond, J. French, & S. P. Garcia-Lopez (Eds.), *Learning to teach for social justice* (pp. 43–51). New York: Teachers College Press.

Udvari-Solner, A., & Thousand, J. (1995). Promises and practices that foster inclusive education. In R. Villa & J. Thousand (Eds.), *Creating an inclusive school* (pp. 87–109). Alexandria, VA: Association for Supervision and Curriculum Development.

The University of New Hampshire Institute on Disability. (1999). *High school inclusion: Equity and excellence in an inclusive community of learners.* Baltimore: Brookes.

U.S. Charter Schools (n.d.). Web site homepage. Available: www.uscharter schools.org/pub/uscs_docs/index.htm

U.S. Department of Education (2000). *To assure the free public education of all children with disabilities. Twenty-second Annual Report to Congress on the Implementation of the Individuals with Disabilities Education Act.* Washington, DC: Author.

U. S. Department of Education (2002). *No Child Left Behind: A desktop reference.* Washington, DC: Author.

Valencia, R. R. (Ed.). (1997). *The evolution of deficit thinking: Educational thought and practice.* London: Falmer.

Vandercook, T., & York, J. (1989). The McGill Action Planning System (MAPS): A strategy for building the vision. *The Journal of the Association for Persons with Severe Handicaps, 14*(3), 205–215.

Vibert, A., & Portelli, J. (2000). School leadership and critical practice in an elementary school. *Exceptionality Education Canada, 10*(1–2), 23–36.

Wasik, B., Bond, M. A., & Hindman, A. (2002). Educating at-risk preschool and kindergarten children. In S. Stringfield & D. Land (Eds.), *Educating at-risk students* (Vol. 101, pp. 89–110). Chicago: University of Chicago Press.

WIDA Consortium. (2006, January 6). Homepage. Retrieved February 6, 2006, from http://www.wida.us

Wigginton, E. (Ed.). (1977). *Foxfire 4.* Garden City, NY: Anchor Press.

Wigginton, E., & Bennett, M. (Eds.). (1986). *Foxfire 9.* Garden City, NY: Anchor Press.

Willig, A. C. (1985). A meta-analysis of selected studies on the effectiveness of bilingual education. *Review of Educational Research, 55*(3), 269–317.

Wisconsin Department of Public Instruction. (2005). *Special Education Index* [Online]. Available at http://www.dpi.state.wi.us/dpi/dlsea/een/hmtopics.html

Wong Fillmore, L., & Snow, C. (2000). *What teachers need to know about language.* Washington, DC: ERIC Clearinghouse on Languages and Linguistics.

Young, B. N., Helton, C., & Whitley, M. E (1997). *Impact of school-related, community-based, and parental-involvement activities on achievement of at-risk youth in the high school setting.* Paper presented at the annual meeting of the Mid-South Educational Research Association, Memphis, Tennessee. (ERIC Document Reproduction Service No. ED 414 533)

Ysseldyke, J. (2001). Reflections on a career: 25 years of research on assessment and instructional decision making. *Exceptional Children, 67*(3), 295–309.

Zhang, D., & Katsiyannis, A. (2002). Minority representation in special education. *Remedial and Special Education, 23*(3), 180–187.

Index